Getting a
Coding Job

FOR

DUMMIES®

A Wiley Brand

by Nikhil Abraham

with Kathleen Taylor and Bud E. Smith

FOR

DUMMIES®

A Wiley Brand

Getting a Coding Job For Dummies®

Published by: **John Wiley & Sons, Inc.,** 111 River Street, Hoboken, NJ 07030-5774, www.wiley.com

Copyright © 2015 by John Wiley & Sons, Inc., Hoboken, New Jersey

Published simultaneously in Canada

No part of this publication may be reproduced, stored in a retrieval system or transmitted in any form or by any means, electronic, mechanical, photocopying, recording, scanning or otherwise, except as permitted under Sections 107 or 108 of the 1976 United States Copyright Act, without the prior written permission of the Publisher. Requests to the Publisher for permission should be addressed to the Permissions Department, John Wiley & Sons, Inc., 111 River Street, Hoboken, NJ 07030, (201) 748-6011, fax (201) 748-6008, or online at http://www.wiley.com/go/permissions.

Trademarks: Wiley, For Dummies, the Dummies Man logo, Dummies.com, Making Everything Easier, and related trade dress are trademarks or registered trademarks of John Wiley & Sons, Inc. and may not be used without written permission. All other trademarks are the property of their respective owners. John Wiley & Sons, Inc. is not associated with any product or vendor mentioned in this book.

For general information on our other products and services, please contact our Customer Care Department within the U.S. at 877-762-2974, outside the U.S. at 317-572-3993, or fax 317-572-4002. For technical support, please visit www.wiley.com/techsupport.

Wiley publishes in a variety of print and electronic formats and by print-on-demand. Some material included with standard print versions of this book may not be included in e-books or in print-on-demand. If this book refers to media such as a CD or DVD that is not included in the version you purchased, you may download this material at http://booksupport.wiley.com. For more information about Wiley products, visit www.wiley.com.

Library of Congress Control Number: 2015941960

ISBN 978-1-119-05094-0 (pbk); ISBN 978-1-119-12101-5 (ebk); ISBN 978-1-119-12102-2 (ebk)

Manufactured in the United States of America

10 9 8 7 6 5 4 3 2 1

Table of Contents

Introduction

· ·

*E*verywhere you turn, people are looking for coders. In offices and board-
rooms, at your neighborhood bar, and around the family table, people
have ideas wanting to become websites, data needing to be analyzed, and
processes waiting to turn into a mobile app. Building a product requires
many people — including designers, product managers, marketers, and
content creators — but finding coders is always at the top of everyone's list
because they are so scarce.

On the supply side of the equation, learning to code and then getting a job
can feel overwhelming. However, there have never been more ways to learn
how to code, including on your own, in school, at a coding boot camp, and on
the job. And companies of every size and type are hiring developers.

Getting a Coding Job For Dummies will help you make sense of all the options
and show you ways to get that first coding job.

About This Book

This book is designed for the person with little to no experience with coding
jobs. In plain English, you discover why coding jobs are so popular, which
technologies to use when coding, ways to learn coding, and how to launch
your career. The topics covered include the following:

- ✔ How coding became such a hot topic and big industry
- ✔ Types of coding jobs
- ✔ Options for learning to code, including coding boot camps
- ✔ Coding technologies used to build websites, analyze data, and create
  mobile apps
- ✔ Building a portfolio and a network
- ✔ Interviewing your way into your first coding job

As you read the book, keep the following in mind:

- ✔ Skip around as much as you like. The book can be read from beginning to end, but if a topic interests you, start there.

- ✔ At some point, you will have questions or something will not make sense. Do not fear! Many resources are available to help, including support forums, free tutorial websites, others on the Internet, and me! Using Twitter, you can send a public message to me at @nikhilgabraham.

Foolish Assumptions

I do not make many assumptions about you, the reader, but I do make a few.

You do not need to have previous programming experience. In this regard, you need to be able to read, type, and follow directions. I explain as many concepts as possible by using examples and analogies you already know.

Before trying to get a coding job, you will spend some time learning how to code. Chapter 5 shows you some basic code examples, and Part III outlines options and resources for learning how to code in greater depth. If you don't have any coding knowledge, keep in mind that it will take at least a few months to learn enough to be able to get a coding job.

You'll need a computer running the latest version of Google Chrome if you want to complete the coding examples. Chrome is a free browser and the examples in the book and in the external resources have been tested and optimized for the Chrome browser, although they may also work in latest version of Firefox. Using Internet Explorer when learning to code is discouraged because its support for coding languages varies and it doesn't always work as expected.

I assume that you have access to an Internet connection. You can read almost all the book without an Internet connection, but you need an Internet connection to access external learn-to-code resources, such as the Codecademy website. Many listed resources are free and can be used without downloading or installing anything.

Icons Used in This Book

Here are the icons used in the book to flag text that should be given extra attention or that can be skipped.

This icon indicates useful information or explains a shortcut to help you understand a concept.

This icon explains technical details about the concept being explained. The details might be informative or interesting but are not essential to your understanding of the concept at this stage.

This icon marks a concept that likely has been explained before. It's flagged to reinforce what you've already learned.

Watch out! This icon indicates common mistakes and problems that can be avoided if you heed the warning.

Beyond the Book

Online resources are available in addition to the ones in this book:

- ✔ **Cheat sheet:** Visit www.dummies.com/cheatsheet/ gettingacodingjob for tips while job searching and during your interviews.

- ✔ **Extras:** Additional articles with extra content are posted for roughly each section of the book. You can access this additional material by visiting www.dummies.com/extras/gettingacodingjob.

- ✔ **Updates:** You can find any updates or corrections by visiting www. dummies.com/extras/gettingacodingjob.

Where to Go from Here

With all the administrative stuff out of the way, it's time to get started. Remember, you can start at the beginning or jump to whatever section interests you the most. Congratulations on taking your first step to getting a coding job!

Part I
Getting a Job in Coding

Check out www.dummies.com/extras/gettingacodingjob for more great content online.

In this part . . .

- ✔ Understand why coding matters
- ✔ Explore coding career paths
- ✔ Follow a coder on the job
- ✔ Learn key coding concepts

Chapter 1

Seeing the Big Picture

· ·

In This Chapter

▶ Seeing the history of coding and where it's headed

▶ Understanding different types of coding jobs and salaries

▶ Learning about companies that hire coders

· ·

If you just focus on the smallest details, you never get the big picture right.

—*Leroy Hood*

Today, many moments in your daily life are affected by code. Code runs the mobile phone alarm that wakes you up in the morning, the word processing and spreadsheet software you use at work or in school to create letters or projections, the games you play on a phone or console, and the web browser you run to check your email and read the news. Many tasks in our lives have remained the same — there will always be people who need help waking up in the morning — but technology is increasingly influencing the way we complete these tasks.

Because you're reading this book, you understand coding's pervasiveness, but you may wonder about the industry's size and future. Is getting a coding job like becoming a horse and buggy driver just as Ford was starting to sell the Model T?

In this chapter, you learn where coding came from, how fast it has grown, and what the future might hold for those who can code. Additionally, you'll see the types of companies that hire coders and find out what recruiting professionals look for when hiring coders.

What Is Coding?

Computer code consists of a set of statements (like sentences in English); each statement directs the computer to perform a single step or instruction. Each step is precise and followed to the letter. For example, if you're in a restaurant and ask a waiter to direct you to the restroom, he might say, "head to the back, and try the middle door." To a computer, these directions are vague and therefore unusable. Instead, if the waiter gave instructions to you as if you were a computer program, he might say, "From this table, walk northeast for 40 paces. Then turn right 90 degrees, walk 5 paces, turn left 90 degrees, and walk 5 paces. Open the door directly in front of you, and enter the restroom."

One rough way to measure a program's complexity is to count its statements or lines of code. Basic applications such as Pong have 5,000 lines of code, while more complex applications such as Facebook currently have over 10 million lines of code. Whether few or many lines of code, the computer follows each instruction exactly and effortlessly, never tiring like the waiter might when asked for the 100th time for the location of the restroom.

Figure 1-1 shows lines of code from the popular game Pong. Don't worry about trying to understand what every single line does.

Be careful when using the number of lines of code as a measure of a program's complexity. Just like when writing in English, 100 well-written lines of code can perform the same functionality as 1,000 poorly written lines of code.

This book describes the ins and outs of careers in coding but will not teach you a programming language. In Part III, you can read about the different ways you can learn to code: by yourself, in a coding boot camp, in college, and on the job.

Figure 1-1:
Computer
code from
the game
Pong.

```
 1
 2  launchPong(function () {
 3      function colour_random() {
 4          var num = Math.floor(Math.random() * Math.pow(2, 24));
 5          return '#' + ('00000' + num.toString(16)).substr(-6);
 6      }
 7
 8
 9      pongSettings.ball.size = 15;
10      pongSettings.ball.color = colour_random();
11      pongSettings.ball.velocity[0] = 15;
12      pongSettings.ball.velocity[1] = 15;
13
14  });
```

Why Coding Matters: Past, Present, Future

Today, programs written with code power so many different activities, and the work they do can almost seem like magic. With a few mouse clicks or finger taps, you can see your current location on a map, have groceries delivered to your door, or video chat with someone in another country. Although the research and development to make these advancements possible has been massive — billions of dollars invested and millions of hours worked — it has been worthwhile. In this section, I briefly describe a history of code and possibilities for the future.

Coding in the past

Unveiled in 1946 at the University of Pennsylvania, ENIAC was the first general-purpose computer. See Figure 1-2. It was the size of a large room, and programmers punched holes in paper cards to code programs that could take hours to complete. Sometimes bugs would crawl inside these large computers, causing the circuits to malfunction and resulting in errors. Removing these bugs from the computer was called *debugging,* which is the name used even today.

Figure 1-2: ENIAC was the size of a large room.

Gradually, with advances in hardware, computers became smaller and more powerful. Whereas the ENIAC's tens of thousands of resistors and capacitors took up almost 2,000 square feet, later microprocessors could fit all these electronics onto a chip the size of a postage stamp. Eventually, these microprocessors would be built using silicon, which is both cheap and plentiful.

Increased computing power from powerful microprocessors allowed programmers to write more complicated and resource-intensive programs. For example, computer games became faster, used more complex graphics, and displayed on-screen smoothly and realistically. Writing code, or software programming, depends on and is constrained by the underlying hardware on which the code runs. As computing power increases, code is written to provide more features at a faster speed to users.

Programming languages were also invented to take advantage of this new computing power. You may remember languages such as Basic, Fortran, Pascal, C++, and Java. Like spoken languages, programming languages were created to fill a need. If other programmers coded using the language, the programming language would survive and thrive; otherwise, it would die.

Popular programming languages can decline in popularity or die, but this can take a long time if the language is used for core processes. For example, Fortran is not nearly as popular as it was 30 years ago, but it continues to be used in the scientific community and in the financial sector, where it powers applications for some of the biggest banks in the world.

Coding today

In 2011, Marc Andreessen, creator of Netscape Navigator and now a venture capitalist, noted that "software is eating the world." He predicted that software companies would rapidly disrupt existing companies. Traditionally, software was used on desktops and laptops. The software had to be installed, and the installation process at a minimum varied by computer type and might not even work or might be incompatible with your computer hardware and software. After the software was installed, you had to supply data to the program.

Four trends have dramatically increased the use of code in everyday life:

> ✔ **Web-based software:** This software operates in the browser without requiring installation. For example, if you want to check email, you previously had to install an email client by downloading the software or from a CD-ROM. Issues arose when the software was not available for your operating system or conflicted with your operating system

version. Hotmail, a web-based email client, rose to popularity in part because it allowed users visiting `www.hotmail.com` to instantly check email without worrying about installation or software compatibility. Web applications increased consumer appetite to try more applications, and developers in turn were incentivized to write more applications.

✔ **Internet broadband connectivity:** Broadband connectivity has increased, providing a fast Internet connection to more people in the last few years than in the previous decade. Today, more than 2 billion people can access web-based software, up from approximately 50 million only a decade ago.

✔ **Coding repositories:** Anyone can publish code for others to view and use. Popular coding repositories, such as Github, are making coding a more collaborative, open, and public process than ever before. Programmers publish code to show others what they can build, to solicit feedback to increase functionality or find vulnerabilities, and to quickly spread software to other programmers.

✔ **Mobile phones:** Today's smartphones bring programs with you wherever you go and help supply data to programs. Many software programs became more useful when accessed on the go than when limited to a desktop computer. For instance, the use of maps apps greatly increased thanks to mobile phones because users need directions the most when lost not just when at home on the computer planning a trip. In addition, mobile phones are equipped with sensors that measure and supply data such as orientation, acceleration, and current location through GPS. Now instead of having to input all the data to programs yourself, mobile devices can help. For instance, a fitness application such as RunKeeper automatically tracks your distance, speed, and time.

The combination of these trends has resulted in software companies that have upended incumbents in almost every industry, especially ones typically immune to technology. Some notable examples include the following:

✔ **Airbnb:** A peer-to-peer lodging company that owns no rooms, yet books more nights than the Hilton and Intercontinental, the largest hotel chain in the world. See Figure 1-3.

✔ **Uber:** A car transportation company that owns no vehicles but books more trips and has more drivers in 200 cities than any other car or taxi service.

✔ **Groupon:** A daily deals company that generated almost $1 billion after just two years in business, growing faster than any other company in history, let alone any other traditional direct marketing company.

Coding in the future

The one constant in technology and coding is change. Improvements in existing computer architecture will lead to the creation of newer, faster, and smaller hardware devices, and developers will then write code to operate and control those hardware devices.

Moore's Law, a rule of thumb used in the computer hardware industry, predicts that the number of transistors per square inch on an integrated circuit will double every year. The prediction has proved to be true for the last 50 years, although some experts doubt whether it will continue to hold true for the next 50 years.

The following technology developments are increasing in popularity and should remain relevant at least for the next five years:

- ✔ **Internet of Things (IOT):** Computing power is transforming dumb hardware devices into smart, connected, self-regulated devices. For example, the Nest thermostat uses a motion detector to record when people are present, and then heats and cools homes when people are expected to be at home instead of all day. Similarly, Lockitron makes a device that allows you to lock and unlock your front door with your smartphone.

Other connected devices, such as the FitBit fitness tracker and the Apple Watch, need coders to add functionality and connect people in new ways.

✔ **Machine learning:** For years, databases just stored data. Now, code is finally being written to analyze the data and make intelligent predictions. For example, mapping applications use real-time and historical data to predict traffic and the time your route will take to complete. 23andme, a genetics company, compares your human genome against its database to predict which diseases you are more likely to have. General Electric has outfitted industrial machines such as hospital equipment and jet engines with sensors, and uses historical data to repair machines before they break, decreasing downtime and increasing revenue. Coders will continue to write analytics programs to crunch large datasets and generate predictions with increasing accuracy.

✔ **Interconnected applications:** An application programming interface (API) allows one program to talk to and request data from another external program, which provides a response. Although APIs are powerful, their functionality can be limited and they rarely talk to one another. For example, Dropbox, the storage provider, has an API to allow third-party applications to back up data, and Facebook has an API that lets third-party applications retrieve a user's photos. However, using just those two APIs, you cannot automatically back up every Facebook photo to Dropbox. Companies such as IFTTT (If This Then That) allows users to create recipes that combine APIs.

✔ **Virtual software containers:** Traditionally, software programs could be described as an interconnected web of your code and code written by others. To incorporate someone else's code into your own program, you had to check that both programs were compatible and that any third-party code used by the external program, called a dependency, was also compatible with your code. The process of resolving conflicts was frequently time-consuming and frustrating. One solution is to move away from the current interconnected system of software programming to an independent self-contained system. Docker is one company that hosts an open-source project to help programmers package software and its dependencies into a self-contained program called a *virtual container*. These virtual containers have standardized inputs and outputs, run on many operating systems, and can connect to each other with little need to check for compatibility. Just like standardized shipping cargo containers make it easier and faster to load and unload ships, so too do virtual containers make it easier and faster to package programs to work easily with other programs.

Tracking the Explosion of Coding Jobs

Creating applications and making computer programs work seamlessly requires many people working many hours because every instruction must be explicit. The Bureau of Labor Statistics estimates that across all industries, about 140,000 jobs in computing are being created every year that pay approximately $80,000. In some industries, computing jobs are growing by over 20 percent, which is two to four times the average growth rate across all occupations.

The demand is great, but computer programmers are in short supply. Colleges train the most computer programmers and graduate about 40,000 computer scientists per year. Using current estimates, by 2020 there will be 1,000,000 more jobs than qualified students, representing a $500 billion opportunity. See Figure 1-4.

Table 1-1 shows some of the coding occupations contributing to this boom. Each job is unique, and generally there is not a great deal of switching between jobs. For example, mobile developers don't suddenly become data scientists, or vice versa. When people do switch between these positions, there is usually a training period.

Web developers are typically self-taught; according to census data, less than 40 percent have earned a four-year college degree. Many developers also enter the profession as a quality assurance analyst and then move into a junior web developer role.

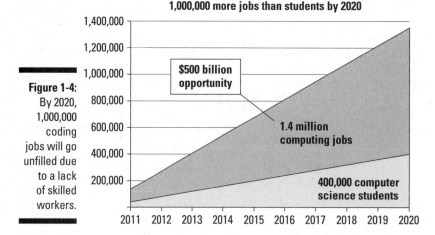

Figure 1-4: By 2020, 1,000,000 coding jobs will go unfilled due to a lack of skilled workers.

Table 1-1	Entry-Level Coding Occupations	
Occupation	*Job Summary*	*Average Salary*
Mobile developer	Code applications that run on mobile devices such as phones and tablets. Also responsible for app performance and user interactions that are easy to complete on a mobile device.	$95,000
Software developer	Develop programs and write code for hardware, software, and network systems.	$93,350
Database administrator	Use specialized software to store and organize data, such as financial information and customer shipping records. Make sure that data is available to users and is secure from unauthorized access.	$77,080
Web developer	Design and create websites. Responsible for both the look and feel of the site, and for technical aspects, such as the website's speed and traffic capacity.	$62,500
Data analyst	Analyze big data using statistics and machine-learning techniques to generate insights and future predictions.	$60,000
Quality assurance analyst	Test programs to ensure that features perform according to specification, and document bugs.	$53,000

Sources: Bureau of Labor Statistics, Indeed.com, Glassdoor.com

Companies Hiring Coding Professionals

There's no way around it — all industries are experiencing a massive shortage of talent who can code. Employers are looking for talent wherever they can find it. People with traditional and nontraditional backgrounds, and those who want to work in an office or work remotely are all finding companies that need help.

The two general types of coding jobs are full-time positions in companies and contract or freelance work.

Full-time jobs

Companies of various sizes hire people who have just learned how to code for full-time positions. The size of the company can have pros and cons when it comes to hiring people who have just learned how to code:

✔ **Large companies:** Companies with more than 1,000 employees, such as Fortune 500 companies and large tech companies including Yahoo!, Google, and Facebook have high standards for hiring employees. Given the number of applications they receive for each open position, recruiters at these companies usually use a strict screening process and grant interviews only to people who have a computer science, math, or engineering-related major. However, for those people who do pass the hiring screen and are eventually hired, there are many resources, both formal programs and people who can help coach and train you to increase your skills.

Almost every large company has an online application. Send in your application online, and then find an advocate, someone at the company who believes in your candidacy, to help your application pass to the interview stage.

✔ **Medium-sized companies:** Of the three types of companies, getting hired at a medium-sized company can be hardest. With their large recruiting departments, candidates have to interview with as many people as in large companies. In addition, medium-sized companies typically do not spend as much money on training as large companies.

One successful strategy to getting hired permanently in a medium-sized company is to freelance first, which helps you build up your reputation and allows the company to assess your skills in a low risk way.

✔ **Startups:** With less than 20 employees, startups often desperately need coding talent and are small enough to make hiring decisions quickly. They don't have a formal recruiting staff, so you should develop a personal connection with the person doing the hiring. Startups don't have extensive training programs, and you are expected to contribute immediately. However, the small company size should help you form personal relationships with your engineering coworkers, who can help answer questions and informally train you.

In the beginning, successful startups often have so much work and are so short staffed that having anyone do the work is better than having no one. For this reason, startups decide on candidates quickly, rather than wait for the best person for each role.

✔ **Government:** City, state, and federal governments and their agencies have thousands of internship and full-time job openings for coders. Depending on the agency, the application process can be time consuming, and require proof of U.S. citizenship, extensive background checks, and completion of qualifying exams. Applicants can use www. usajobs.gov to search across all federal opportunities, and individual state government websites for opportunities in a specific state or city government.

From the source: Tips from a tech recruiter

Yoonie Kim has been a recruiter for technology companies for almost 15 years. She has held recruiting roles at Codecademy, Ning, Meetup, Google, Amazon, and Microsoft. I asked her the following questions:

✔ *Can you share a little about your work experiences?*

I've worked at tech companies of all sizes and stages. I started my career at Microsoft, and worked at large established companies like Amazon and Google, all the way to small and early-stage companies like Ning and Codecademy. I also cofounded my own recruiting company to help smaller startups build out their initial engineering teams. In 2014, I joined Dropbox to help build out the New York and Seattle presence and offices.

✔ *How do you attract and screen candidates?*

People use and have heard of your product, that helps, but I also reach out to candidates when employees refer them to me, and when I see candidates' work online in a blog post, open source project, or talk. When I screen candidates, I'm usually looking for what they've accomplished, and whether they have actually built something meaningful or just maintained a product. Most interview processes start with a phone screen and then on-site interviews, but I try to personalize the interview as much as possible for the candidate. If you have less coding experience, you might be asked about something you just built, while more experienced candidates will jump into a hard problem the company is currently solving.

✔ *What do you screen for?*

At the resume stage, I'm always looking for something interesting that will excite the team and make people want to have a conversation with the candidate. In the actual interview, I'd say 70 percent of the evaluation is technical ability, and the rest of the evaluation is a combination of soft skills and cultural contribution. I used to look for a specific candidate profile, usually a computer science degree and previous tech experience, but I've become more open to people without college degrees, career switchers, and people who have taught themselves to code. I have recruited a few self-taught programmers, and they have gone on to have incredibly successful careers within companies.

✔ *What is a mistake everyone makes in the recruiting process?*

Have a story both about what you have done previously and what you want to do at the company where you are now interviewing. Sometimes candidates don't have much to say about a topic they should know a lot about — themselves! Also, have a product or a feature you want to work on if you're given an offer. It can be hard to advocate for candidates who don't express any preferences.

Freelancing and contract jobs

Companies of all sizes hire freelancers to do discrete projects that are not overly complex and have a definite end date. For example, freelancers often build a website with a few defined pages, create mobile apps, or scrape and store data from websites into databases. Getting some of the initial work performed by a freelancer helps a company see how much time and money a project will cost and whether there is a need to hire a full-time employee.

Contract work also provides freelancers with some valuable benefits. Even for full-time coders, doing some contract work is a great way to build up skills in a new programming language or framework. Also, because coding work can be done from anywhere, freelancers have a good deal of flexibility and don't necessarily have to sit behind a desk in an office. For example, some freelancers travel often for pleasure, and can be found working in cities such as Boston one month and Bali the next month. Finally, some coders freelance full-time, and build their business by doing work for existing clients and pitching new work to client referrals.

One issue with freelancing is that you are always looking for the next job. A few websites, such as Freelancer (www.freelancer.com) and Upwork (www.upwork.com), formerly odesk.com, help provide freelancers with steady work by creating communities that connect employers and freelancers. See Figure 1-5.

These sites create online reputations for both freelancers and companies, which helps each side feel more confident that the work will be completed and the agreed upon amount will be paid.

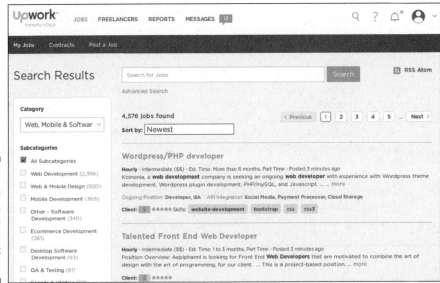

Figure 1-5: Upwork helps freelancers find and bid on contract coding jobs.

Chapter 2

Exploring Coding Career Paths

We shall not cease from exploration, and the end of all our exploring will be to arrive where we started and know the place for the first time.

—T.S. Elliot

For many people, the words "coding career" evoke an image of a person sitting in a dimly lit room typing incomprehensible commands into a computer. The stereotype has persisted for decades — just watch actors such as Matthew Broderick in *War Games* (1983), Keanu Reeves in *The Matrix* (1999), or Jesse Eisenberg in *The Social Network* (2010). Fortunately, these movies are not accurate representations of reality. Just like a career in medicine can lead to psychiatry, gynecology, or surgery, a career in coding can lead to an equally broad range of options.

In this chapter, you see how coding can augment your existing job across a mix of functions, and you explore increasingly popular careers based primarily on coding.

Augmenting Your Existing Job

Many people find coding opportunities in their existing job. It usually starts innocently enough, and with something small. For example, you may need a change made to the text on the company's website, but the person who would normally do that is unavailable before your deadline. If you knew how to alter the website's code, you could perform your job faster or more easily. This section explores how coding might augment your existing job.

Choosing a career path

Coding career paths are extremely varied. For some people, the path starts with using code to more efficiently perform an existing job. For others, coding is a way to transition to a new career. As varied as the career path is, so too are the types of companies that need coders.

As more people carry Internet-capable mobile phones, businesses of every type are turning to coders to reach customers and to optimize existing operations. No business is immune. For example, FarmLogs is a company that collects data from farm equipment to help farmers increase crop yields and forecast profits. FarmLogs needs coders to build the software that collects and analyzes data, and farmers with large operations may need coders to customize the software.

To build or customize software, you'll need to learn new skills. Surprisingly, the time required to learn and start coding can range from an afternoon of lessons to a ten-week crash course to more time-intensive options, such as a four-year undergraduate degree in computer science.

Creative design

Professionals in creative design include those who

- ✔ Shape how messages are delivered to clients
- ✔ Create print media such as brochures and catalogs
- ✔ Design for digital media such as websites and mobile applications

Traditionally, digital designers, also known as visual designers, created *mockups*, static illustrations detailing layout, images, and interactions, and then sent these mockups to developers who would create the web or mobile product. This process worked reasonably well for everyday projects, but feedback loops started becoming longer as mockups became more complex. For example, a designer would create multiple mockups of a website, and then the developer would implement them to create working prototypes, after which the winning mockup would be selected. As another example, the rise of mobile devices has led to literally thousands of screen variations between mobile phones and tablets created by Apple, Samsung, and others. Project timelines increased because designers had to create five or more mockups to cover the most popular devices and screen sizes.

As a designer, one way to speed up this process is to learn just enough code to create working prototypes of the initial mockups that are responsive, which means one prototype renders on both desktop and mobile devices. Then project managers, developers, and clients can use these early prototypes to decide which versions to further develop and which to discard. Additionally, because responsive prototypes follow a predictable set of rules across all devices, creating additional mockups for each device is unnecessary, which further decreases design time. As mobile devices have become more popular, the demand for designers who understand how to create good user interactions (UI) and user experiences (UX) has greatly increased.

Prototyping tools such as InVision and Axure provide a middle option between creating static illustrations and coding clickable prototypes by allowing designers to create working prototypes without much coding. Still, a person with basic coding skills can improve a prototype generated with these tools by making it more interactive and realistic. Designers who can design and code proficiently are referred to as "unicorns" because they are rare and in high demand.

Content and editorial

Professionals in content and editorial perform tasks such as the following:

- Maintain the company's presence on social networks such as Twitter and Facebook
- Create short posts for the company blog and for email campaigns
- Write longer pieces for articles or presentations

At smaller companies, content creation is usually mixed with other responsibilities. At larger companies, creating content is a full-time job. Whether you're blogging for a startup or reporting for *The Wall Street Journal,* writers of all types face the same challenges of identifying relevant topics and backing it up with data.

Traditionally, content was written based on a writer's investigation and leads from a small group of people. For example, you might write a blog post about a specific product feature because a major customer asked about it during a sales call. But what if most of your smaller customers, who you don't speak with regularly, would benefit from a blog post about some other product feature?

As a writer, you can produce more relevant content by writing code to analyze measurable data and use the conclusions to author content. I Quant NY (http://iquantny.tumblr.com), an online blog, is one shining example of data driving content creation. In 2014, the site author, Ben Wellington, analyzed public data on New York City parking tickets, bike usage, and traffic crashes, and wrote about his conclusions. His analysis led to original stories and headlines in major newspapers such as *The New York Times* and *New York Post* (see Figure 2-1).

Figure 2-1:
Article
about a
ticket-
generating
fire hydrant.

Human resources

Those who work in human resources might be expected to do the following:

- ✔ Source and screen candidates for open company jobs
- ✔ Manage payroll, benefits, performance, and training for employees
- ✔ Ensure company compliance with relevant laws, and resolve disputes

Traditionally, HR professionals have not performed much coding in the work-place. The human- and process-driven components of the job generally out-weighed the need for automation that coding typically provides. For example, a dispute between coworkers is usually resolved with an in-person meeting organized by HR, not by a computer program. However, the recruiting function in HR may benefit from coding. Hiring employees has always been challenging, especially for technical positions where the demand for employees far exceeds the supply of available and qualified candidates.

If you are responsible for technical recruiting and want to increase the number of candidates you reach out to and source, one solution is to learn some coding to discover people who may not meet the traditional hiring criteria. For example, a company might ordinarily look for developers from a specific university with at least a 3.0 grade point average.

However, increasingly developers are self-taught and may have dropped out or not attended university at all. A technical recruiter who can evaluate code that self-taught developers have written and made publicly available on sites such as Github or Bitbucket can qualify candidates who previously would have been rejected. Additionally, recruiters working with technical candidates improve outcomes by being able to speak their language.

Companies such as Google and Facebook have taken a technical approach to managing the expensive and difficult problem of finding and retaining employees. These companies perform people analytics on their employees by looking at everyone that applies and analyzing factors that contribute to hiring, promotion, and departure, such as undergraduate GPA, previous employer, interview performance, and on-the-job reviews. At Google, this analysis requires some serious coding because more than two million people apply each year.

Product management

Product managers, especially those working on software and hardware products, perform tasks like the following:

- ✔ Manage processes and people to launch products on time and on budget, maintain existing products, and retire old products
- ✔ Connect all departments that create a product, including sales, engineering, marketing, design, operations, and quality control
- ✔ Guide the product definition, roadmap, and business model based on understanding the target market and customers

The product manager's role can vary greatly because it is a function of the company culture and the product being built. This is especially true for technical products; in some companies, product managers define the problem and engineers design hardware and software to solve those problems. In other companies, product managers not only define the problem but also help design the technical solution.

One of the hardest challenges and main responsibilities of a product manager is to deliver a product on time and within budget. Timelines can be difficult to estimate, especially when new technology is used or existing technology is used in a new way. When you manufacture, say, a chair, it has a set product definition. For a product with a technical component, additional features can creep into the project late in development, or a single feature might be responsible for the majority of time or cost overruns. The product manager helps to keep these variables in check.

The product manager working on a technical product who has some coding skill will be able to better estimate development cycles and anticipate the moving pieces that must come together. In addition, solving technical challenges that arise and understanding the tradeoffs of one solution versus another are easier with some coding background.

Business analysts or integration specialists translate business requirements from customers into technical requirements that are delivered to project managers and that are eventually implemented by back-end engineers.

Sales and marketing

Sales and marketing professionals perform tasks like

- ✔ Segment existing customers and identify new potential customers
- ✔ Generate and convert prospective leads into sold customers
- ✔ Craft product and brand images to reflect company and customer values

Salespeople and marketers expend a great deal of effort placing the right message at the right time to the right customer. For decades, these messages were delivered in newspapers, in magazines, on television, and in radio. Measuring their effect in these channels was difficult, part art and part science. With the movement of messages to the Internet, we can now measure and analyze every customer view and click. Online marketing has created another problem: Online customers generate so much data that much of it goes unanalyzed.

The salesperson or marketer who can code is able to better target customers online. If you're a salesperson, generating leads is the start of the sales funnel, and coding enables you to find and prioritize online website visitors as potential customers. For example, when Uber launched their mobile application, it was available only in San Francisco. The company tracked and analyzed the location of users who opened the app to decide which city to launch in next.

If you are in marketing, identifying *who* to market to is as important as identifying *what* message to market. Website visitors reveal behavioral and demographic data about themselves, including location, web pages visited, visit duration, and often gender, age, employer, and past online purchases. Even moderately successful websites generate tens of millions of records a month, and coding can help spot trends such as the 25-to-29-year-old females in Nebraska who are suddenly interested in but are not purchasing your product. Marketing messages become more efficient when you know the segments you are targeting and how they are responding.

Legal

Professionals providing legal services might perform the following tasks:

- ✔ Identify and manage legal risks in agreements and transactions
- ✔ Ensure ongoing compliance with relevant laws and regulations
- ✔ Review documents such as prior cases, business records, and legal filings
- ✔ Resolve disputes through litigation, mediation, and arbitration

Historically, the legal profession has been resilient to advances in technology. I include it here because if lawyers who code are able to more efficiently perform their jobs, professionals in any other industry should be able to benefit from coding as well.

Coding knowledge may not assist a lawyer with delivering a passionate argument in court or finalizing a transaction between two Fortune 500 companies, but the bulk of a lawyer's time is spent on document review, a task that could benefit from coding knowledge.

When reviewing legal documents, a lawyer might read previous cases in a litigation, check existing patent filings before filing a new patent, or examine a company's contracts in preparation for a merger. All these tasks involve processing large amounts of text, and current legal tools enable, for example, wildcard searching (such as using *new** to find New York, New Jersey, and New Hampshire).

However, the use of *regular expressions* — code that searches for patterns in text — could help lawyers review documents faster and more efficiently. See Figure 2-2.

For example, suppose you are a government lawyer investigating an investment bank for fraudulently selling low-quality mortgages. The investment bank has produced two million documents, and you want to find every email address mentioned in these documents. You could spend months reviewing every page and noting the email addresses, or you could spend a few minutes writing a regular expression that returns every email address automatically.

As the government lawyer reviewing those documents, one of many regular expressions you could use to find email addresses is `.+@.+\..+`. Much like the * wildcard character, each symbol represents a pattern to match. I show it here only as an example, so don't let the code intimidate you. This regular expression first looks for a least one character before and after the @ symbol, and at least one character before and after a period that appears following the @ symbol. This pattern matches the username@domain.com email address format.

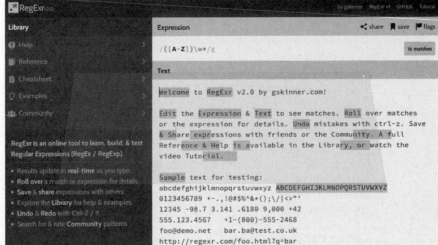

David Zvenyach, a government lawyer and computer programmer, has created two websites of interest to lawyers. The first site, SCOTUS Servo, logs a message whenever the Supreme Court changes an already issued opinion and is available at `https://twitter.com/scotus_servo`. The second site, Coding for Lawyers, teaches lawyers code that could be helpful in the practice of law and is available at `http://codingforlawyers.com`.

Finding a New Coding Job

The career changer looking to transition to a coding job can choose from a variety of roles. This section describes the most popular coding jobs today. In these roles at the entry level, your coding knowledge will be used daily. As you become more skilled and senior, however, your people-management responsibilities will increase while the number of lines of code you write will decrease. For example, Mark Zuckerberg wrote the code for the initial version of Facebook and continued to write code for two years after the website launched, after which he stopped coding for almost six years to focus on managing the team's growth.

Some coding roles may appeal to you to more than others. In addition to understanding jobs available in the market, some self-reflection can help you make the best choice possible. As you review the role descriptions in this section, take a personal inventory of the

✔ Tasks you enjoy and dislike in your current role

✔ Skills you already possess, and the skills you will need to learn

✔ Interests you want to pursue that will make you excited about working every day

Although no job is completely secure, the demand for technical roles is high and continues to grow. The US government estimates that by 2020, more than 1 million computer science related jobs will be unfilled, with 1.4 million available jobs and only 400,000 computer science students trained to fill them.

Front-end web development

Web developers create websites. There are two types of web developers:– front-end developers and back-end developers. Each requires different skills and tasks, which are discussed in this section.

Front-end web developers code everything visible on the web page, such as the layout, image placement and sizing, input features including buttons and text boxes, and the site's general look and feel. These effects are created with three major programming languages: HTML (Hypertext Markup Language), which is used to place text on the page, CSS (Cascading Style Sheet), which styles the text and further contributes to its appearance, and JavaScript, which adds interactivity.

In addition to these three languages, front-end developer job postings reveal a common set of skills that employers are looking for:

✔ **SEO (search engine optimization):** Creating web pages for humans might seem like the only goal, but machines, specifically search engines, are the primary way most users find websites. Search engines "view" web pages differently than humans, and certain coding techniques can make it easier for search engines to index an individual web page or an entire website.

✔ **Cross-browser testing:** Users navigate web pages by using four major browsers (Chrome, Firefox, Internet Explorer, and Safari), each with two or three active versions. As a result, a web developer must be skilled in testing websites across eight or more browser versions. Developing for older browsers is typically more difficult because they support fewer features and require more code to achieve the same effect as modern browsers.

✔ **CSS tools:** Developers use precompilers and CSS frameworks to make coding in CSS easier. *Precompilers* extend CSS functionality with features such as variables and functions, which make it easier to read and maintain CSS code. *CSS frameworks,* such as Bootstrap and Base, provide prewritten HTML and CSS code that makes it easier to develop a website with a consistent look across desktop and mobile devices. Proficiency in all precompilers and frameworks is unnecessary, but knowledge of one precompiler and framework can be helpful.

✔ **JavaScript frameworks:** Developers use prewritten JavaScript code called a *JavaScript framework* to add features to web pages. Some popular JavaScript frameworks are Angular.js and Ember.js. Proficiency in the over thirty JavaScript frameworks is unnecessary, but knowing one or two can be helpful.

Words like HTML, CSS, and JavaScript might seem intimidating at first, especially if you have no prior experience in web development. I mention some terminology here and also in the glossary because knowing these programming language names is the first step to learning more about each of them.

None of the work a web developer does would be possible without product managers and designers. Developers work with product managers to ensure that the product scope and timelines are reasonable. Additionally, product managers make sure that the technical and nontechnical teams are communicating and aligned. Developers also work with designers who create *mockups,* or illustrations of the website, images, and the flow users take to move between web pages. After the mockups are created, front-end developers code the website to match the mockups as closely as possible.

Back-end web development

Back-end web developers code everything that is not visible on the web page but is necessary to support the front-end developer's work. Back-end development happens in the following three places:

✔ **Server:** The *server* is the computer hosting the coding files that include the website application and the database. When you visit www.google.com, for example, your web browser requests the web page from Google servers, which respond with a copy of the web page you see in your browser.

✔ **Application:** The *application* handles the content in web pages sent to users and the changes made to the database. Applications are written using programming languages like Ruby, Python, and PHP, and only run on the server. Proficiency is one language is usually sufficient.

✔ **Database:** The *database* stores website and user data so it is available for future browsing sessions. The simplest database is an Excel spreadsheet, which is ill suited for web development. Databases such as Postgres and MongoDB are optimized for website use; usually only one these databases is used per website.

As an example of back-end web development, suppose that you visit www. amazon.com using your web browser. Your computer makes a request to the Amazon server, which runs an application to determine what web content to serve you. The application queries a database, and past purchases and browsing show that you have an interest in technology, legal, and travel books. The application creates a web page that displays books matching your interests, and sends it to your computer. You see a book on bike trails in New York, and click to purchase it. After you enter your credit card and shipping details, the application stores the information in a database on the server for easy checkout in the future.

For back-end developers, one major part of the job is writing code for the application and database to render web pages in the browser. Employers are interested in additional skills such as these:

- ✔ **Scaling:** Back-end developers must change and optimize application code, servers, and databases to respond to increases in website traffic. Without the right planning, a mention of your website on a morning talk show or in the newspaper could results in a "website not available" error message instead of thousands of new customers. *Scaling* involves balancing the cost of optimizing the website with leaving the configuration as-is.

- ✔ **Analytics:** Every online business, whether large or small, has key website performance indicators, such as new user signups and retention of existing users. Back-end developers can implement and track these metrics by querying information from the website database.

- ✔ **Security:** Websites with a substantial number of users become a target for all types of security risks. Attackers may automate signups, in which fake profiles post spam that promotes unrelated products. Additionally, you may receive a massive amount of traffic in a short period of time, called a *denial of service attack,* which prevents legitimate customers from accessing your website. Or attackers might try to detect weaknesses in your servers to gain unauthorized access to sensitive information such as email addresses, passwords, and credit card numbers. In 2014, major data breaches were uncovered at large corporations including Sony, Target, and JP Morgan. Prevention of these attacks rests, in part, with back-end developers.

The back-end developer is a part of the product team and works closely with front-end developers and product managers. Unlike front-end developers, back-end developers do not interact frequently with designers because the job is not as visual or based on website appearance.

Mobile application development

Mobile application developers create applications that run on cellphones, tablets, and other mobile devices. Mobile applications can be more challenging to create than browser-based websites because users expect the same functionality on a device without a dedicated keyboard and with a smaller screen. In 2014, users purchased and spent more time on mobile devices than traditional PC desktops, marking a major milestone and the continuation of a trend years in the making.

Users today prefer to download and use native mobile applications from an app store, though it is possible to create mobile optimized websites that run in the browser using HTML, CSS, and JavaScript. The two most popular app stores are the Apple App Store, which hosts apps for iOS devices such as iPhones and iPads, and the Google Play Store, which hosts apps for phones that tables running the Android operating system. Developers code apps for iOS devices by using the Objective-C and Swift programming languages, and code apps for Android devices by using Java.

Objective-C, which was invented in 1983, is traditionally and currently used to create iOS apps. Swift is a new programming language created by Apple and released in 2014. This programming language was designed from the ground up as a replacement for Objective-C.

Mobile developers are in high demand as mobile usage overtakes browsing on traditional PCs. In addition to creating apps, employers also value these skills:

- ✔ **Location services:** The service most frequently integrated into and used in mobile applications is location. Maps, reservation, and transportation applications all become more useful when they take into account our current location. However, location services consume battery life rapidly, although specialized techniques can reduce battery drain. Mobile developers who understand these techniques will have a leg up on the competition.

- ✔ **Application testing:** The number of devices that a mobile developer has to consider is staggering. In addition, an errant line of code can cause a mobile application to not install correctly or to leak memory until the application crashes. Mobile application testing software automates the process of testing your application across a variety of device types, saving a huge amount of time and a drawer full of phones. Mobile developers who can integrate testing software such as Crashlytics into their applications will get the data needed to continuously improve their application code.

Mobile application developers work with designers to create easy and intuitive mobile experiences, with back-end developers to ensure that data submitted by or received from the phone is in sync with data on the website, and with product managers so that the application launches smoothly.

Data analysis

Data analysts sift through large volumes of data, looking for insights that help drive the product or business forward. This role marries programing and statistics in the search for patterns in the data. Popular examples of data analysis in action include the recommendation engines used by Amazon to make product suggestions to users based on previous purchases and by Netflix to make movie suggestions based on movies watched.

The data analyst's first challenge is simply importing, cleaning, and processing the data. A website can generate millions of database entries of users' data daily, requiring the use of complicated techniques, referred to as *machine learning*, to create classifications and predictions from the data. For example, half a billion messages are sent per day using Twitter; some hedge funds analyze this data and classify whether a person talking about a stock is expressing a positive or negative sentiment. These sentiments are then aggregated to see whether a company has a positive or negative public opinion before the hedge fund purchases or sells any stock.

Any programming language can be used to analyze data, but the most popular programming languages used for the task are R, Python, and SQL. Publicly shared code in these three languages makes it easier for individuals entering the field to build on another person's work. While crunching the data is important, employers also look for data analysts with skills in the following:

- ✔ **Visualization:** Just as important as finding insight in the data is communicating that insight. Data visualization uses charts, graphs, dashboards, infographics, and maps, which can be interactive, to display data and reduce the complexity such that one or two conclusions appear obvious, as shown in Figure 2-3 courtesy of I Quant NY. Common data visualization tools include D3.js, a JavaScript graphing library, and ArcGIS for geographic data.

- ✔ **Distributed storage and processing:** Processing large amounts of data on one computer can be time intensive. One option is to purchase a single faster computer. Another option, called *distributed storage and processing*, is to purchase multiple machines and divide the work. For example, imagine that we want to count the number of people living in Manhattan. In the distributed storage and processing approach, you might ring odd-numbered homes, I would ring even-numbered homes, and when we finished we would sum our counts.

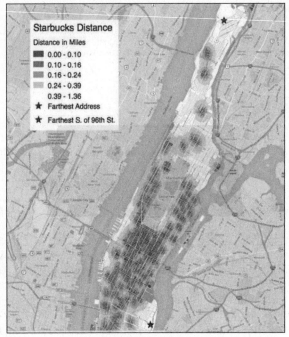

Figure 2-3:
The two
Manhattan
addresses
farthest
away from
Starbucks.

Data analysts work with back-end developers to gather data needed for their work. After the data analysts have drawn conclusions from the data, and come up with ideas on improving the existing product, they meet with the entire team to help design prototypes to test the ideas on existing customers.

Chapter 3

Working as a Coder

> *Work is about a search for daily meaning as well as daily bread, for recognition as well as cash, for astonishment rather than torpor . . .*
>
> —*Studs Terkel*

Some people are born into their occupation. The Queen of England didn't interview for her position as head of state, but for most of us, considerable effort goes into obtaining a job. Every job has many variables that involve much more than just the work, such as compensation, relationships with colleagues, and the potential for career growth. If you understand these variables before your start a new job, you'll increase your chances for success, and potentially save yourself from recruiting or training for a job that won't be a good fit.

In this chapter, you explore the process developers use to write code, who they interact with, and other factors beyond the daily work.

Writing Code by Using a Process

Writing code is much like painting, furniture making, or cooking — it isn't always obvious how the end product was created. However, all programs are created using a process, and two of the most popular processes, as shown in Figure 3-1, used today are

✔ **Waterfall:** A set of *sequential* steps followed to create a program

✔ **Agile:** A set of *iterative* steps followed to create a program

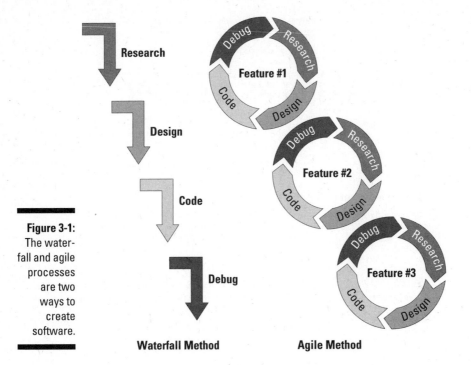

Figure 3-1:
The water-
fall and agile
processes
are two
ways to
create
software.

Let me describe a specific scenario to explain how these two processes work. Imagine you want to build a restaurant app that does the following two things:

✔ It displays restaurant information, such as the hours of operation and the menu.

✔ It allows users to make or cancel reservations.

Using the waterfall method, you'd define everything the app needs to do: You'd design the information display and reservation parts of the app, write documentation for every feature, code the entire app, and then release the app to users.

By contrast, using the agile method, you would define, design, and code only the information-display portion of the app, release it to users, and collect feedback. Based on that feedback, you'd redesign the information display to address major concerns. When you were satisfied with the information-display portion, you'd define, design, and build the reservation part of the app. Again, you would collect feedback and refine the reservation feature to address major concerns. Finally, as product development was finishing you would write the least amount of documentation necessary for the features you actually created.

The agile methodology stresses shorter development times, and has become more popular as the pace of technological change has increased and the cost of creating software has decreased. The agile methodology works especially well in environments where the customer's needs are unclear and product requirements and features change frequently. For example, Instagram started as a photo-sharing app that allowed users to check-in to locations, post pictures, and earn points. Initial feedback was that the app felt cluttered, and so over eight weeks the app was redesigned twice to only include photos and commenting. The newly designed version received one million user signups in ten weeks.

With the waterfall approach's one long development cycle, technology or user preferences may change midway through the project. Still, the waterfall approach remains popular in certain contexts, such as with financial and government software, in which requirements and approval are obtained at the beginning of a project.

The healthcare.gov website, released in October 2013, was developed using a waterfall process. All code testing occurred in September 2013, when the entire system was assembled. Unfortunately, the tests occurred too late and were not comprehensive, so there was not enough time to correct errors before the site was launching publicly.

Regardless of whether you choose the agile or waterfall methodology, coding involves four steps:

1. Research
2. Design
3. Code
4. Debug

On average, you will spend much more time researching, designing, and debugging your app than doing the actual coding, which is the opposite of what you may expect.

Each of these steps is described in the sections that follow.

Researching what you want to build

Your manager comes to you with a feature or product she wants you to build. Before writing any code, it helps to do some investigating. Consider the possibilities for your project as you answer the following questions:

✔ What similar website or app already exists? What technology was used to build it?

✔ Which features should I include — and more importantly exclude — in my work?

✔ Which providers can help create these features? For example, companies such as Google, Yahoo, and Microsoft may have software already built that you could incorporate into your app.

To illustrate, consider the restaurant app mentioned earlier. When conducting market research and answering the preceding three questions, a Google search is usually the best resource. When I searched for *restaurant reservation app,* the results included OpenTable, SeatMe, and Livebookings. The OpenTable app, for example, allows users to reserve a table from restaurants displayed on a map using Google Maps.

In the restaurant app example, you'd want to clarify beforehand the type of restaurant information to provide and how extensive the reservation system portion of the app should be. Defining your program's scope is one of the most important tasks before you begin.

In addition, for each of these questions, you must decide whether to build the feature from scratch or use an existing provider. For example, when providing restaurant information, do you want to just show the name, cuisine, address, telephone number, and hours of operation, or do you also want to show restaurant menus and reviews? When displaying restaurant data, do you prefer extensive coverage of a single geographical area, or do you want coverage in many cities even if that means you'd cover fewer restaurants in any specific area?

MenuPage, a site that aggregated restaurant menus, initially took the first approach and extensively covered a few major cities such as New York, Chicago, Los Angeles, and San Francisco. By contrast, Savored, a company that offered a 30 percent discount on food during restaurant off-peak times, used the second approach and worked with twenty to thirty restaurants in each of twenty to thirty cities.

Designing your app

Your app's visual design incorporates all your research and describes how your users will interact with every page and feature. Because your users will be accessing your site from desktop, laptop, and mobile devices, you want to make sure that you create a *responsive* (multidevice) design and carefully consider how your site will look on all these devices.

At this stage of the process, a general web designer, illustrator, or user interface specialist will help create visual designs for the app.

The type types of visual designs, which are shown in Figure 3-2, are

- ✔ **Wireframes:** Low-fidelity website drawings that show structurally the ways your content and your site's interface interact

- ✔ **Mockups:** High-fidelity website previews that include colors, images, and logos

Figure 3-2:
Wireframes (left) are simple site renderings, whereas mockups (right) show full site previews.

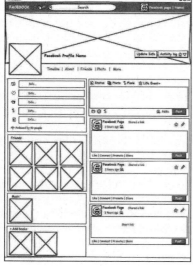

Balsamiq is a popular tool used to create wireframes. For creating mockups, professionals often use Adobe Photoshop, Adobe Illustrator, or Sketch. However, you can create your app designs and avoid paying for additional software by using PowerPoint (PC), Keynote (Mac), or the free and open-source OpenOffice.

Professional designers often create mockups using graphic *layers*, which isolate individual site elements. A properly created layered file helps developers more easily write the code for those website elements.

In addition to visual design, complex apps will also have technical designs and decisions to finalize. For example, if your app stores and retrieves user data, you need a database to perform these tasks. Initial decisions at this stage include choosing the type of database, the database provider, and the method for integrating the database into the application.

Coding your app

When the research and design are complete, you're ready to code your application. In everyday web development, you would begin by coding certain pages and features. Knowing how much to code and when to stop can be tough. Developers call the first iteration of an app the *minimum viable product* — meaning you've coded just enough to test your app with real users and receive feedback. If no one likes your app or thinks it's useful, it's best to find out as soon as possible.

An app is the sum of its features, and for any individual feature it's a good idea to write the minimum code necessary and then add to it. For example, your restaurant app may have a toolbar at the top of the page with drop-down menus. Instead of trying to create the entire menu at once, it's better to create the toolbar menu options first, and create the drop-down menu effect later.

Another timesaving approach is to reuse your own or other people's code. For example, a programmer may have already written code for drop-down menus, and published that code under an open-source license. Use a search engine to find code others have written, rather than reinvent the wheel.

Projects can involve *front-end developers,* who code the appearance of the app, and *back-end developers,* who code the logic and create the databases. A *full-stack developer* can do both front-end and back-end development. On large projects, it's common to have specialized front-end and back-end developers, along with project managers who ensure that everyone is communicating with each other and adhering to the schedule.

Debugging your code

Debugging is a natural part of any application. The computer always follows your instructions exactly, and yet no program ever works as you expect it to.

Debugging can be frustrating. Three of the more common mistakes to watch out for are

- ✔ **Syntax errors:** These errors are caused by misspelling words or commands, omitting characters, or including extra characters. Some languages, such as HTML and CSS, are more forgiving of these errors and your code will still work even with some syntax errors. Other languages, such as JavaScript, are more particular and your code won't run when any such error is present.

- ✔ **Logic errors:** With a logic error, your syntax is correct but the program behaves differently than you expected. One example of a logic error is when the prices of the items in a shopping cart of an e-commerce site do not sum up to the correct total. Logic errors are harder to fix than syntax errors.

- ✔ **Display errors:** With display errors, your program might run and work properly but won't appear properly. This type of error occurs mostly in web applications. Because web apps run on many types of devices, browsers, and screen sizes, extensive testing is the only way to catch this type of error.

The word *debugging* was popularized in the 1940s by Grace Hopper, who fixed a computer error by removing a moth from a computer.

Compensating a Coder

"Do what you love and you'll never work a day in your life" is the common saying, but money, not love, pays the bills. Companies compensate coders not only with a salary, but also with benefits, equity, advancement, and perks. Compensation packages vary based on seniority and role. You can negotiate some types of compensation, but will largely have to accept the market standard for others.

To understand whether an offer is fair or competitive, you must first determine your market value if you were paid only in cash. Variables such as location, industry, title, and job description affect your perceived market value. In this section, you find resources to help you make your own assessment.

After you know your market value, decrease the cash value of that offer as you increase the other dimensions. For example, suppose one job pays $100,000 but has little opportunity for advancement. Another pays $80,000 per year but the company is growing so fast that you'll likely be promoted quickly. To choose between the two offers, you would need to determine the value of the opportunity for promotion.

Salary and equity

Salary and *equity* (an ownership stake in the company) are the most visible and widely used benchmarks when looking for a job. Measuring and comparing salaries is easy but doing so with equity can be more complicated. Equity is either granted as *common stock,* which is an outright ownership stake in the company, or as *options,* which are the right to purchase for cash an equity stake in the company.

According to the Department of Labor, entry-level software developers across all companies earn between $60,000 and $80,000 per year. Compensation at startups is similar, with junior software engineers earning $50,000 to $100,000 and up to 0.25 percent in equity. See Figure 3-3.

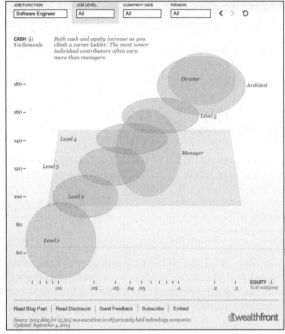

Figure 3-3: Compensation data for junior software engineers by Wealthfront.

The greater the risk of joining a company, the more equity you receive. A well-capitalized and profitable company that pays a market salary will offer far less equity than a startup company without a revenue model or funding. Expect as much as 50 percent equity if you join someone else in a garage, less than 1 percent if you receive a competitive salary, and somewhere between 1 percent and 50 percent if you receive a below-market salary. See more salary and equity details at www.wealthfront.com/tools/startup-salary-equity-compensation.

Equity is used more frequently in the technology industry than in other industries. For companies that eventually mature and go public on a stock exchange, equity compensation can generate individual employee wealth. Bill Gates and Mark Zuckerberg, for example, both made their billions not from their annual salaries but from equity. For public companies and late-stage private companies, the equity issued to you has a relatively stable and predictable value.

Cash is scarce in new private technology companies, such as startups, so they pay employees lower than market salaries but grant more equity than a public company. They figure that the equity will be worth more in the future when the company is successful. The caveat: Greater than 90percent of early-stage private companies fail, so the value of your equity is volatile. When accepting a job at a startup, you may feel like you're joining the next Facebook, but you should treat your equity as a lottery ticket — worth nothing today but potentially worth something in the future.

For information on different types of equity a company can grant and the resulting tax consequences, go to www.nceo.org/articles/stock-options-restricted-phantom-sars-espps.

Equity documents are always long and confusing, and slight wording changes can greatly favor the company instead of the employee. If the amount of equity is a large portion of your total compensation, seek qualified legal counsel to review your employment documents before you sign.

Benefits and perks

The demand for coders is so high that companies, especially in the technology sector, provide numerous employee benefits and perks. For example, Google famously provides employees with gourmet meals, free massages, and on-site daycare.

Although benefits and perks should not be the reason for joining a company, they help make daily life more comfortable. Here are some common perks:

- ✔ **Healthcare:** Medical and dental coverage with a low deductible and low copay is standard at large companies and at startups that have received funding.

- ✔ **Parental leave:** Large tech companies offer more than 15 weeks of paid leave for the birth of a child, more than any other industry. Depending on the company size, parental leave may be either paid or unpaid.

- ✔ **Flexible work and vacation policies:** Companies of all sizes offer flexible start times, remote work, and generous vacation policies. Some smaller startups even have unlimited vacation time policies, allowing you to take as much leave as you like, although presumably your vacation may become permanent if you take too much time.

- ✔ **401(k):** Company-sponsored retirement accounts are common among larger public companies but rarely seen at startups except for late-stage large ones.

- ✔ **Catered meals:** Large and small tech companies alike provide meals prepared by chefs in-house or ordered from local vendors.

- ✔ **Transportation:** Large companies have shuttle buses to make commuting easier, and some smaller companies provide transportation vouchers.

- ✔ **Continuing education:** Companies want you to keep learning and will often subsidize expenses for classes to help you learn new technologies and for conferences so you can promote the company and meet other developers.

- ✔ **Equipment purchases:** Except at the smallest startups, companies will provide you with a work laptop and often let you customize it to your specifications.

Many of these perks are non-negotiable. The ability to work remotely, however, is one perk with flexibility. Because coding work can be done anywhere, you may be able to work remotely and appear in person one week a month or even less frequently.

Advancement

Company size, industry, and market growth affect your advancement, which should be considered when benchmarking your overall compensation package. In fast growing industries such as healthcare, insurance, and technology, people can join a company near its inception and lead major divisions just a few years later. For example, Marissa Mayer, an early Google employee, became the VP of Search after five years at the company, left Google after thirteen years to become the CEO of Yahoo!, and at the age of thirty-seven is the youngest CEO of a Fortune 500 company.

Restrictions on employment

The compensation and benefits detailed previously are usually subject to the following restrictions:

- ✔ **Vesting and clawback:** When you start coding for a company, they make a significant investment in you to bring you up to speed. To make sure that investment pays off, companies incentivize you to stay by *vesting*, or granting your equity package in installments.

Usually, your equity will vest over four years, with 25 percent granted after one year of employment, and the remaining equity granted on a monthly basis. If you leave before four years, you keep only your vested equity and forfeit the unvested equity. Similarly, some companies *claw back*, or require partial repayment of, salary and upfront bonuses if you leave before some time limit, usually one year.

✔ **Noncompete:** The enforceability of a noncompete restriction varies from state to state, but generally the clause prevents you from working in the future at a company that competes with your current employer. The employer wants to prevent an employee from using sensitive intellectual property to aid a competitor; the employee wants to continue using and developing specialized skills. Usually, to decrease the burden on the employee, the noncompete clause is limited either by time or by geography. For example, the language may say that you cannot work for any competitor for up to one year or for any competitor within 50 miles of any company location. In either case, negotiate to minimize the effect of a noncompete clause.

Noncompete agreements governed by California law are generally void, except in a narrow set of circumstances involving the sale or shutdown of an entire business.

Joining a company versus freelancing

Formally joining a company and enjoying the benefits just described may be ideal for some. Others, however, want the flexibility provided by freelancing, or working as a contractor-for-hire.

For someone just beginning a coding career, taking on smaller freelance jobs is a great way to build up a portfolio to show potential future full-time employers. For more experienced coders, freelancing can supplement income and provide higher pay than full-time work, especially when the employer is short staffed and on a tight deadline.

For highly experienced coders who know the latest cutting-edge programming languages, so many companies demand their skills that freelance work can become a full-time job. For example, when Apple first released the iPhone (and even today), so many companies wanted an iPhone app that programmers with the necessary skills could engage multiple companies at once. In addition to higher pay, freelancers can also work anywhere — a beach in Bali or a sailboat in Saint-Tropez — but the work comes with less job security and fewer benefits, and can be lonely.

TIP

Visit www.remoteok.io for a listing of companies advertising jobs that can be performed remotely. Similarly, www.nomadlist.com lists the best cities for the remote worker, ranked by cost of living, weather, Internet access, and safety.

A Week in the Life of a Coder

Coders hold a variety of jobs, from developer to data analyst. Regardless of their role, all coders spend many hours writing code, debugging errors, meeting with teammates (virtually or in-person), and reviewing feedback from customers. Whether you're a full-time developer at a startup like Instacart or a big technology company like Amazon, your typical week might look like the following:

Monday

I have no set start time to go into work, but I usually get there by 9 a.m. on Monday because the company has a 10 a.m. all-hands meeting, where the team shares work updates, new hires, and events during the week. I spend the rest of the morning catching up on email from the weekend and reviewing code that developers have submitted before it is pushed, or uploaded, to the web server. I find a few lines of code that might create bugs, so I write email the developers who wrote the code for more information and schedule a meeting if needed.

After lunch, I'm supposed to be working a new feature: an email alert that is sent when an item goes on sale that was in the customer's shopping cart but did not result in a purchase. This feature is part of a planned website overhaul that the company will be launching at the end of the week. Instead, I check a few of my favorite websites, such as Hacker News (news.ycombinator.com), Techcrunch (www.techcrunch.com), and Reddit (www.reddit.com). I get sucked into reading some articles about the sensors on Apple Watch. After an hour, I'm back on track. I've planned how this feature will work technically, but I need to resolve a few issues. I need to know how far back in time I should check the shopping cart, and whether an email alert should happen for all sales or only deep discounts. I send a few emails to my product manager, write some more code, and leave by 7 p.m.

Tuesday

Tuesday starts off normally, and I'm in my desk at 10 a.m. After my routine check of email, I pick up where I left off yesterday coding the alert feature. I need to complete the code and test it before I present it at the Wednesday afternoon product meeting.

I eat lunch at my desk, and watch an Amazon presentation on their new content delivery network, thinking about how it could improve our site speed and prevent attacks.

Mid-afternoon, I receive numerous alerts and email messages saying that the website is down. I drop everything and spend the rest of the afternoon with the four other developers reviewing and reversing changes made to the website in the last 24 hours. The pressure is on to find what is causing the error. Eventually, we find that our website server software automatically upgraded database drivers to a new version that conflicted with the software used on the rest of the site. We roll back the software, using an older version of the driver, and turn off automatic updates. It's late at night before I work to finish coding the email alert feature.

Wednesday

I spend Wednesday morning in a race to test the email alert feature, and finalize the remaining details, such as choosing the address from which the email should originate, dealing with bounced emails, and implementing tracking to see whether customers click and purchase products shown in the emails.

The product meeting starts. See Figure 3-4. I haven't completely finished — some emails are not being sent and I'm not sure why. But for now, I've met the internal deadline.

Figure 3-4:
Product meetings usually occur weekly to discuss progress and obstacles.

Courtesy of wwworks via Flickr

The rest of the day is spent on my least favorite activity — bug squashing. One monitor displays my code editor, and the other monitor displays a list of all site bugs and their priority. I scan the list looking for a high-priority bug that I can fix today.

After four hours of squashing bugs, I head home. Usually, on Wednesday nights, a company engineer or an external speaker gives an engineering talk, but tonight I'm going to work on one of my side projects. Inspired by a $180 flight I took from New York to Milan, I'm creating an app that will send an email and text message when a deeply discounted or mistaken airfare is published.

Thursday

On Thursday, I hear back from the product manager, and have a list of updates to make to the email alert feature. One main issue is that the feature specification calls for animated effects on the website along with the email alert. These effects are easy to implement on newer browsers, but some customers use Internet Explorer 8 and supporting that browser is difficult. I meet with the product manager and designer to discuss a few comprises. I keep testing and fixing bugs that pop up.

In the afternoon, I have four candidates to interview for a junior back-end developer position. I need to choose a few challenging code examples to see how the candidates solve problems. I'll also assess whether the candidates have researched the company and whether they would fit in with the culture.

Friday

I've tested the email alert feature, and on Friday I think I've fixed all the bugs. I check one of the email alerts, and it appears correctly on an Android phone but has incorrectly sized figures on an iPhone. I find another developer more experienced with HTML and CSS, and we work together to debug the issue. By 4 p.m. we've solved all the major problems. I put the email alert feature in the queue to be reviewed by another developer. With that developer's approval, the app will be released to all users.

Over the weekend, I'll check email deliverability rates, and whether users have sent feedback through email or on Twitter. For now, I'm off to a happy hour with other coworkers to close out the week.

Chapter 4

Understanding Key Coding Concepts

> *Thoughts without content are empty, intuitions without concepts are blind.*
>
> —*Immanuel Kant*

As you continue learning about coding careers, whether researching on the Internet or having conversations with other programmers, you'll hear some words and phrases repeatedly. You might hear a developer say, "I started on the back end, but front end work is more visual and definitely my style." Or "Merging my branch with master, deployed to production, seeing your work live is what makes this so much fun."

A few key coding concepts crop up in almost every conversation on coding. After you understand these concepts, you'll be better equipped to participate in the conversation. Much like following a baseball game, you might not know what the infield fly rule is, but knowing the basics of strikes, outs, walks, and runs makes it easier to understand the more obscure rules.

In this chapter, you discover key coding concepts such as developing for the front end and back end, storing data in databases, version control, and big data basics.

Developing for the Front End and Back End

When browsing a website or using an application, the experience is seamless and cohesive as you move from one screen to another, reading and entering information as needed. The code for websites and programs can be divided into four categories, as shown in Figure 4-1, according to the code's function:

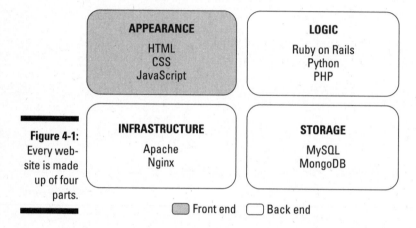

Figure 4-1: Every website is made up of four parts.

- ✔ **Appearance:** The visible part of the website, including content layout and any applied styling, such as font size, font typeface, and image size. This category is called the *front end* and is created using languages such as HTML, CSS, and JavaScript.

- ✔ **Logic:** Determines the content to show and when to show it. For example, a New Yorker accessing a news website should see New York weather, whereas Chicagoans accessing the same site should see Chicago weather. This category is part of the group called the *back end* and is created using languages such as Ruby on Rails, Python, and PHP. These back-end languages can modify the HTML, CSS, and JavaScript displayed to the user.

- ✔ **Storage:** Saves any data generated by the site and its users. User-generated content, preferences, and profile data must be stored for retrieval later. This category is part of the back end and is stored in databases such as MongoDB and MySQL.

✔ **Infrastructure:** Delivers the website from the server to you, the client machine. When the infrastructure is properly configured, no one notices it. But it can become noticeable when a website becomes unavailable due to high traffic from events such as presidential elections, the Super Bowl, or natural disasters. Web servers such as Apache and Nginx receive requests from clients and respond by sending copies of website code. Without the proper configuration a surge of traffic will generate requests faster than the web server can respond, resulting in error messages.

Usually, website developers specialize in one or at most two of these categories. For example, a developer might understand the front end and logic languages, or specialize in only databases. Website developers have strengths and specializations, and their expertise outside these areas is limited, much in the same way that Kanye West, a terrific rapper, would likely make a terrible harp player in a symphony orchestra.

The rare website developer proficient in all four of these categories is referred to as a *full stack developer*. Usually, smaller companies hire full stack developers, whereas larger companies require the expertise that comes with specialization.

Each feature you see on a web page requires set up for the front end and back end. For example, let's say you're building a social network, and you want to include user profiles. First, on the front end you'll need to design how each profile screen looks and functions. Next, on the back end, you'll need to select, install, and set up a database that will allow you to create, retrieve, update, and delete profiles as needed. Finally, you'll need to make your database accessible to web and mobile applications. Depending on which operating system your server is using, you may need to upgrade the entire operating system or key libraries to resolve compatibility issues before you can install the database.

Back end as a service (BAAS) providers reduce the time and effort you spend on back-end installations and setup by maintaining ready-to-use servers, which you can rent. To install a service, like a database, you click a button; the installation happens automatically on the server and you don't need to worry about software incompatibilities. Any libraries or dependencies needed by the database are installed by the BAAS provider, which also handles keeping the servers up and running, upgrades, and security patches. Some of the more popular BAAS providers are Heroku, for web apps, and Parse, for mobile apps.

Storing Data in SQL and NoSQL Databases

Website and applications use databases to permanently store data to be retrieved at a later time. The data to be stored could be user credentials, pictures, product information, status updates, tweets, or just about anything else. The key consideration for any type of database is its *scalability,* or the capability to handle more data with increasing frequency. Over the last forty years, two types of databases have emerged for storing data — SQL databases and NoSQL databases.

SQL databases

SQL, or *Structured Query Language,* is the standard language for relational databases. A *relational database* stores data in tables of columns and rows, with a unique key assigned to each row. This unique key is then used to create relationships between data in related tables. For example, if a university were building a student database, they might create the following:

- ✔ Student table with student first and last names, address information, phone number, and emergency contact information. Each student would also have a unique key (student ID).

- ✔ Student_Courses table with each student's unique key, the course's unique key (course ID), and the student's final grade.

- ✔ Courses table with the course's unique key, course name, professor's name, location, and meeting time.

The tables and the predefined relationship between data elements, as shown in Figure 4-2, make a database relational. You might wonder why multiple tables are needed, when instead you could represent all the information in one big table. Two reasons are data consistency and data accuracy. If the name of a course changed and you were using one big table, you would have to find and change all instances of the course name. With one course table, you could change the course name just once. SQL databases work best when data is not repeated and is instead linked using multiple tables.

The SQL programming language accesses and modifies databases by using SQL queries. A SQL query is inserted into the code of the programming language you're using (Ruby, Python, or PHP), and the results of the query are then output to your website or data analytics program. If you're setting up the database yourself, you might want to install a popular database management systems such as MySQL or PostgreSQL. Alternatively, if you're using a BAAS provider for your application, your database can be installed automatically.

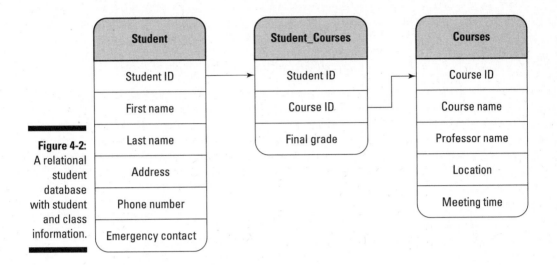

Figure 4-2:
A relational
student
database
with student
and class
information.

NoSQL databases

NoSQL databases take advantage of advances in hardware to build faster and more efficient databases. Historically, CPUs and storage were expensive, so databases were designed to minimize cost and resources used. If the database grew too large, or the queries started running slowly, the database was moved to a more powerful computer with additional storage.

Today, two things have happened that challenge assumptions used by SQL databases. First, hardware prices of storage and CPUs have dropped, while hard drives have become bigger and CPUs have become more powerful. Second, the amount of data that needs to be stored has increased, and it is not always clear in advance what data will be collected and stored. For example, Google processes 24 petabytes (1000 terabytes) of data daily — the average consumer hard drive is a little over 1 terabyte.

NoSQL databases are distributed, which means they are stored and processed across multiple servers. Popular NoSQL databases include MongoDB, CouchDB, and Redis. A NoSQL database system has the following advantages:

- ✔ **No schema:** Unlike with a SQL database, you do not define the data relationships beforehand. NoSQL databases allow you to change the format or type of data being stored at any time.

- ✔ **Scalable:** If your database becomes too large, you can easily add another relatively cheap server without any downtime. For SQL databases, scaling your database requires buying an expensive server and experiencing downtime to migrate and install the database on a new system.

> ✓ **Cheap:** You can use inexpensive consumer-level hardware for a NoSQL database. For even greater ease, you can use a product such as Amazon Web Services (AWS) to cheaply rent storage space and set up a NoSQL database with just a click, without buying physical servers.

NoSQL databases also spread the processing load across multiple CPUs. In a process called MapReduce, a large data set is divided into smaller data sets, which are each processed independently. The results from these individual data sets are then reduced back into a single data set or result. For example, suppose you want to find the Facebook user with the most friends. Instead of using one computer to search Facebook's 1.5 billion users, you could split the users into fifteen data sets of 100,000 users each, and then map each data set to one of fifteen computers. Each computer would process its list to find the user with the most friends, after which each result would be reduced into one smaller data set of fifteen names. The final operation would find the user with the most friends from this smaller list of fifteen users.

NoSQL databases have many advantages, but there are some obstacles as well. The database system is relatively new, so there is less technical support and fewer people with expertise to set up, administer, and develop NoSQL databases. Additionally, because running simple queries in NoSQL databases can be difficult, doing analytics and business reporting for NoSQL databases is not as developed and is much harder than doing similar work for SQL databases.

Saving Your Code in a Repository

Version control systems and code repositories allow developers to work together. The code for the front end or back end, along with the queries you write to retrieve data from databases, are initially stored on your own computer. However, if you work on a team — and most coding jobs are team based — you need a version control system so that code on your computer can be shared with other developers without creating conflicts from differing versions.

If you've ever had a folder with filenames like Resume_Nov_2014_v1, Resume_Nov_2014_v2, and Resume_Jan_2015_v1, you've created a version control system for files. Similarly, the track changes feature in word processors is a version control system for content in a file. Version control systems for code track files and their content, and store code in centralized code repositories that are shared with other programmers. Typically, each developer has a local copy of the code, and everyone uses one centralized code repository.

Git is one of the most popular version control systems, and GitHub is one of the most popular code repositories. Other version control systems are CVS, SVN, and Mercurial.

The most basic version control system commands are *checking in* and *checking out* files. You check in a file when you add it to the code repository, and you check out a file by making a local copy of a file from the code repository. After you check out and change a file, you can either check in the updated file back to the code repository, or discard your copy and leave the original as-is.

Every time you check in a file, add comments to the file so others can easily see at a glance what has changed without reading the entire file.

Sometimes conflicts can occur. For example, suppose you checked out a file with code for a restaurant's home page, and you changed the image on the front page from a hotdog to a cheeseburger. While you were working on the file, a coworker changed the image on the front page from a hotdog to a milk shake and added an image of an ice cream cone. If your coworker checks in the file before you, and you try to check in your version of the file, you would receive a warning from the version control system alerting you to a conflict. You would either need to overwrite your coworker's changes with your own, or check out the version of the file with the milk shake and ice cream cone, replace the milk shake image with the cheeseburger image, delete the ice cream cone, and check in the file again.

Advanced version control system commands include branching and merging files. Imagine you had a crazy idea to add a cooking school to the restaurant web page. Instead of changing the existing files, you can make a copy of the master version of the files in the code repository called a *branch,* as shown in Figure 4-3. You can keep checking in and checking out files from the branch as you add code and content for the cooking school. After you finish and the restaurant owner approves your cooking school addition, you can then *merge* the changes back into the master version of the files.

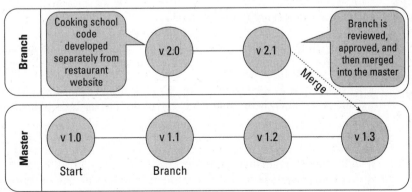

Figure 4-3: Branching code, making changes, and merging it back to the master version.

Before merging your changes, your coworkers may do a *code review* to check the quality of your code, typically making sure your code is bug-free and well documented.

Optimizing Code for Search Engines

The phrase "If you build it, they will come" was used in the movie *Field of Dreams* about an Iowa corn farmer who built a baseball field and suddenly players appeared to use the field. Although viral hits do happen, for the most part the saying does not hold true for technology products. Just building a website or an app will result in thousands of visitors, downloads, or substantial other traffic.

The most reliable way to bring in traffic is to rank highly in a search engine for certain keywords. People using search engines such as Google, Bing, or Yahoo! enter keywords and typically click one of the first ten results. The technique of increasing your site's visibility to be within the top ten search engine results for a particular set of keywords is called *search engine optimization (SEO)*.

Search engines rank results by using two factors: domain authority and page authority. *Domain authority* describes how high a particular domain ranks in search results, based on the domain's trustworthiness, and the number of links from other highly ranked domains. *Page authority* describes how high a specific page will rank in search results. Page authority is based on how many other highly ranked sites link to this specific web page, the keywords used in hyperlinks on other pages, and the keywords on the page itself.

One of the most reliable ways to improve your search ranking is to get more links from other highly ranked pages.

Strategies that follow search engine guidelines and focus on attracting a human audience are called *white hat SEO techniques,* while strategies that use borderline unethical techniques to trick the programs that crawl websites are called *black hat SEO techniques.* When search engines discover sites that use black hat SEO techniques, they are penalized in the rankings.

Because web pages are automatically crawled for content, search engines generally recommend creating keyword-rich text content, using the title and headings, and not displaying important information in an image. These tips directly affect how you write the code for a web page because presenting information with complex code may affect the capability of search engines to read your web page. Analytics packages such as Google Analytics track visitors so you can see over time the effect SEO is having on your website.

Part II
Technologies Used When Coding

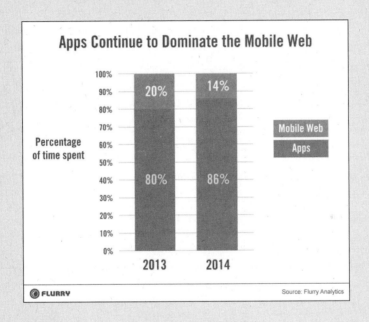

Apps Continue to Dominate the Mobile Web

Check out www.dummies.com/extras/gettingacodingjob for tips on choosing an API.

In this part . . .

- ✓ Learn how basic websites are made
- ✓ Understand advanced programming languages
- ✓ Differentiate between mobile web and native apps
- ✓ See the programming languages used to analyze data

Chapter 5

Creating a Website

• •

• •

> *The web as I envision it, we have not seen it yet. The future is still so much bigger than the past.*
>
> —*Tim Berners-Lee, inventor of HTML*

Many people start learning to code by building basic websites using HTML, CSS, and JavaScript. These easy-to-learn programming languages are visual, so you can see the product of your hard work displayed on the page. In addition, these languages form the basic building blocks of all websites used on the Internet.

You start by building static web pages with content that does not change often or at all, such as the menu page on a restaurant website. As you gain experience, you'll build more complex websites with dynamic content, which changes based on user preferences and inputs.

In this chapter, you learn the basics involved in using HTML, CSS, and JavaScript.

What Do HTML, CSS, and JavaScript Do?

HTML, or *HyperText Markup Language,* tells the browser how to display text and images on a web page. Think about how you create a document with a word processor. Whether you use Microsoft Word, WordPad, Apple Pages, or another application, your word processor has a main window in which you type text, and a menu or a toolbar with multiple options to structure and style that text (see Figure 5-1). You can create headings, insert pictures, underline text, and much more. Similarly, you can use HTML to structure and style text and other elements that appear on a website.

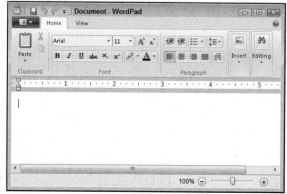

Figure 5-1:
The layout
of a word
processor.

Markup language documents, such as HTML documents, are just plain text files. Unlike documents that can be viewed only with the word processor used to create the document, you can view an HTML file using any web browser on any type of computer.

HTML files are plain text files that appear styled only when viewed with a browser.

CSS, or *Cascading Style Sheet*, styles HTML elements with greater control than HTML. Take a look at Figure 5-2. On the left is a Facebook page as you'd see it in your browser. On the right is the same Facebook page without the CSS styling; all the images and text appear left-justified, borders and shading disappear, and the text has minimal formatting.

Figure 5-2:
Facebook
with CSS
(left) and
without
(right).

JavaScript creates and modifies web page elements, and interacts with the existing web page HTML and CSS. See Figure 5-3. When you visit a web page containing JavaScript, your browser downloads the JavaScript code and runs it *client side* (on your machine).

JavaScript is different from another programming language called Java. In 1996, Brendan Eich, at the time a Netscape engineer, created LiveScript. As part of a marketing decision, LiveScript was renamed to JavaScript to try and benefit from the reputation of the then-popular Java.

JavaScript has continued to evolve. In the last decade, its most important innovation has allowed developers to add content to web pages without requiring the user to reload the page. This technique, called *AJAX* (asynchronous JavaScript), might sound trivial, but it has led to the creation of cutting-edge browser experiences, such as Gmail (shown in Figure 5-4).

Before AJAX, the browser would display new data on a web page only after waiting for the entire web page to reload. This technique slowed down the user experience, especially when viewing web pages with frequent real — time updates, such as news, sports updates, and stock information. With AJAX, the browser could communicate with a server in the background, and update the current web page with new information.

Figure 5-3: JavaScript can create the date picker found on travel websites.

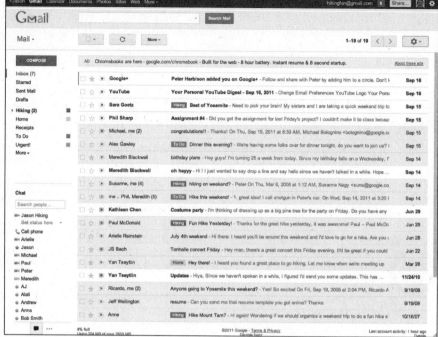

Figure 5-4:
Gmail uses
AJAX,
which lets
users read
new emails
without
reloading
the web
page.

Here is an easy way to think about AJAX: Imagine you're at a coffee shop and have just ordered a coffee after waiting in a long line. Before asynchronous JavaScript, you would have to wait patiently at the coffee bar until you received your coffee before doing anything else. With asynchronous JavaScript, you can read the newspaper, find a table, phone a friend, and do multiple other tasks until the barista calls your name, alerting you that your coffee is ready.

Common HTML Tasks and Tags

HTML is used on every page you browse on the Internet. The purpose of HTML is to create the basic page layout and put text and images on the web page.

In a word processor, you typically style text by highlighting it with your cursor, and then applying an effect, such as bold or italics. With HTML, instead of pointing and clicking, you use special text keywords called *elements*, which apply a special effect.

The browser recognizes an element and applies its effect if the following three conditions exist:

✔ The element is a letter, word, or phrase with special meaning. For example, h1 is an element that applies a header effect, with bold text and a large font size.

✔ The element is enclosed with a left-angle bracket (<) and a right-angle bracket (>), such as <h1>. An element enclosed in this way is called a *tag*.

✔ An opening tag (such as <h1>) is followed by a closing tag (</h1>). Note that the closing tag differs from the opening tag by the addition of a forward slash after the first left bracket and before the element.

When all three conditions are met, the text between the opening and closing tags is styled with the tag's defined effect.

For a better understanding of these three conditions, check out the following example code:

```
<h1>This is a big heading with all three conditions</h1>
h1 This is text without the < and > sign surrounding the tag /h1
<rockstar>This is text with a tag that has no meaning to the browser</rockstar>
This is regular text
```

You can see how a browser would display this code in Figure 5-5.

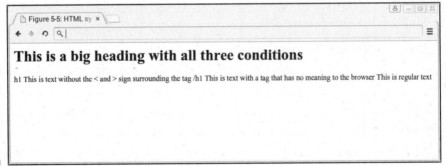

Figure 5-5: The example code displayed in a browser.

The browser applies a header effect to "This is a big heading with all three conditions" because h1 is a header tag and all three conditions for a valid HTML tag exist:

✔ The browser recognizes the h1 element.

✔ The h1 element is surrounded with a left (<) and right angle bracket (>).

✔ The opening tag (<h1>) is followed by text and a closing tag (</h1>).

Note how the `h1` tag itself does not appear in the heading. The browser only displays text between a properly formatted opening and closing HTML tag.

The remaining lines of code are displayed as plain text because they do not fulfill all three conditions. On the second line of code, the `<h1>` tag is missing the left and right brackets, which violates the second condition. The third line of code violates the first condition because `rockstar` is not a recognized HTML element. (After you finish this chapter, however, you may feel like a rock star!) Finally, the fourth line of code is displayed as plain text because it has no opening tag preceding the text and no closing tag following the text, which violates the third condition.

Every left-angle bracket must be followed after the element with a right-angle bracket. In addition, every opening HTML tag must be followed with a closing HTML tag.

Your browser can interpret over a hundred HTML tags, but most websites use just a few tags to do most of the work. To understand this, let's try a little exercise: Think of your favorite news website. Have one in mind? Now connect to the Internet, open your browser, and type the address of that website. Bring this book with you, and take your time — I can wait!

In the event you can't access the Internet right now, take a look at the article from my favorite news website, *The New York Times,* in Figure 5-6.

Figure 5-6: A *New York Times* article with headline, paragraphs, hyperlinks, and images.

Look closely at the news website on your screen (or look at mine). Four HTML elements are used to create the majority of the page:

- ✔ **Headlines:** Headlines are displayed in bold and have a larger font size than the surrounding text.
- ✔ **Paragraphs:** Each story is organized into paragraphs with white space dividing each paragraph.
- ✔ **Hyperlinks:** The site's home page and article pages have links to other stories, as well as links to share the story on social networks such as Facebook, Twitter, and Google+.
- ✔ **Images:** Writers place images throughout the story. Also look for site images such as icons and logos.

In the following sections I explain how to write code to create these common HTML features.

Writing headlines

Use headlines to describe a section of your page. HTML has six levels of headings:

- ✔ h1, which is used for the most important headings
- ✔ h2, which is used for subheadings
- ✔ h3 to h6, which are used for less important headings

The browser renders h1 headings with a font size larger than h2, which in turn is larger than h3. Headings start with an opening heading tag, the heading text, and then the closing heading tag, as follows:

```
<h1>Heading text here</h1>
```

Here are some code examples showing various headings:

```
<h1>Heading 1: "I'm going to make him an offer he can't refuse"</h1>
<h2>Heading 2: "Houston, we have a problem"</h2>
<h3>Heading 3: "May the Force be with you"</h3>
<h4>Heading 4: "You talking to me?"</h4>
<h5>Heading 5: "I'll be back"</h5>
<h6>Heading 6: "My precious"</h6>
```

The result of these examples is shown in Figure 5-7.

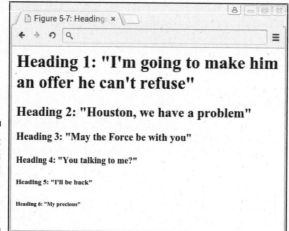

Figure 5-7:
Headings
created
using ele-
ments h1
through h6.

Always close what you open. With headings, remember to include a closing heading tag, such as `</h1>`.

Organizing text in paragraphs

To display text in paragraphs, you can use the p element. Place an opening `<p>` tag before the paragraph and a closing tag after it. The p element takes text and inserts a line break after the closing tag.

To insert a single line break after any element, use the `<br>` tag. The `<br>` tag is self-closing, so no closing tag is used.

Paragraphs start with an opening paragraph tag, the paragraph text, and then the closing paragraph tag:

```
<p>Paragraph text here</p>
```

Following are examples of coding a paragraph.

```
<p>Armstrong: Okay. I'm going to step off the LM now.</p>
<p>Armstrong: That's one small step for man; one giant leap for mankind.</p>
<p>Armstrong: Yes, the surface is fine and powdery. I can kick it up loosely
            with my toe. It does adhere in fine layers, like powdered
            charcoal, to the sole and sides of my boots.</p>
```

The result is shown in Figure 5-8.

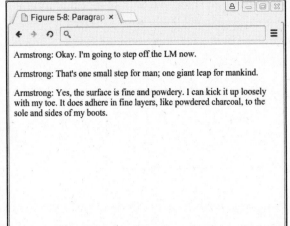

Figure 5-8:
Text displayed in paragraphs using the p element.

Linking to your (heart's) content

Hyperlinks are one of HTML's most valuable features. Web pages that include hyperlinked references to other sources allow the reader to access those sources with just a click, a big advantage over printed pages.

A hyperlink has two parts:

- **Link destination:** The web page the browser visits after the link is clicked. The link destination can be for another section of the same page or to another external web page.
- **Link description:** The words used to describe the link, which are more readable and descriptive than the link destination.

To create a hyperlink in HTML, start with an opening anchor tag (`<a>`) with an `href` attribute. Attributes modify HTML elements and are placed inside the opening HTML tag. Then add the value of the `href` attribute, which is the link destination. Then add text to describe the link after the opening anchor tag, and finally include a closing anchor tag.

The resulting HTML should look something like this:

```
<a href="website url">Link description</a>
```

Three examples of coding a hyperlink follow:

```
<a href="http://www.amazon.com">Purchase anything</a>
<a href="http://www.airbnb.com">Rent a place to stay from a local host</a>
<a href="http://www.techcrunch.com">Tech industry blog</a>
```

The resulting links are shown in Figure 5-9.

When rendering a hyperlink, the browser underlines the link and colors it blue by default.

Google's search engine ranks web pages on many factors but primarily based on the words used to describe a web page between the opening and closing `<a>` tags. This method was a big improvement over previous search-indexing methods, which tried to analyze an individual web page's content.

Adding images

Images spruce up plain HTML text pages. To include an image on your web page — your own or someone else's — you must obtain the image's web address. Websites such as Google Images (`images.google.com`) and Flickr (`www.flickr.com`) allow you to search for online images based on keywords. When you find an image you like, right-click the image and select Copy Image URL.

If you want to use an image that has not already been uploaded to the Internet, you can use a site such as `www.imgur.com` to upload the image. After uploading, you will be able to copy the image URL and use it in your HTML.

To include an image, start with an opening image tag `<img>`, define the source of the image using the `src` attribute, and include a forward slash at the end of the opening tag to close the tag. For example:

```
<img src="http://upload.wikimedia.org/wikipedia/commons/5/55/Grace_Hopper.jpg"/>
<img src="http://upload.wikimedia.org/wikipedia/commons/b/bd/Dts_news_bill_
          gates_wikipedia.JPG"/>
```

Figure 5-10 shows the result, with US Navy Rear Admiral Grace Hopper on the left and Bill Gates on the right.

TIP

The image tag is self-closing, so you don't use a separate `</img>` closing image tag. The image tag is one of the exceptions to the always-close-what-you-open rule!

Figure 5-10:
Images
of Grace
Hopper and
Bill Gates
rendered
using
`<img>`.

Common CSS Tasks and Selectors

CSS can style almost any HTML tag that creates a visible element on the page, including all the HTML tags you just saw to create headings, paragraphs, links, and images. With CSS, you can style the following:

- ✔ Text size, color, style, typeface, and alignment
- ✔ Link color and style
- ✔ Image size and alignment

Using CSS instead of HTML

You may wonder why creating a separate language such as CSS to handle styling was considered a better approach than expanding the capabilities of HTML. The three main reasons for that decision follow:

✔ **History:** CSS was created four years after HTML as an experiment to see whether developers and consumers wanted extra styling effects. At the time, it was unclear whether CSS would be useful, and only some major browsers supported it. As a result, CSS was created separately from HTML to allow developers to build sites using just HTML.

✔ **Code management:** Initially, some CSS functionality overlapped with existing HTML functionality. However, specifying styling effects in HTML resulted in cluttered and messy code. In addition, separating the styling of the content from the content itself has allowed search engines and other automated website agents to more easily process the content on web pages.

✔ **Inertia:** Millions of web pages use HTML and CSS separately, and every day that number grows. CSS remains a separate language because its popularity continues to grow and integrating now would require too much effort to convert existing sites.

CSS modifies HTML elements with rules that apply to each element. These rules are written as follows:

```
selector {
property: value;
}
```

A CSS rule is comprised of three parts:

✔ **Selector:** The HTML element you want to style.

✔ **Property:** The feature of the HTML element you want to style, such as font typeface, image height, or color.

✔ **Value:** The options for the property that the CSS rule sets. For example, if `color` is the property, the value might be `red`.

The selector identifies which HTML element you want to style. In HTML, an element is surrounded by angle brackets, but in CSS the selector stands alone. The selector is followed by a space, an opening left curly bracket ({), the property with a value, and then a closing right curly bracket (}).

A line break after the opening left curly bracket and before the closing right curly bracket is not required by CSS. In fact, you could put all your code on one line with no line breaks or spaces. Developers follow the convention of using line breaks to make CSS easier to modify and read.

Looking for curly braces on your keyboard? Most keyboards have the left and right curly brace to the right of the P key. Make sure you choose the curly braces and not the square brackets, which are on the same key.

The following code shows you an example of CSS modifying a specific HTML element. The CSS code appears first, followed by the HTML code that it modifies. First, the CSS:

```
h1 {
    font-family: cursive;
}
```

And now the HTML:

```
<h1>
    Largest IPOs in US History
</h1>
<ul>
    <li>2014: Alibaba - $20B</li>
    <li>2008: Visa - $18B</li>
</ul>
```

The CSS selector targets and styles only the HTML element with the same name. For example, the preceding code is displayed in Figure 5-11. The heading "Largest IPOs in US History" was created using the opening and closing `<h1>` tag. It was styled with the h1 selector, where the `font-family` property with the `cursive` value is used to style only the text between the opening and closing `<h1>` tag, and not any items in the bulleted list. Font families are further described later in this chapter.

Figure 5-11: CSS targeting the heading h1 element.

CSS uses a colon instead of the equals sign (=) to set values against properties. Multiple values for the same property are separated using a comma, and a semicolon is placed after the final value.

CSS lets you control text in many HTML elements. The most common text-related CSS properties and values are shown in Table 5-1. I describe these properties and values more fully in the sections that follow.

Table 5-1		Common CSS Properties and Values for Styling Text	
Property name	**Possible values**	**Description**	**Example**
`font-size`	*pixels (#px)* *%* *em (#em)*	Specifies the size of text measured in pixels, as a percentage of the containing element's font size, or with an em value, which is calculated by dividing the desired pixel value by the containing element's font size in pixels.	`font-size: 16px;`

`color`	*name*
	 hex code
	 rgb value
		Changes the color of the text specified using a name, a hexadecimal code, or RGB (red, green, and blue) value.	`color: blue;`
			
			 `color: #0000FF;`
			
			 `color: rgb(0,0, 255);`

`font-style`	*normal* *italic*	Sets font to appear in italics (or not).	`font-style: italic;`
`font-weight`	*normal* *bold*	Sets font to appear as bold (or not).	`font-weight: bold;`
`font-family`	*font name*	Sets the font typeface.	`font-family: "serif";`

Setting the font size

You can set the size of the font you're using with CSS's `font-size` property. You have a few options for setting the font size, and the most common is to use pixels, as in the following:

```
p {
   font-size: 16px;
}
```

In this example, I used the p selector to size the paragraph text to 16 pixels. Percentage sizing and em values, the other options to size your fonts, are considered more accessibility friendly because they scale and resize more accurately on various devices. The default browser font size for normal text is 16 pixels. With percentage sizing and em values, fonts can be sized relative to the user-specified default. For example, the CSS for percentage sizing looks like this:

```
p {
   font-size: 150%;
}
```

In this example, I used the p selector to size the paragraph text to 150% of the default size. If the browser's default font size was set at 16 pixels, this paragraph's font would appear sized at 24 pixels (150% of 16).

A font-size equal to 1px is equivalent to one pixel on your monitor, so the size of the text displayed varies according to the size of the monitor. Accordingly, for a fixed font size in pixels, the text appears smaller as you increase the screen resolution.

Setting the color

The color property sets the color in one of three ways:

- ✔ **Name:** You can reference 147 colors by name, including common colors, such as black, blue, and red, as well as uncommon colors, such as burlywood, lemon chiffon, and thistle.

- ✔ **Hex code:** You can define more than 16 million colors by using hexadecimal code to specify their component parts of red, green, and blue.

- ✔ **RGB value:** Just like hex codes, RGB values specify the red, green, and blue component parts for over 16 million colors. RGB values are the decimal equivalent to hexadecimal values.

Don't worry about trying to remember hex codes or RGB values. You can easily identify colors using an online color picker such as the one at www.w3schools.com/tags/ref_colorpicker.asp.

Following are examples of each of the three types of color changes:

```
p {
   color: red
}
h1 {
   color: #FF0000
}
h2 {
   color: rgb(255,0,0)
}
```

In the first example, `color: red`, I set the paragraph color to red using the common color name . In the second example, I set the `h1` color equal to #FF0000. After the hashtag (#), the first two digits (FF) refer to the red in the color, the next two digits (00) refer to the green in the color, and the final two digits (00) refer to the blue in the color. In the last example, `color: rgb(255,0,0)`, each decimal value is separate by commas. The first decimal value of 255 is equivalent to the first two hexadecimal FF digits in the second example, and the second and third decimal values of 0 are equivalent to 00 in hexadecimal.

All three colors in the preceding example reference the same shade of red. For the full list of colors that can be referenced by name, go to www.w3.org/TR/css3-color/#svg-color.

Setting the font style and font weight

The `font-style` property can set text to italics, and the `font-weight` property can set text to bold. For each of these properties, the default is `normal`, which doesn't need to be specified. In the following example, the paragraph is styled so that the font appears italicized and bold:

```
p {
   font-style: italics;
   font-weight: bold;
}
```

Setting the font family

The `font-family` property sets the typeface used for text. The property is set equal to one font or to a list of fonts separated by commas. Your website visitors will have a variety of fonts installed on their computers, and the browser displays the first specified font in the `font-family` property only if that font is already installed on their system. If the font is not installed, the browser tries the remaining specified fonts until an installed font is found. If no specified fonts are installed, a default font is used.

The font-family property can be set equal to two types of values:

✔ **Font name:** Specific font names such as Times New Roman, Arial, and Courier.

✔ **Generic font family:** Modern browsers usually define one installed font for each generic font family:

- serif (such as Times New Roman or Palatino)
- sans-serif (such as Helvetica or Verdana)
- monospace (such as Courier or Andale Mono)
- cursive (such as Comic Sans or Florence)
- fantasy (such as Impact or Oldtown)

When using font-family, it's best to define two or three specific fonts followed by a generic font family as a fallback in case the fonts you specify aren't installed. For example:

```
p {
    font-family: "Times New Roman", Helvetica, serif;
}
```

In this example, the paragraph's font family is defined as Times New Roman. If Times New Roman isn't installed on the user's computer, the browser uses Helvetica. If Helvetica isn't installed, the browser will use any available font in the generic serif font family.

When using a font name with multiple words (such as Times New Roman) enclose the font name in quotes.

Common JavaScript Tasks and Commands

JavaScript can be used to perform many tasks, from simple variable assignments to complex data visualizations. The following tasks, here explained in a JavaScript context, are core programming concepts that haven't changed in the last twenty years and won't change in the next twenty. They're applicable to any programming language.

JavaScript can do any of the following:

✔ Control web page appearance and layout by changing HTML attributes and CSS styles

✔ Easily create web page elements such as date pickers and drop-down menus

✔ Take user input in forms, and check for errors before submission

✔ Display and visualize data using complex charts and graphs

✔ Import and analyze data from other websites

Understanding JavaScript structure

JavaScript has a different structure and format than HTML and CSS and allows you to do more than position and style text on a web page. With JavaScript, you can store numbers and text for later use, decide what code to run based on conditions in your program, and even name pieces of your code so you can easily reference them later.

As with HTML and CSS, JavaScript has special keywords and syntax that allow the computer to recognize what you're trying to do. Unlike HTML and CSS, however, JavaScript is intolerant of syntax mistakes. If you forget to close an HTML tag or to include a closing curly brace in CSS, your code may still run and your browser will try its best to display the code. When coding in JavaScript, on the other hand, forgetting a single quote or parenthesis can cause your entire program to fail to run.

HTML specifies the content type and applies an effect to the text between opening and closing tags. For example, the HTML code <h1>This is a header</h1> signals that the text between the two tags is a text header. CSS styles the HTML element using properties and values between opening and closing curly braces. For example, the CSS code h1 { color: red;} styles the text header to be the color red.

Using semicolons, quotes, parentheses, and braces

The following code illustrates common punctuation used in JavaScript, specifically, semicolons, quotes, parentheses, and braces:

```
var age=22;
var planet="Earth";
if (age>=18)
{
  console.log("You are an adult");
  console.log("You are over 18");
}
else
{
```

```
console.log("You are not an adult");
console.log("You are not over 18");
}
```

General rules of thumb to know while programming in JavaScript include the following:

✔ Semicolons separate JavaScript statements.

✔ Quotes enclose text characters or *strings* (sequences of characters). Any opening quote must have a closing quote.

✔ Parentheses are used to modify commands with additional information called *arguments*. Any opening parenthesis must have a closing parenthesis.

✔ Braces group JavaScript statements into blocks so that they execute together. Any opening brace must have a closing brace.

These syntax rules can seem arbitrary and may be difficult to remember initially. With some practice, however, the rules will feel like second nature to you.

Storing data with variables

Variables, like those in algebra, are keywords used to store data values for later use. The variable name usually starts with a letter. Although the data stored in a variable may change, the variable name remains the same.

Think of a variable like a gym locker — what you store in the locker changes, but the locker number stays the same. Table 5-2 lists some types of data that JavaScript variables can store.

Table 5-2	Data Stored by a Variable	
Data Type	*Description*	*Examples*
Numbers	Positive or negative numbers with or without decimals	156
		−101.96
Strings	Printable characters	Holly Novak
		Señor
Boolean	True or false value	true
		false

For a list of rules on variable names, see the "JavaScript Variables" section at www.w3schools.com/js/js_variables.asp.

The first time you use a variable name, you use `var` to declare the variable name. Then you can optionally assign a value to variable using the equals sign. In the following code example, I declare three variables and assign values to those variables:

```
var myName="Nik";
var pizzaCost=10;
var totalCost=pizzaCost * 2;
```

Programmers say you have *declared a variable* when you first define it using the `var` keyword. Declaring a variable tells the computer to reserve space in memory and permanently store values using the variable name. You can view these values by using the `console.log` statement. For example, after running the preceding code, typing the statement `console.log(totalCost)` would return the value 20.

After declaring a variable, you change its value by referring to just the variable name and using the equals sign, as shown in the following examples:

```
myName="Steve";
pizzaCost=15;
```

Variable names are case sensitive, so when referring to a variable in your program, remember that `MyName`, for example, is a different variable than `myname`. In general, it's a good idea to give your variable a name that describes the data being stored.

Making decisions with if-else statements

After you've stored data in a variable, it is common to compare the variable's value to other variable values or to a fixed value, and then to make a decision based on the outcome of the comparison. In JavaScript, these comparisons are performed by using a *conditional statement*. The `if-else` statement is a type of conditional. Its general syntax is as follows:

```
if (condition) {
    statement1 to execute if condition is true
}
else {
    statement2 to execute if condition is false
}
```

In this statement, the if is followed by a space, and a condition enclosed in parentheses evaluates to true or false. If the condition is true, statement1, located between the first set of curly brackets, is executed. If the condition is false and I include else, which is optional, statement2, located between the second set of curly brackets, is executed. When the else is not included and the condition is false, the conditional statement simply ends.

Note there are no parentheses after the else — the else line has no condition. JavaScript executes the statement after else only when the preceding conditions are false.

The condition in an if-else statement is a comparison of values using operators. Common operators are described in Table 5-3.

Table 5-3	Common JavaScript Operators		
Type	*Operator*	*Description*	*Example*
Less than	<	Evaluates whether one value is less than another value	(x < 55)
Greater than	>	Evaluates whether one value is greater than another value	(x > 55)
Equality	===	Evaluates whether two values are equal	(x === 55)
Less than or equal to	<=	Evaluates whether one value is less than or equal to another value	(x <= 55)
Greater than or equal to	>=	Evaluates whether one value is greater than or equal to another value	(x >= 55)
Inequality	!=	Evaluates whether two values are not equal	(x != 55)

Here is a simple if statement, without the else:

```
var carSpeed=70;
if (carSpeed > 55) {
  alert("You are over the speed limit!");
}
```

I declare a variable called carSpeed and set it equal to 70. Then an if statement with a condition compares whether the value in the variable carSpeed is greater than 55. If the condition is true, an alert (a pop-up box) states

"You are over the speed limit!" In this case, the value of `carSpeed` is 70, which is greater than 55, so the condition is `true` and the alert is displayed. If the first line of code instead were `var carSpeed=40;`, the condition would be `false` because 40 is less than 55, and no alert would be displayed.

Let us expand the `if` statement by adding `else` to create an `if-else`, as shown in this code:

```
var carSpeed=40;
if (carSpeed > 55) {
    alert("You are over the speed limit!");
}
else {
    alert("You are under the speed limit!");
}
```

In addition to the `else`, I added an `alert` statement inside the curly brackets following the `else`, and set `carSpeed` equal to 40. When this `if-else` statement executes, `carSpeed` is equal to 40, which is less than 55, so the condition is `false`. Because the `else` has been added, an alert appears stating, "You are under the speed limit!"(See Figure 5-12) If the first line of code instead had been `var carSpeed=70;` as before, the condition would be `true`, because 70 is greater than 55, and the first alert would be displayed.

Figure 5-12:
JavaScript
alert for an
`if-else`
statement.

JavaScript Alert

You are under the speed limit

OK

Our current `if-else` statement allows us to test for one condition, and to show different results depending on whether the condition is `true` or `false`. To test for two or more conditions, you can add one or more `else if` statements after the original `if` statement. The general syntax is as follows:

```
if (condition1) {
    statement1 to execute if condition1 is true
}
else if (condition2) {
    statement2 to execute if condition2 is true
}
else {
    statement3 to execute if all previous conditions are false
}
```

The if-else is written as before, and the else if is followed by a space and a condition enclosed in parentheses that evaluates to either true or false. If condition1 is true, statement1 (located between the first set of curly brackets) is executed. If condition1 is false, condition2 is evaluated and is found to be either true or false. If condition2 is true, statement2 (located between the second set of curly brackets) is executed. At this point, additional else if statements could be added to test additional conditions.

As you can see, statement3 is executed only when all if and else if conditions are false and an else is included. Only one statement is executed in a block of code, after which the remaining statements are ignored and the next block of code is executed.

When writing the if-else, you must have one and only one if statement; you may have only one else statement if you choose to include one. The else if is optional, can be used multiple times in a single if-else statement, and must come after the original if statement and before the else. You cannot have an else if or an else by itself, without a preceding if statement.

Here is another example else if statement:

```
var carSpeed=40;
if (carSpeed > 55) {
    alert("You are over the speed limit!");
}
else if (carSpeed === 55) {
    alert("You are at the speed limit!");
}
```

When this if statement executes, carSpeed is equal to 40, which is less than 55, so the condition is false, and then the else if condition is evaluated. The value of carSpeed is not exactly equal to 55, so this condition is also false; no alert is shown, and the statement ends.

If the first line of code were instead var carSpeed=55; the first condition would be false because 55 is not greater than 55. Then the else if condition would be evaluated, and because 55 is exactly equal to 55, the second alert would be displayed, stating "You are at the speed limit!"

Look carefully at the preceding code. When setting the value of a variable, you use one equals sign. But when comparing whether two values are equal, you use three equals signs (===).

The final example is an `if-else` statement with an `else if` statement:

```
var carSpeed=40;
if (carSpeed > 55) {
    alert("You are over the speed limit!");
}
else if (carSpeed === 55) {
    alert("You are at the speed limit!");
}
else {
    alert("You are under the speed limit!");
}
```

As the diagram in Figure 5-13 shows, two conditions, which appear in the figure as diamonds, are evaluated in sequence. In this example, `carSpeed` is equal to 40, so the two conditions are `false`, and the statement after the `else` is executed, showing the alert, "You are under the speed limit!" Here `carSpeed` is initially set to 40, but depending on the initial `carSpeed` variable value, any one of the three alerts could be displayed.

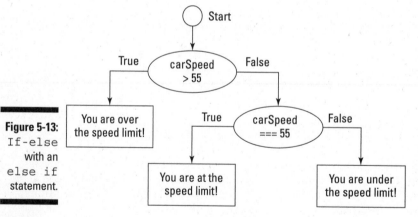

Figure 5-13: If-else with an else if statement.

The condition is always evaluated first, and every condition must either be `true` or `false`. Independent from the condition is the statement that executes if the condition is `true`.

Working with string and number methods

The most basic data types are strings and numbers. They are usually stored in variables. Programmers often need to manipulate strings and numbers to perform basic tasks, such as the following:

✔ Rounding a number to a *fixed* numbers of decimal points, such as when getting a subtotal in an online shopping cart, calculating the tax, rounding the tax to two decimal points, and adding the tax to the subtotal

✔ Determining the *length* of a string, such as for a password

Tasks like these are so common that JavaScript includes shortcuts called *methods* that make performing these tasks easier. The general syntax to perform these tasks is to follow the affected variable's name or value with a period and the name of the method, as follows for values and variables:

```
value.method;
variablename.method;
```

Table 5-4 shows examples of JavaScript methods applied to values, such as strings, and to variables.

Table 5-4	Common JavaScript Methods		
Method	*Description*	*Example*	*Result*
`.toFixed(n)`	Rounds a number to *n* decimal places	`var jenny=8.675309;` `jenny.toFixed(2);`	8.68
`.length`	Represents the number of characters in a string	`"Nik".length;`	3

When using a string, or assigning a variable to a value that is a string, always enclose the string in quotes.

For a list of additional string and number methods see W3Schools at `www.w3schools.com/js/js_number_methods.asp` and `www.w3schools.com/js/js_string_methods.asp`.

Alerting users and prompting for input

Displaying messages to the user and collecting input are the beginnings of the interactivity that JavaScript provides. Although more sophisticated techniques exist, the `alert()` method and `prompt()` method are easy ways to show a pop-up box with a message and prompt the user for input.

The syntax for creating an alert or a prompt is to write the method with text in quotes placed inside the parentheses, like so:

```
alert("You have mail");
prompt("What do you want for dinner?");
```

Figure 5-14 shows the alert pop-up box created by the `alert()` method and the prompt for user input created by the `prompt()` method.

Figure 5-14:
A Java-
Script alert
pop-up box
and a user
prompt.

Practicing Your HTML, CSS, and JavaScript

You can practice your HTML, CSS, and JavaScript online by using the Codecademy website. Codecademy is a free website created in 2011 to allow anyone to learn how to code right in the browser, without installing or downloading any software. Practice the tags and commands that you learned in this chapter by following these steps:

1. **Open your browser, and go to** `www.codecademy.com`.

2. **Sign up for or sign into your Codecademy account.**

   Creating an account is optional, but doing so means you can save your work. To use the website without creating an account, scroll down the bottom of the page, and click the lessons under the Learn to Code heading.

3. **Under the Language Skills section, click the HTML & CSS card or the JavaScript card, and then click a lesson.**

   You see background information in the upper-left part of the screen and instructions in the lower left.

4. **Complete the instructions in the main coding window.**

   A green check mark appears and you can proceed to the next exercise.

If your code has an error, a warning appears with a suggested fix. If you run into a problem or have a bug you can't fix, click the hint, use the Q&A forums, or tweet me at @nikhilgabraham and include hashtag #codingFD.

Chapter 6

Programming with Ruby and Python

The sooner you start to code, the longer the program will take.

—Roy Carlson

R uby and Python are server-side programming languages that allow developers to create complex applications and web experiences. HTML, CSS, and JavaScript have been used to display static information to users, but could not store user data after the user navigates away from the page or closes the browser. Using Ruby or Python, user information can be stored centrally, and then programmers can customize the information shown to users on the website.

In this chapter you learn the basics of using languages such as Ruby and Python, you write some simple code, and you discover resources to learn more advanced Ruby and Python topics.

Introducing Ruby and Python

Ruby is a general-purpose programming language typically used for web development. The programming language makes it easy to create, update, store, and retrieve data in a database. For example, suppose you want to create a social networking website like Twitter. The content you write in your tweet will be stored in a central database. You can exit the browser and turn off your computer, but when you come back to the website later, you can still access your tweets. Additionally, if someone searches for keywords in the tweets you've written, this same central database will be queried, and any matches will be displayed.

Ruby developers frequently perform tasks such as storing information in a database, and a Ruby framework called *Rails* speeds development by including prebuilt code, templates, and easy ways to perform these tasks. For these reasons, websites frequently use Ruby and Rails together.

A website using the Rails framework is referred to as being "built with Rails" or "built using Ruby on Rails."

Twitter's website was one of the most trafficked websites to use Ruby on Rails, and until 2010 used Ruby code for its search and messaging products. Following are other types of websites currently using Ruby on Rails:

- ✔ E-commerce websites such as those on the www.shopify.com platform
- ✔ Music websites such as www.soundcloud.com
- ✔ Social networking sites such as www.yammer.com
- ✔ News websites such as www.bloomberg.com

As you can see, Ruby and Rails can create a variety of websites. Although Rails emphasizes productivity, allowing developers to quickly write code and test prototypes, some developers criticize Ruby and Rails for not being scalable and cite as evidence Twitter rewriting their code to stop using Rails for many core features in an effort to improve the website's speed and increase the website's capability to handle more users at the same time.

I can't resolve the scalability debate here, but I can say that Rails can adequately handle millions of visitors per month. And no matter the language used, significant work must be done to scale a website to properly handle tens or hundreds of millions of monthly visitors.

You can confirm the programming language used by any major website with BuiltWith, which is available at www.builtwith.com. After entering the website address in the search bar, look under the Frameworks section for the programming language used. An example is shown in Figure 6-1.

Like Ruby, Python is a general-purpose programming language used for web development. Both languages are more alike than they are different. Python, like Ruby but unlike HTML, CSS, and JavaScript, allows for storing data after the user has navigated away from the page or closed the browser. Python includes prebuilt code to easily create and query these databases.

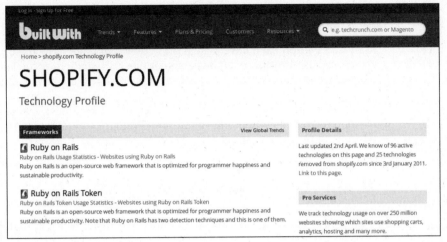

Figure 6-1: Shopify, the e-commerce platform, uses Ruby on Rails for its website.

SQLite is a free lightweight database commonly used by Python programmers to store data.

Many highly trafficked websites, such as YouTube, were created using Python. Other websites currently using Python include

- ✔ Quora, for its community question and answer site
- ✔ Spotify, for internal data analysis
- ✔ Dropbox, for its desktop client software
- ✔ Reddit, for generating crowd-sourced news
- ✔ Industrial Light & Magic and Disney Animation, for creating film special effects.

From websites to software to special effects, Python is a versatile language, powerful enough to support a range of applications.

Python programmers help spread Python code by creating *libraries,* which are standalone prewritten code that performs certain tasks. For example, a library called Scrapy performs *web scraping* (data extraction from websites), and another library called SciPy performs math functions used by scientists and mathematicians. The Python community maintains thousands of libraries like these; most are free to use as well as open-source, so anyone may modify them.

In addition, just like the Rails framework makes developing Ruby applications for the web easier, Django and Flask are two frameworks that make it easier to code web applications in Python.

Coding Advanced Functionality

Ruby and Python each have design principles that guide how the language is structured. In addition, each has conventions that guide how the language is written, like the curly braces in JavaScript or opening and closing tags in HTML.

In this section, I describe the design principles and show you what the code looks like. After this basic overview, you can learn more by checking out the referenced resources, along with Part III of this book.

Ruby design principles and code

Ruby was created by Yukhiro "Matz" Matsumoto, a developer with experience programming in Perl and Python, Unsatisfied with both and wanting an easy-to-use scripting language, he created Ruby.

When designing Ruby, Matsumoto's explicit goal was to "make programmers happy." He created the language so that programmers could learn and use it easily. Today, Ruby is a popular way for startups and companies to quickly create prototypes and launch websites on the Internet.

A few design principles make programming in Ruby less stressful and more fun than other programming languages. These design principles follow:

- **Conciseness:** In general, short and concise code helps create faster and easier-to-read programs. The initial set of steps written in English to run a program is referred to as *pseudocode*. Ruby is designed so that little additional effort is needed to translate pseudocode into actual code. Even existing Ruby commands can be made more concise. For example, Ruby's `if` statement can be written in three lines or just one.

- **Consistency:** A small set of rules governs the entire language. Sometimes this principle in referred to as the principle of least astonishment or the principle of least surprise. In general, if you're familiar with another programming language, the way Ruby behaves should feel intuitive. For example, when working with string methods in JavaScript, you can chain them together as follows:

```
"alphabet".toUpperCase().concat("Soup")
```

This JavaScript statement returns "ALPHABETSoup" by first making the string "alphabet" uppercase by using the `.toUpperCase()` method, and then concatenating "soup" to "ALPHABET". Similarly, the following Ruby statement chains methods just as you would expect, also returning "ALPHABETSoup":

```
"alphabet".upcase.concat("Soup")
```

✔ **Flexibility:** There are multiple ways to accomplish the same thing, and even built-in commands can be changed. For example, when writing an `if-else` statement, you can use the words `if` and `else`, or you can use a single `?`. The following versions of code both perform the same task:

Version 1:

```
if 3>4
    puts "the condition is true"
else
    puts "the condition is false"
end
```

Version 2:

```
puts 3>4 ? "the condition is false" : "the condition is true"
```

Ruby generally uses less punctuation than other programming languages you may have previously tried. Some sample code follows:

```
print "What's your first name?"
first_name = gets.chomp
first_name.upcase!

if first_name=="NIK"
    print "You may enter!"
else
    print "Nothing to see here."
end
```

If you ran this code, it would do the following:

1. Print a line asking for your first name.
2. Take user input (`gets.chomp`) and save it to the `first_name` variable.
3. Transform any inputted text into uppercase.
4. Test the user input. If the input equals "NIK" then the code would print "You may enter!"; otherwise, it prints "Nothing to see here."

Don't worry if these statements and commands seem foreign to you. For now, as you look at the code, notice some of its styling characteristics:

✔ **Less punctuation:** Ruby, unlike JavaScript, does not have curly braces, and unlike HTML, does not have angle brackets.

✔ **Space, tab, and indentation are ignored:** These whitespace characters do not matter unless they are in a text string.

- **A newline indicates the end of a statement:** Although you can use a semicolon to put more than one statement on a line, the preferred and more common method is to put each statement on its own line.

- **Dot notation is frequently used:** The period (for example, `.chomp` or `.upcase`) signals the use of a *method,* which is a set of instructions that carry out a particular task. In this code example, `.chomp` removes carriage returns from user input, and `.upcase` transforms the user input into uppercase.

- **An exclamation point signals danger:** A method applied to a variable, such as `first_name.upcase`, by default transforms a copy of the variable's value, not the value itself. An exclamation point signals a permanent change, so `first_name.upcase!` permanently changes the value of the variable `first_name`.

To learn more Ruby, see Chapters 9 and 10 for additional resources. You might also want to check out `www.codecademy.com` and `www.tryruby.org` for some free, short, self-taught lessons.

Python design principles and code

Python was created by Guido van Rossum, a developer who was bored during the winter of 1989 and looking for a project to do. Van Rossum had helped create one language, ABC, and the experience had given him many ideas that he thought would appeal to programmers. He executed these ideas when he created Python.

Although ABC never achieved popularity with programmers, Python was a runaway success. Python is one of the world's most popular programming languages, used by those just starting out as well as professionals building heavy-duty applications.

The *Zen of Python,* a poem that is part of the Python documentation, contains nineteen design principles that describe how the Python language is organized. Some of the most important principles include the following:

- **Readability counts:** This is possibly Python's most important design principle. Python code looks similar to English and even enforces certain formatting, such as indenting, to make the code easier to read. With highly readable code, you'll find it much easier to fix a bug or add a feature months later. Readable code also means others can use your code or help debug your code with ease.

Reddit.com is one of the top 10 most visited websites in the US, and one of the top 50 most visited websites in the world. Its cofounder, Steve Huffman, initially coded the website in Lisp but switched to Python because it is "extremely readable, and extremely writeable."

✔ **There should be one — and preferably only one — obvious way to do it:** This principle is directly opposite Perl's motto, "There's more than one way to do it." In Python, two programmers may approach the same problem and write two different programs, but the ideal is that the code will be similar and easy to read, adopt, and understand. Although Python may allow you to perform a task (such as combining two strings) in multiple ways, you should use the most obvious and common option.

✔ **If the implementation is hard to explain, it's a bad idea:** Programmers have been known to write esoteric code to increase performance. However, Python was designed to be easy to use, and this principle reminds programmers that easy-to-understand implementations are preferable over faster but harder-to-explain ones.

Access the full list of design principles, which is in the form of a poem, by typing `import this;` in any Python interpreter, or by visiting `www.python.org/dev/peps/pep-0020`. These principles, written by Python community member Tim Peters, describe the intentions of Python's creator, Van Rossum, who is also referred to as the Benevolent Dictator for Life (BDFL).

Python generally uses less punctuation than other programming languages you may have previously tried. Some sample code is included here:

```
first_name=raw_input("What's your first name?")
first_name=first_name.upper()

if first_name=="NIK":
    print "You may enter!"
else:
    print "Nothing to see here."
```

The examples in this book are written for Python 2.7. Two popular versions of Python are currently in use: Python 2.7 and Python 3. Python 3 is the latest version of the language but it is not backwards compatible, so code written using Python 2.7 syntax does not work when using a Python 3 interpreter. Initially, Python 2.7 had more external libraries and support than Python 3, but this is changing. For more about the differences between the two versions, see `https://wiki.python.org/moin/Python2orPython3`.

If you ran this code, it would do the following:

1. Print a line asking for your first name.

2. Take the user input (`raw_input(What's your first name?)`) and save it to the `first_name` variable.

3. Transform any inputted text into uppercase.

4. Test the user input. If the input equals "NIK," the code will print "You may enter!" Otherwise it prints "Nothing to see here."

These commands are similar to Ruby. For now, as you look at the code, note some of its styling characteristics:

- **Less punctuation:** Python, unlike JavaScript, does not have curly braces, and unlike HTML, does not have angle brackets.

- **Whitespace matters:** Statements indented to the same level are grouped together. In the preceding example, note how the `if` and `else` align, and the `print` statements below each are indented the same amount. You can decide the amount of indentation, and whether to use tabs or spaces, as long as you are consistent. Four spaces from the left margin is considered the norm.

  See Python style suggestions on indentation, whitespace, and commenting by visiting `www.python.org/dev/peps/pep-0008`.

- **A newline indicates the end of a statement:** Although you can use semicolons to put more than one statement on a line, the preferred and more common method is to put each statement on its own line.

- **A colon separates a code block:** Some new Python programmers wonder why they should use colons to indicate code blocks, like the one at the end of the `if` statement, when using newlines would suffice. Early user testing with and without the colons showed that beginner programmers better understood the code with the colon.

To learn more about Python, see Chapters 9 and 10. If you can't wait, check out `www.codecademy.com` or `developers.google.com/edu/python` for some free, short, self-taught lessons.

Choosing between Ruby and Python

When you're just starting out, decide which language to learn first can be difficult. Ruby and Python are two popular programming languages for web development, so you can't go wrong with learning either one first. (PHP and Java are two additional programming languages that can be used for web development, but they aren't usually recommended for beginners.)

When choosing whether to learn Ruby, Python, or any other programming language, consider the following factors:

- **Domain-specific use:** Some languages have better functionality for certain domains and purposes. For example, Python has built-in features and libraries that make it a strong choice for statistics or scientific applications. Ruby is popular among startups because you can quickly create and modify prototypes.

✓ **Company preference:** Companies usually choose one or two programming languages and frameworks with which to develop applications. To find out which languages a company uses, search their website by using www.builtwith.com, review their job postings to see which types of developers they are hiring, or search for blog posts they've written about the technology used. For example, Airbnb's blog post on Large Scale Payment Systems and Ruby on Rails, which is available at nerds. airbnb.com/large-scale-payments-systems-ruby-rails, is a good clue that Ruby on Rails is used at the company. Many companies will hire developers who don't know the company's preferred language if the developer is willing to learn it.

✓ **Feature support:** If you're building an app with a must-have feature, look into how you would build that feature. You can search for online tutorials, how other companies built the same or similar feature, and open source libraries that offer support. For example, the Python libraries NumPy and SciPy make doing data analysis much easier in Python than in Ruby, though in recent years Ruby developers have created SciRuby to bridge this gap.

✓ **Community:** Inevitably, you'll get stuck while coding and need others to help you make progress. When evaluating the strength of a community around a programming language, see what discussion sites exist, how active they are, and how quickly people respond to questions. In addition, the existence of mailing lists, blog posts, Meetup groups, and conferences all help create a sense of community and support.

View a list of Ruby community resources by visiting www.ruby-lang. org/en/community. For a list of Python community resources, go to www. python.org/community.

Chapter 7

Creating Mobile Apps

● ●

In This Chapter

▶ Uncovering the difference between mobile web apps and native apps

▶ Knowing when to build a hybrid native app

▶ Seeing the different parts of an app

● ●

> *Three objects were considered essential across all participants, cultures, and genders: keys, money, and mobile phone.*
>
> —*Jan Chipchase, Nokia*

Mobile phones are increasing the reach of web applications and those connected to the Internet. Every year, people buy 300 million desktop computers but almost 2 billion mobile phones — and the number is steadily increasing.

With all these mobile phones users, it takes less time than ever to build a massive user audience. Facebook, which initially started as a website, reached 1 billion users after eight and a half years. Whatsapp, a mobile messaging app, registered the same number of users in just six years.

In this chapter, you learn about the creation of mobile applications that run in a browser on any mobile device as well as applications that are downloaded from an app store and run directly on only one type of mobile device, such as an iPhone or Android phone.

Defining Types of Mobile Apps

Web applications are websites you visit using a web browser on any device. Websites optimized for use on a mobile device, such as a phone or a tablet, are called *mobile web applications*. By contrast, *native mobile applications* cannot be viewed using a web browser. Instead, native mobile applications are downloaded from an app store such as Apple's App Store or Google's Play Store, and designed to run on a specific device such as an iPhone or an Android tablet. Historically, desktop computers outnumbered and outsold mobile devices, but two major trends in mobile usage have occurred recently:

- ✔ In 2014, people with mobile devices outnumbered people with desktop computers. This gap is projected to continue increasing, as shown in Figure 7-1.

- ✔ Mobile-device users spend 80 percent of their time using native mobile applications, and 20 percent of their time browsing mobile web applications.

Figure 7-1: Mobile devices have increased at a faster pace than desktops.

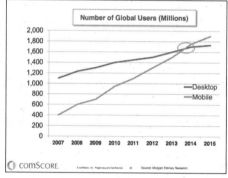

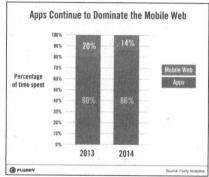

Credit: Flurry Analytics (2014), comScore (2012)

Companies are called *mobile first* when they design and develop the mobile version of their applications before the desktop version. For example, Instagram first built a mobile application, which continues to have more functionality than their regular website.

When coding mobile applications, developers can build either

- ✔ **Mobile web applications** by using web development languages such as HTML, CSS, JavaScript for the front end and Python, Ruby, or another server-side language for the back end.

- ✔ **Native mobile applications** by using a specific language. For example, Apple devices are programmed using Objective-C or Swift, and Android devices are programmed using Java.

The choice between these two options may seem simple, but a few factors are at play. Consider the following:

- ✔ Companies developing mobile web applications must make sure the mobile version works across different browsers, screen sizes, and manufacturers, such as Apple, Samsung, RIM, and Microsoft. All these variables result in thousands of possible phone combinations, which can greatly increase the complexity of testing before launch. Native mobile apps run on only one phone platform, so you need to account for less variation.

✔ Despite running on only one platform, native mobile apps are more expensive and take longer to build than mobile web apps.

✔ Some developers have reported that mobile web applications have more performance issues and load more slowly than native mobile applications.

✔ As mentioned, users are spending more time using native mobile applications and less time using browser-based mobile web apps.

✔ Native mobile apps are distributed through an app store, which may require approval from the app storeowner, whereas mobile web apps are accessible from any web browser. For example, Apple has a strict approval policy and takes up to six days to approve an app for inclusion in its App Store, but Google has a more relaxed approval policy and approves an app within two hours.

In one famous example of an app rejected from an app store, Apple blocked Google from launching the Google Voice app in Apple's App Store because it overlapped with Apple's own phone functionality. Google responded by creating a mobile web app accessible from any browser, and Apple could do nothing to block it.

If you're making the choice between building a mobile web or a native app, consider the complexity of your application. Simple applications, like schedules or menus, can likely be cheaply developed with a mobile web app, whereas more complex applications, like messaging and social networking, may benefit from having a native mobile app. Even well established technology companies struggle with this choice. Initially, Facebook and LinkedIn created mobile web applications, but both have since shifted to primarily promoting and supporting native mobile apps. The companies cited better speed, memory management, and developer tools as some of the reasons for making the switch.

Creating Mobile Web Apps for Any Phone

To build a mobile web app, you use the front-end languages HTML, CSS, and JavaScript. CSS controls the website appearance across devices based on the screen width. Screens with a small width, such as those on phones, are assigned a vertically based layout; screens with a larger width, such as those on tablets, are assigned a horizontally based layout. Because mobile web apps are accessed from the mobile browser and are not installed on the user's device, these web apps usually can't send push notifications (alerts) to the phone, can't run in the background while the browser is minimized, and can't communicate with other apps.

Although you can write the HTML, CSS, and JavaScript for your mobile web app from scratch, mobile web frameworks enable you to develop from a base of pre-written code, much like the frameworks for programming languages (such as Rails for Ruby). These mobile web frameworks include a collection of generic components that are reused frequently, and allow developers to build, test, and launch websites more quickly. Twitter Bootstrap is one such mobile web framework, allowing your websites to have a consistent look across devices.

For applications that have additional complexity, such as storing user data or payment mechanisms, you can use back-end languages such as Ruby, Python, or PHP.

As you increase feature complexity, keep in mind that phones typically have limited to poor bandwidth, a small screen size, and finite battery power.

Any website can be viewed with a mobile browser, but websites not optimized for mobile devices look weird, with the regular website font size and image dimensions either improperly scaled down to fit on a mobile screen or not adjusted at all (as shown in Figure 7-2, left). By contrast, websites optimized for mobile devices with CSS have fonts that are readable, images that scale to the mobile device screen, and a vertical layout suitable for a mobile phone (as shown in Figure 7-2, right).

Figure 7-2:
The Starbucks site not optimized (left) and optimized (right) for mobile.

Coding Native Mobile Apps for iPhones and Android Devices

Native mobile apps can be faster, more reliable, and look more polished than mobile web apps, as shown in Figure 7-3, left. Built using Java for use on Android devices, and Objective-C or Swift for use on Apple devices (iOS), native mobile apps must be uploaded to an app store, which may require approval.

The main benefits of an app store are its centralized distribution and capability to curate, catalog, and feature apps, which can drive downloads. Also, because native mobile apps are programs that are installed on the mobile device, they can be used in more situations without an Internet connection. Finally, and most importantly, users appear to prefer native mobile apps to mobile web apps by a wide margin, one that continues to increase.

Native mobile apps can take advantage of features that run in the background while the app is minimized, such as push notifications, and can communicate with other apps. These features are not available in a mobile web app. Additionally, graphics-intensive apps, such as games, perform better as a native mobile app.

Figure 7-3: Facebook's native mobile app (left) and mobile web app (right).

Although native mobile apps offer better performance and a greater number of features, they require longer development time and are more expensive to build than mobile web apps.

Another way to build a native mobile app is to use a hybrid approach that involves building an app with HTML, CSS, and JavaScript, packaging that code using a *wrapper,* and then running the code inside a native mobile app container.

The most popular wrapper is a product called PhoneGap, which recognizes specific JavaScript commands that allow access to device-level functionality that's normally inaccessible to mobile web applications. After one version of the app is built, native mobile app containers can be launched for up to nine platforms, including Apple, Android, Blackberry, and Windows Phone. The major advantages to using this hybrid approach follow:

- ✔ You can code the app using languages you already know, resulting in a much smaller learning curve.
- ✔ You can build your app once, and then release it to many platforms simultaneously.
- ✔ You can prototype, test, and receive feedback on your app quickly and more easily than when building a native app from scratch.

Major apps, such as the BBC's Olympics app, have been built using this approach. However, if the app takes off, it is often rebuilt into a purely native version to increase speed and reliability.

Imagine you know how to play the piano, but you also want to learn how to reproduce the sound of a violin. One way you could do this is to buy a violin and start learning how to play. Another option is to buy a synthesizer keyboard, set the tone to violin, and play the keyboard so that it sounds like a violin. This second option is similar to the hybrid approach, except in this example, the piano is HTML, CSS, and JavaScript, the violin is a native iOS app, and the synthesizer keyboard is a wrapper such as PhoneGap. Just like the synthesizer keyboard can be set to violin, cello, or guitar, so too can PhoneGap create native apps for Apple, Android, and other platforms.

Identifying the Parts of an App

Whether you're building a mobile web app or a native app, the component parts of an app run on both the client and the server.

The client is your personal mobile device that runs a local version of the app. The server stores the master copy of the app code and related databases.

Client components or processes affect the look, feel, and functionality on the mobile device. The following are typical components and processes that affect the client:

- **User interaction and user experience (UI/UX) design:** The small screen and virtual keyboard require a good amount of thought around how the app will receive user input and what to display. UI/UX design is the process of designing how the app will look, feel, and operate. Minor changes and design choices can have a huge effect on the ultimate success of the app. For example, when the Tinder dating app launched, it differed from other dating apps because users browsed through short picture profiles of people by using a simple left-right swipe gesture instead of viewing lengthy detailed textual profiles. This change helped Tinder capture 90 percent of the online dating market in less than one year.

- **Wireframes:** After you determine the main user interactions and displays, you use wireframes to display each screen and exactly how the users will interact with the app. Initially, these wireframes can be rough sketches. Then, usually before writing any code, high-fidelity versions with images are created for developers to use.

- **Caching:** Because mobile devices typically have limited bandwidth and speed, you can improve performance if you locally *cache,* or save, certain data onto the phone. For example, if you were creating a restaurant reservation app, you might store on the phone the restaurants where the user makes the most reservations instead of requesting these frequently visited restaurants from the server each time the app is launched.

- **Synchronization:** Users often expect that a mobile app, unlike websites built for desktops, will work even when no Internet connection is present. This expectation creates an issue because changes made to the app when offline must be uploaded to the server, and any conflicts must be reconciled. For example, suppose you lose your Internet connection while you are accepting a meeting invite using the calendar app on your phone. The app needs to have code that decides how often and when to upload your accepted meeting invite to the server.

Server components or processes occur on the company's server, in the background or in real-time, and support the app's functionality. The following are typical components that run on the server and processes that affect the code or components running on the server:

- **Logic:** Code must be written to decide what information to permanently save for later retrieval and what to display to the user and when.

- **Storage:** Databases must be created to store user-generated data and anything else your app will display to users.

✔ **Notifications:** These pop-ups appear even when the app is closed, keeping users engaged by reminding them to use the app. Notification events can be trigged by time, user activity (for example, you just made a payment), or an external event (such as someone just shared a photo and tagged you in it).

✔ **User accounts:** Creating and deleting user accounts, authenticating users, and allowing access to some or all app features are necessary for any app that stores sensitive information.

✔ **Referrals and sharing:** Integration with email providers and social networks are another way apps gain new users. Each social network, such as Facebook or Twitter, has its own steps to authenticate and share user content.

✔ **Versions:** Unlike software you install on a desktop, mobile software is typically updated more frequently with new features and security fixes. Some users will not upgrade to the latest version of your app, so you need to make sure that any new versions of your app do not conflict with older versions.

Chapter 8

Analyzing Big Data

· ·

· ·

Data is one of the most powerful mechanisms for telling stories. I take a huge pile of data, and I try to get it to tell stories.

—Steven Levitt, author of Freakonomics

Although all coding jobs are in high demand, the big data and data analytics professions continue to be at the top. This jobs explosion has happened, in part, because sensors and systems can measure much more data than before. Big data professionals analyze data to create useful insights.

Traditionally, the data captured from cellphones consisted of only phone call information, such as caller number, time of call, and duration. Today's smartphones have additional sensors that capture location, speed, direction, ambient light, and elevation. The trend around increased data generation and collection isn't limited to physical devices — our online behavior generates data as well, and the volume of data increases as more people gain access to the Internet.

Although machines generate the data, people must analyze it to come up with useful insights.

In this chapter, you find out what big data is. Then you discover some of the tools used to analyze big data to create useful insights. You also see how programming languages, such as Python and R, can be used to perform the analysis, and how visualization techniques can communicate insights quickly and easily.

Understanding Big Data

Over the last few years, many companies have announced significant plans to capture and monetize big data. In 2012, the CEO of GE (General Electric), Jeffrey Immelt, committed over a billion dollars to the company's big data division. They installed 10 million sensors on machines such as medical equipment and jet engines, which gathered 50 million data points. The data was used to avoid breakdowns by predicting when repairs were needed. Two years later, the initiative had generated over $1 billion, a level of sales achieved more quickly than in any other division.

All this data by itself, however, is not worth much. Its value comes from visualizing the data to spot trends, connecting data sources to find new patterns, and doing all this faster than ever before. For example, Target collects and analyzes customer purchasing behavior, and has found a correlation between pregnancy and purchases of 25 specific products, including unscented lotion, mineral supplements, and cotton balls. Now when customers start buying increasing quantities of these products, Target sends coupons for diapers and infant clothes to spur purchasing.

Defining big data

Big data is typically defined as data so large that it is impractical to manage with traditional software tools. If that definition sounds vague and ambiguous, that's because it is!

Three factors are typically used to describe big data:

- ✔ **Volume:** The amount of data being generated in aggregate. For example, does all the data fit on a USB thumb drive, or does it require dedicated servers?

- ✔ **Velocity:** The rate or speed of the data being generated. For example, every day, Facebook users generate 5 billion likes per day, which is almost 60 thousand likes per second.

- ✔ **Variety:** The different types of data being created. For example, an online e-commerce site such as Amazon has transaction data (such as purchases and returns), social media data (such as tweets and likes on products), and visitor data (for example, visitor country and time on the site).

Table 8-1 shows these three factors and examples of big data in 2000 and 2014.

Some industry commentators evaluate data using additional factors such as veracity, which measures data accuracy, and value, which considers the value of the data.

Table 8-1	Big Data in 2000 versus 2014	
Factor	*2000*	*2014*
Volume	10 GB hard drives. Today, the same size drives are sold as USB storage sticks.	Facebook processes 500 TB of data per day, more than any one hard drive can handle.
Velocity	E-commerce sites such as Amazon served 10 to 20 million customers per year.	Online ad exchanges process 1 million events per ad per second to display the right ad to a visitor.
Variety	Metadata (basic summary information about data), such as file size, creator, and date of creation were considered cutting-edge and complex to process.	Websites such as Yelp and Foursquare generate multiple data types, such as social, geolocation, and transaction data.

Preparing your data for analysis

Real-world data can rarely be used right away. The real world is messy, and so too is the data it produces. Frequently, data has incorrect or missing values, fields that are no longer applicable, or multiple data sets in different formats. Before starting your analysis, you need to do the following:

✔ Import your data

✔ Clean your data

When you import data using Excel or another spreadsheet application, the process requires just a few mouse clicks. However, large amounts of data cause problems for most spreadsheet applications. For instance, the latest version of Excel supports approximately 1 million rows of data, but the entire application starts to slow down with 50,000 rows of data. Additionally, if your data is constantly changing you will need an automated way to keep importing it. Later in this section, you discover tools you can use. Regardless of the tool, you still need to make sure that the data is importing correctly.

The majority of your time will be spent cleaning the data. For example, suppose you are downloading sales data from two applications. One data source spells out the month but the other uses numerals. This situation requires that you make the data consistent. You also must check for and delete duplicate data and outliers, both of which are likely errors. Similarly, if you have a row of data and some of the fields are missing, you must decide whether to delete the entire row or fill in the missing data.

Surveying techniques to analyze data

When they think of data analysis, many people imagine complex mathematical models. Those equations certainly have their place, but there are other data analysis techniques. This section describes some of the ones used to analyze large data sets.

Summarizing data trends and examining outliers

One simple data analysis technique is to graph the data, and see whether there are any extreme outliers or interesting trends. The challenge with this task is finding all the relevant data, and knowing enough about the underlying data set to spot anomalies.

For example, the New York City Department of Health assigns to each of its 24,000 restaurants a letter grade of A (13 or fewer points), B (14 to 27), or C (28 or more, which can close a restaurant until the violations are corrected) based on health code compliance. Ben Wellington, a data analyst and blogger, charted all the restaurant letter grades and noticed that three times as many restaurants scored 13 points, the lowest score that still receives an A, than 14 points, a B grade. See Figure 8-1. In other words, health inspectors may be inflating grades for those restaurants on the edge of an A or a B score. The finding generated newspaper coverage and responses from the NY Health Department.

Figure 8-1:
Three times as many NYC restaurants scored 13 points than 14 points

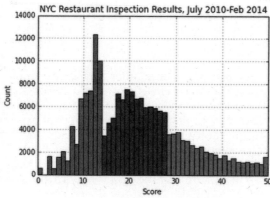

Segmenting and aggregating data

Another data analysis technique is to filter your data for certain criteria, and then aggregate the data to see whether there's an interesting story.

Google, for example, created a flu map called Flu Trends by filtering all their search queries for flu-related search terms. They aggregated the queries by location and highlighted abnormal increases, as shown in Figure 8-2.

Traditionally, the U.S. Centers for Disease Control monitors flu outbreaks by reporting on physician visits. In 2009, Flu Trends predicted the flu outbreak in the U.S. in real time, two weeks before the official CDC reports.

Figure 8-2:
Google
Flu Trends
predicted a
flu outbreak
before offi-
cial reports
did.

Combining two or more data sets

The mash up of two different data sets can create unexpected and interesting results. Whenever you combine data sets, the challenges are cleaning the data and understanding how to combine it.

For example, over half of New York City's drains were clogged, and the city wanted to find restaurants that were illegally dumping grease into the city's sewers. Ordinarily, the city would be able to inspect only a fraction of its 20,000 restaurants. Instead, city data analysts mapped the location of the clogged drains and restaurant locations that did not have waste management services. Although mapping locations may sound simple, agencies in NY report location in different ways, such as by GPS, block, or parcel. The resulting list was small enough for city inspectors to tackle, and the initiative resolved 95 percent of the illegal dumping.

Modeling

Much of the advanced big data work, and work you'll likely do if you become a data analyst, involves some type of modeling. A *model* is a name given to a math formula used to represent real world data, and many different types of models and formulas exist.

In general, models typically either predict some future value or classify data into categories. For example, models can predict how the US Supreme Court will rule on a particular case, or what movies to watch next given the movies you've already seen. In addition, models can classify whether the email you just received is a spam message or a legitimate message, and where the faces are in pictures of people.

Kaggle.com hosts competitions involving real data analysis in which anyone can practice their data skills. Some people use extremely complex models and techniques, but the people who consistently win Kaggle competitions comment that the simple models usually do best. I provide more resources for learning data science topics in Chapter 9, but don't let any of these additional resources intimidate you.

Improving the models used to predict judicial opinions and classify email require human intervention. *Machine learning* is the term that describes a set of models that learn and improve performance automatically. There are two categories of learning:

- **Supervised learning:** Data with a known structure and relationship is examined.

  For example, the book *Moneyball* chronicles how Billy Bean, the general manager of the Oakland Athletics, used a player's on-base percentage and walks as predictors for how many runs the player would score in a game.

- **Unsupervised learning:** Data without a known structure or relationship is analyzed to try and find some relationship.

  For example, suppose that you run a dating website and want to divide your users into three to six groups so that you can match people in each group with similar interests. Before looking at people's profiles, you won't know how many groups you'll have in the end or what they will be. After you starting dividing your users, you find that you have a group of people working at startups, a group of middle-aged people interested in art and theater, and a group who likes running and skiing.

Decoding Data with R and Python

Numerous tools can be used to analyze data. In addition to Python, which is described in other chapters, you may have heard of R, SAS, Stata, and SPSS. SPSS does not have all the capabilities of the other tools, but beginners can use it to perform straightforward statistical tasks easily.

SAS and Stata, which are programming languages, are powerful for some types of tasks but can be limited for more advanced data analysis. Generally, R and Python are considered the most powerful languages to use for modern data analysis. Both languages have strong statistical capabilities, increased functionality through external packages and libraries, and a growing community of users that provide support.

Using R for data analysis

R is a programming language developed in the early 1990s. Created for statisticians, the language quickly spread to other fields such as finance, biology, epidemiology, and social sciences. R has a few attributes that have contributed to its popularity:

- ✔ **Free and open source:** Download R and use it at no charge. It's hard to beat free, especially when SAS, Stata, and SPSS charge for either the software package or annual licenses to use the software. (The fee often includes technical support.) R also allows you to freely modify the software.

- ✔ **Interoperable:** Interface R with other statistical packages such as SAS, Stata, and SPSS.

- ✔ **Multiplatform:** Use R on a variety of operating systems, including Windows, Mac, and Unix operating systems.

- ✔ **Visualizations:** R comes with built-in visualization capabilities that make it easy to create colorful, professional looking charts and graphs.

- ✔ **Expanded functionality:** Download freely available packages that add functionality and features such as text cleanup, visualization, and geolocation mapping.

R uses a command-line interface; you type your code one line at a time. You can also store the code in a script file and reference it when necessary. R is made friendlier by a number of code editors and graphical user interfaces, including RStudio, shown in Figure 8-3, and R Commander.

Using Python for data analysis

Python is a general-purpose programming language that was developed in 1989 and has become popular for application, web development, games, and data analytics. Much of Python's strength in analyzing data comes from external code libraries that have expanded Python's functionality, and the community of users who continue supporting and maintaining these libraries.

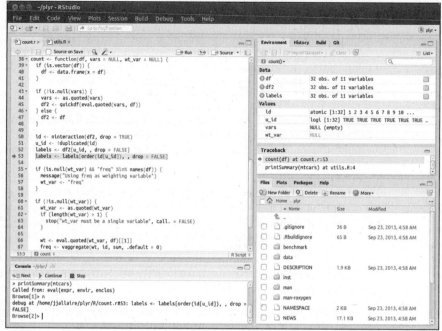

Figure 8-3:
RStudio is a
code editor
to make pro-
gramming in
R easier.

Compared to R, Python is similar in many respects that make it popular among data scientists, including the following:

- **Free and open source:** Download and use Python for free, and freely modify the program.

- **Interoperable**: Use plug-ins to integrate Python with other statistical packages, such as SAS, Stata, and SPSS. Note, however, that these integrations are experimental in many cases.

- **Multiplatform:** Run Python on a variety of operating systems such as Windows, Macintosh, and Unix.

- **Visualizations:** Python includes support for charts and graphs, but it is not as developed as R. However, this functionality is improving through the use of external APIs.

- **Expanded functionality:** Expand Python's feature set by installing libraries. This capability is Python's biggest strength due to the sophisticated and well-developed Python libraries that are available, such as the following:

  - NumPy: Performs linear algebra calculation, and is required by many other libraries

  - SciPy: Builds upon the NumPy libraries and does integration, optimization, and signal and image processing

- Pandas: Deals with time-series data and works with large data sets; replicates much of R's functionality

- Scikit-learn: Used for data mining and data analysis, including regressions and more complex machine learning technique

If you're wondering whether to learn R or Python first, think of your goal and what project you want to complete. Then do some research to find the language preferred by your employer or coworkers and the language in which other similar projects were coded. Also check the online forums for discussions relevant to your topic area or goal.

You can see an example of Python and R used to solve the same problem, with all the steps from setup to conclusion. In the blog post at www. theswarmlab.com/r-vs-python-round-1, the authors created a graph of the top 25 most violent films, ordered by number of screen deaths per minute, using Python and R.

Visualizing and Interacting with Data

Data is most persuasive when used to tell a story. And if words are used to tell a story, adding pictures can help you be more convincing. Many of the analytic tools mentioned in this chapter can create static graphs and charts. However, the creation of interactive charts and graphs, or showing data in motion often requires additional programming.

The motion chart was popularized in a 2006 Ted Talk on economic development given by Swedish professor Hans Rosling. Viewed over 10 million times, his talk included a moving graph of life expectancy versus income from the 1800s to modern day. See Figure 8-4. The animation in his visualization makes it easy to see how the sickest and poorest countries in Asia have caught up in just the last few decades to be as wealthy and healthy as the top countries in Europe and North America.

Rosling had to build his own software from scratch to show his early data visualizations. Today, there are two primary ways to create interactive web-based data visualizations that anyone can view:

- **Visualization libraries:** Many interactive web-based visualizations are created using JavaScript, and one of the most popular visualization libraries is D3.js. This library gives you an extremely high degree of control over the way the data reacts to mouse and keyboard input. In Figure 8-5, D3.js is used to compare the Facebook IPO to other technology IPOs, allowing the reader to zoom in on any particular data point or zoom out for the larger picture.

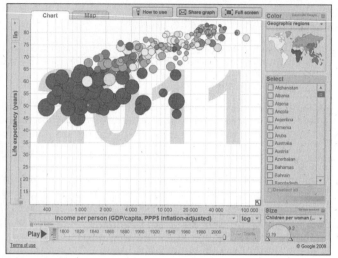

Figure 8-4:
Animated
life expec-
tancy
versus
income chart.

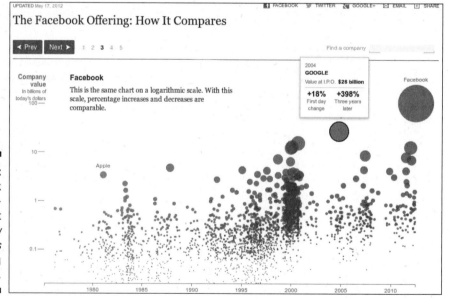

Figure 8-5:
Facebook
IPO compar-
ison chart
for the *New
York Times*
built using
D3.js.

Other popular visualization libraries include Paper.js, which creates
vector images and transformations, and Chart.js, an easy way to create a
number of basic charts.

✔ **Application Programming Interfaces (APIs):** APIs allow public web-based
access to private programs by taking requests and responding with data.
`Plot.ly` is a popular API that can be accessed in a variety of different
languages, and is used to create charts and graphs online.

Part III
Getting Your Coding Education

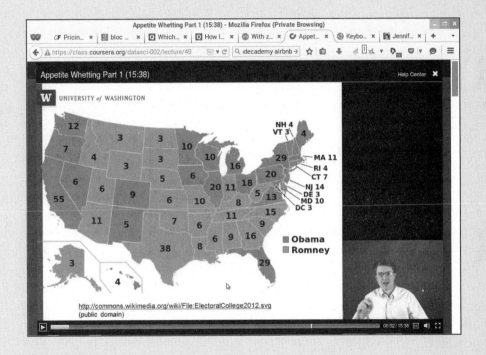

Check out www.dummies.com/extras/gettingacodingjob for ten websites where you can practice coding.

In this part . . .

- ✔ Find out different ways you can learn to code on your own
- ✔ Learn what a coding boot camp is and whether it is for you
- ✔ Explore ways to learn to code on the job and in school

Chapter 9

Coding on Your Own

· ·

· ·

I am always doing that which I cannot do, in order that I may learn how to do it.

— Pablo Picasso

When you decide that a career in coding is for you, there are many ways to take the plunge and start learning. You can learn by yourself, in modern high-intensity coding schools, in traditional environments such as a university or college, or on the job.

Unlike learning subjects like biology or chemistry, learning to code doesn't require lots of expensive equipment or many years before you see results. You can learn how to code a feature or a function, and start implementing it right away. No matter what route you take to learn how to code, it's a good idea to try learning a little bit on your own to see how you like it.

In this chapter, you choose a goal, discover the hardware and software you'll need to start coding, and see the various free and low-cost resources available to learn coding on your own. Learning to code, especially on your own, is not easy — this chapter provides a roadmap to make the journey easier.

Assessing Your Goal, Time, and Budget

Whenever you start learning any new subject you should ask yourself the following questions"

- ✔ What is your goal after you finish learning? Do you want a full-time job or part-time work? Do you want to perform your existing job more efficiently?
- ✔ How much time you can commit?
- ✔ How much money are you willing to spend?

Choosing your goal

The goal for many people is to do their existing job more efficiently. Chapter 2 covered different ways coding could improve your ability to do your job across a variety of roles. For example, you may love your job in sales, and you want to analyze the large volumes of data that your company has on which product the customers use the most, so you can find similar customers and build a list of prospects to solicit. Gradually, as you increase your proficiency, other companies may ask you to consult for them and build some similar capabilities. The commitment and resources required for a gradual change like this are low and constant, because you are learning over a long period of time.

For others, the goal might be more dramatic. You may want a full career change in the next six to twelve months. The commitment and resources required to make this type of switch are significant, but employers are becoming more comfortable with self-taught programmers.

Making time to learn how to code

To achieve your goal it is important to understand how much time is required in total and how you will plan your learning. If your goal is to learn a tool or complete a task at work more efficiently, you may need only a day to a week of training, along with some practice, to start seeing results. Learning to code in a week or less to complete simple tasks is possible for many coding fields, including web development, data analysis, and database management.

To switch careers and be employable as a full-time developer requires between 700 to 1,000 hours. That sounds like a lot, but you can complete that in about ten weeks with intense practice, or in six months to one year with less commitment.

Completing 700 hours of learning in 10 weeks requires a full-time commitment. However, if you want to learn during the course of a year, you might be able to devote 15 hours per week to study while working full-time, depending on your job.

When learning introductory coding topics, which take 50 hours to complete, the time you spend can be more sporadic — an hour between meetings at work, an hour each weeknight at home, and several hours during the weekend. As the topics become more complex, you'll need dedicated blocks of time for learning and for debugging.

Book your dedicated time in your calendar now so you can keep progressing even when holidays, vacations, and birthdays pop up.

Spending money to learn how to code

Learning how to code on your own is the cheapest option in terms of cash spent, though you'll need more time to set up your system and troubleshoot issues that arise. The good news is that putting aside hardware costs, the software and learning resources are free or inexpensive. In addition, you'll find a community of experts and people learning like you who want to share information and support each other.

Purchasing computer hardware

Computer hardware can be expensive, but options exist at a variety of price ranges. Here are some options when purchasing a computer to learn to code:

- ✔ **Cheapest:** Use your existing computer, whether PC or Macintosh. The software is usually harder to install on Windows-based systems than on computers running Linux, Unix, or Mac OS (which runs a version of Unix).

  For $89, Symple (at `www.symplepc.com`) sells a computer with a preinstalled Linux-based operating system and enough power to perform your coding tasks. You need to supply your own monitor, keyboard, and mouse.

- ✔ **Cheap:** Chromebook laptops (see Figure 9-1) are portable and light but powerful enough to run coding software. They run Google's Chrome operating system and are designed to be used while connected to the Internet. You can't install traditional Mac, PC, or Linux applications, but you can install extensions made for the Chrome browser. These laptops typically retail for $200, and are manufactured by major companies such as Acer, HP, and Samsung.

Figure 9-1:
Google
Chrome-
books pack
enough
power to
do serious
coding.

Codestarter (at Codestarter.org), a nonprofit that provides laptops to kids learning to code, has publicly released the script to turn a Chromebook Acer C720 into a coding machine complete with modern programming languages such as Python, Ruby, and NodeJS. Use the script by visiting github.com/codestarterorg/ubuntu-chromebook-installer.

✔ **Moderate:** The computers in the previous categories are fine to learn with but are rarely used in professional development environments. The most popular computers in this category are $600 lightweight PCs called ultrabooks and made by Dell, Acer, and Asus, and the $900 MacBook Air. These laptops have high-resolution screens with sharp contrast and crisp colors, important features when coding website or data visualizations.

✔ **Expensive:** The standard machines used in professional development environments have at least a 21-inch resolution screen, 8 gigabytes of RAM, 500-megabyte hard drive, and 2GHz dual-core or quad-core processors. Some Windows PCs meet these specifications, but most popular among developers are the MacBook Pro laptops and the iMac desktop computers, both of which cost at least $2,000. Apple computers are popular in this category for several reasons:

• **Display:** Apple's retina display screen has such a high resolution that the individual pixels are imperceptible to the human eye at an average distance with normal vision. This high resolution gives Mac displays a strong advantage when doing visual work.

• **Hardware:** Developers who use the Linux or Unix operating system often have to deal with hardware devices (such as graphics cards, sound cards, or USB ports) that don't install or function properly. The Mac operating system, which runs a version of Unix, has few hardware issues because all parts are manufactured and tested by Apple.

- **Software:** Mac computers are preinstalled with the most popular programming languages, including Python, Ruby, PHP, and Perl. In addition, for mobile apps, you can use a PC or a Mac to develop Android apps, but you can use only a Mac to develop apps for iOS devices such as iPhones and iPads.

When learning how to code, you likely don't need the best or fastest computer. If you do decide to purchase a higher-end computer, remember that the majority of people using your programs won't have a computer as fast or a monitor with as high-resolution as you. Developers who forget this create websites and visualizations that others find slow or difficult to read.

Computer software

After you have a computer, you need to install software to help you write computer programs. The software is basically free, though it can take longer than expected to make sure it installs correctly.

Initially, you should install the following types of software:

- ✔ **Programming languages:** Popular programming languages such as Rails and Python are used for everything from web development to data analysis. These languages are usually free to download, install, and use. Use a search engine to find installation guides for the Windows, Mac, or Linux environment.

To install Ruby, Rails, Git, Sublime Text, and more on Windows, Mac, or Linux machines, use the guide at `installrails.com`. Thousands of people have used this guide; if you get stuck, check out the comments at each step.

- ✔ **Code editors:** You can start programming right away with built-in applications such as Notepad on Windows and TextEdit on a Mac. Notepad and TextEdit were not designed for coding, and other code editors provide enhancements such as code syntax highlighting and code autocomplete such as Notepad++ on a PC, Text Wrangler on a Mac, and Geany on Linux environments. To develop mobile applications, you can download and use XCode from Apple for iOS apps, or Android Studio from Google for Android apps. All of this software is freely available for you to use.

Some popular and useful code editors are not free. Sublime Text (`www.sublimetext.com`), which sells for $70, works across multiple platforms and includes advanced editing, highlighting, and code completion features. You can download and trial an unrestricted copy before purchasing. Another code editor is Cloud9 (`c9.io`), which you access in the browser without downloading anything. The main advantage here is that everything is automatically updated, always works, and you can access your work and code from any Internet-connected machine. Cloud9 has a free plan, and paid plans start at $9 per month.

- **Versioning software:** Whether working alone or in team, it can be useful to save backup versions of your code and merge changes and updates from others working on the same program. Git (`git-scm.com`) is a popular free tool to manage backups, versioning, and multiple versions of code when working on a team.

Free cloud-based services interact with Git to back up your code on the Internet. Popular providers include `Github.com` and `Bitbucket.com`. Both allow you and others to view and update code you publicly post.

Learning to Code Online and Offline

An incredible number of resources are available for learning how to code. Do a Google search for *learn to code,* and you will find millions of websites and more content than you could ever consume. To not feel overwhelmed, first ask yourself what kind of coder or coding job you want. Would you like to learn to be a

- **Front-end developer:** Create the look, feel, and appearance of websites accessed on desktops or laptops.
- **Back-end developer:** Write the behind-the-scenes code that supports functionality and features visitors use on your website.
- **Mobile developer:** Build apps for smartphones and mobile devices.
- **Data analyst:** Analyze data, and generate insights to improve outcomes.
- **SEO specialist:** Improve how search engines find and index websites.

This section presents resources you can use to learn more about each of these subject areas.

Using blogs and books

Traditionally, a self-learner used blog posts to dip a toe into a topic, and books to dive deeper into a programming language. Blogs highlight inspirational stories that document people's journeys, and books serve as valuable reference tools. The following are some favorite blogs and books in each subject area:

- **Front-end and back-end development:**
  - `blog.jenniferdewalt.com`: An artist by trade, Jennifer Dewalt (see Figure 9-2) learned to code by building a different website every day for 180 days, writing a blog post about it, and posting the code publicly on GitHub. On day 52, she created an Etch a Sketch program; on day 97 she created a text-to-Braille converter.

Figure 9-2:
Jennifer Dewalt on day 180 after building her 180th website.

- `joshuakemp.blogspot.com`: Joshua Kemp, a blacksmith, seriously injured his hand while shoeing a horse. He decided to learn to code, and wrote about going from a blacksmith to a developer.

- *HTML and CSS* by John Duckett: For front-end developers, this full-color book is the number-one programming book on Amazon and a good introduction to what you can do with HTML and CSS.

- `learncodethehardway.org`: Zed Shaw has written two books for back-end developers titled *Learn Ruby the Hard Way* and *Learn Python the Hard Way*. Both, which are freely available online, provide instructions and real coding examples aimed at beginners.

For a community-sourced list of all freely available, online programming books, visit `http://github.com/vhf/free-programming-books`. The list covers over 25 programming languages and environments, so focus first on the popular and easier languages such as HTML, CSS, Ruby, and Python.

✔ **Mobile development:**

- `app.itize.us`: Half the challenge when creating a mobile app is cramming the functionality you need into a small mobile screen. Visit this site for a curated selection of the best-designed apps.

- • `twotoasters.com/blogs/ideas`: TwoToasters creates mobile apps for some of the largest brands in the country. They maintain an iOS and Android blog on industry news and programming tidbits.

- • *The Swift Programming Language* by Apple, Inc.: Apple recently released a new programming language, and new and experienced developers alike are learning how to use it. This free book, which can be downloaded from iTunes, is long but a good place to start.

✔ **Data analytics:**

- • *Visual Display of Quantitative Information* by Edward Tufte: Finding great insights is most powerful when you can communicate them effectively. This classic book has no code but shows the different ways data can be graphically displayed.

- • *Python for Data Analysis* by Wes McKinney: Data analysis always starts with cleaning, merging, and transforming your underlying data. This book shows you Python techniques to whip your data into shape so you can analyze it.

- • IBM Big Data Hub: Available at `ibmbigdatahub.com/blogs`, IBM's blog has consistent coverage of big data trends, industry news, and the latest technologies.

✔ **Search engine optimization:**

- • Moz: Available at `moz.com/learn/seo`, this blog is the best place to go to start your SEO education. You'll learn all the factors that influence search rankings.

- • `cutroni.com`: To track and measure the effectiveness of any SEO campaign, you need an analytics tool such as Google Analytics. Google's Analytics Advocate blogs about cohort analysis, user identifiers, and other analytics-specific topics.

- • *The Art of SEO* by Enge et al: The authors have been doing SEO work for decades and provide general advice along with specific suggestions for updates made to search engine algorithms.

Learning from online websites

With the demand for coders so high, many companies have created websites with engaging and interactive experiences that are easier to complete than just reading a blog post or a book. Some sites gamify the experience, encouraging you to keep learning by earning points and badges. Most sites have community support, which can include discussion boards, live chat, or tutors to help when needed. The cost for these services varies per website; some are free and others charge a monthly or per-course fee.

When choosing a resource, check how much content is on the site, whether the materials are up-to-date, and the level of community engagement. Nothing beats having a strong online community to answer your questions quickly, and nothing is worse than spending hours trying to debug a problem with your code only to discover that the website you were using had a typo in the instructions.

Here are some favorite online websites in each subject area:

✔ **Front-end and back-end development:**

- codecademy.com (free): Learn basic web programming languages to create complete websites from front end to back end (see Figure 9-3). You can start immediately with only a web browser; you don't have to download or installing any software.

- codeschool.com ($29/month): Initially, Code School became popular with its Rails for Zombies series, but the site also has a niche among intermediate developers. The site features video lessons with in-browser coding challenges for a wide range of programming topics and languages. There are also *screencasts* (recoded coding sessions) with guest speakers teaching various skills.

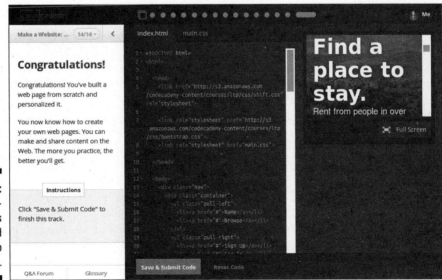

Figure 9-3: Codecademy helps you to build the Airbnb homepage.

- ✔ `teamtreehouse.com` ($25 or $45/month): Treehouse has a slightly larger content library than Code School, and includes all the usual front-end and back-end courses along with mobile app courses for iOS and Android as well as business classes on how to freelance and market your app or business.

Bento (`bentobox.io`) is a community-sourced curated listing of the best free resources for learning how to program and, most importantly, the order in which to take these topics to maximize your learning. The site has grown to include over 100 lessons on programming languages, frameworks, libraries, and APIs.

- ✔ **Mobile development:**

  - Stanford's Developing iOS 8 Apps (free): Stanford's School of Engineering has released on iTunes an online course with over 20 hours of instruction and slides so you can learn to code apps for iPhones and iPads. Go to `itunes.apple.com/us/course/developing-ios-8-apps-swift`.

  - Intro to iOS App Development by Udacity (free): Video lectures teach Swift programming by building an app that records your voice and then transforms it into Darth Vader or a chipmunk. Visit `www.udacity.com/course/ud585`.

  - Android and Swift Immersive by Bitfountain ($150): These two separate courses each have over 300 videos on developing iOS and Android apps. Available at `bitfountain.io`.

- ✔ **Data analytics:**

  - `datasciencemasters.org` (free): This open-source data-science curriculum has curated free and paid online courses, books, and tutorials.

  - Introduction to Data Science (free): Hosted on Coursera (see Figure 9-4), and taught by the University of Washington, this online course covers introductory big data concepts, along with data analysis and visualization. Available at `www.coursera.org/course/datasci`.

  - `datacamp.com` (free to $25/month): This interactive online course teaches you R, a statistical programming language, in the browser. Courses include introductory lessons to advanced data manipulation and visualization using R and specialized libraries.

Find a curated list of 250 free online video courses across a variety of coding topics from universities such as Stanford, MIT, and Princeton by visiting Class Central, available at `www.class-central.com/subject/cs`.

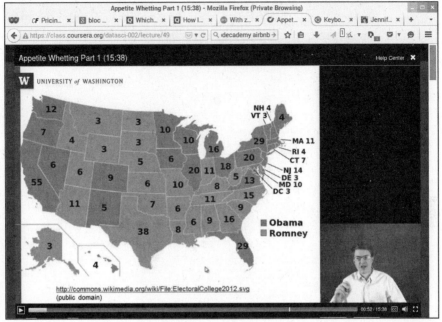

Figure 9-4:
Coursera data science course analyzing 2012 presidential election data.

Adding support with mentors

As you can see, there is no shortage of content or coding topics to learn. As you start your path down any one of these roads, you'll have questions, get stuck, or just need encouragement. Although you are learning by yourself, you can find mentors to support you on your journey and help you make progress.

Mentoring can be expensive, but the cost depends on how much time and assistance you need. If you're taking a Codecademy course or viewing a lecture on Coursera and need an hour or two of ad-hoc help occasionally, check out these hourly services to connect with a mentor:

- ✔ `airpair.com`: Over 2,000 expert developers are available to help you debug and review your code. Experts set their own rates, which range from $60 to $300 per hour.

- ✔ `codementor.io`: Experts in over 800 categories, including HTML, JavaScript, and Ruby, connect with you instantly for one-on-one help. Rates start at $10 for a 15-minute session, and the website displays experts who are online and available to help. (See Figure 9-5.)

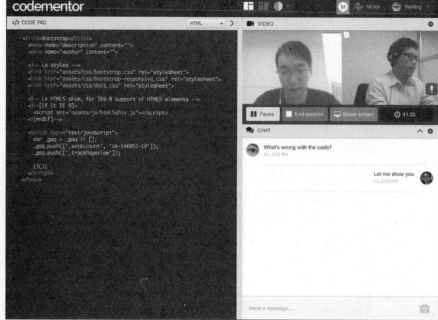

Figure 9-5:
Expert coding mentor services provide live video, chat, and screen sharing.

✔ hackhands.com: Users pay $1 per minute for on-demand help across a variety of programming languages. After you connect to an expert, you have an initial 5-minute grace period at no charge to assess whether the expert is the right person to assist with your problem.

You may want to occasionally ask for help from mentoring sites such as AirPair. Expert-led coding instruction typically involves a curriculum along with mentor check-ins, office hours, a discussion group, and live chat. These fuller and more supported services work well if you have some money to spend on your coding education but don't want to pay $10,000 for a high-intensity coding boot camp (discussed in Chapter 10).

Some options for mentor-led coding instruction include the following:

✔ thinkful.com: Along with courses in web development, design, data science, iOS, and Android programming, Thinkful matches you with a mentor for weekly 45-minute sessions and offers open office hours. Students pay $500 per month, and typically finish one subject in three months.

✔ careerfoundry.com: Similar to Thinkful but with fewer classes, CareerFoundry has a custom curriculum for web development and design, along with weekly mentor sessions and a group chat. The course includes 12 mentor sessions and costs $1,680.

✔ bloc.io: Bloc has programs in web and mobile development as well as design. The fee is $4,500 per course and includes 36 mentor sessions over 12 to 36 weeks.

Staying on Target to Achieve Your Goal

You have a computer, found a website, and even did a few lessons, but you feel stuck. Learning anything on your own, especially coding, can be tough! It's easy to lose motivation, get frustrated, feel confused, and spend way more time on a concept or topic than you had planned. All these feelings are normal when learning a new subject.

This section provides some tips to keep your learning on track and a process to help you get going again when you're stuck.

Pick a language, any language

As a novice coder, you may not be sure where to start. Should you learn Python, Java, Swift, Ruby, PHP, and JavaScript at the same time or sequentially? Or should you just choose a few?

If you've never programmed before, I recommend learning a language used to create web pages, because it's easy to get started and publish work for others to see. Start with HTML and CSS. These are markup languages, which are the easiest to learn. You put content on a web page with HTML, and style that content with CSS.

After you understand some of the basics of presenting content, learn a programming language to manipulate that content. Keep in mind that you don't need to learn every programming language — JavaScript, which adds interactivity to a web page, is a common starting point for beginners, along with either Ruby or Python, which add advanced features such as user accounts and logins.

Learning to code is similar to learning to drive a car. When you first learned to drive, you probably didn't worry too much about the type of car you were driving. After passing the driving test, you could operate just about any car, even one you hadn't driven before, because you knew to look for the ignition, accelerator, and brake. Learning a programming language works the same way: After you learn one language, you know what to look for, and learning and using another language becomes easier. Just start somewhere!

Define a goal

To stay motivated, create a concrete, well-defined goal. You can choose any goal you like, but make sure it's something you would be excited to accomplish. Good goals for beginners include the following:

- ✔ Build your coding vocabulary so you can understand what developers or designers say in meetings at work.

- ✔ Create a small website — consisting of one to four different pages — for yourself, a business, or a group.

- ✔ Analyze a public data set that is too large for Excel (such as all the subway riders or cab riders in New York) and create one simple graph. This type of data is freely available and low-stakes, and you can check your work against blog posts written by others who have used the same data set.

Tilt the odds in your favor by making your goal SMART. You're more likely to accomplish any goal that is specific, measurable, attainable, realistic, and time bound.

You can start practicing by doing small coding tasks, such as bolding a headline. At first, you may feel disconnected from your goal. But as you start to piece together individual coding skills, you'll see a path towards accomplishing your goal.

It can be difficult to know whether your goal is easy and attainable or too hard. Use a search engine to type your goal with *tutorial* at the end. If you can't find any short and easy-to-read tutorials on the subject, try choosing another goal.

Google is a coder's best friend

At some point, you'll get stuck — your program won't run, or it runs but returns incorrect results. Professional developers face these same problems. Developers constantly use the Google search engine to research general questions on how to code a feature or specific questions on syntax for a command or a tag. For example, imagine that a few months from now, you need to add an image to a website. You remember that HTML has a tag to insert images on a website, but you don't recall the syntax. To quickly and efficiently find the answer, follow these steps:

1. **Go to** `www.google.com`.

2. **Search for** *HTML image syntax.*

    The programming language, the intended command, and the word *syntax* should be sufficient to find a good set of resources.

3. **Review trusted websites for answers.**

    For many coding questions you'll likely see the following domain names in the top ten search results:

    - `www.w3schools.com` is one of the best resources for beginners who want to find basic information on developing web pages.

    - `https://developer.mozilla.org` is a crowd-sourced documentation and tutorial site for developing web pages. Its documentation is accurate, although some content is not beginner friendly.

    - `http://stackexchange.com` and `http://stackoverflow.com` are crowd-sourced discussion sites where developers can ask and answer questions about a variety of coding topics. You can find information on everything from front-end and back-end web development to data analysis and operating systems.

You can use this same process to research questions in other coding languages, or to find code examples from other developers who are building programs similar to yours.

Zap those bugs

While you're doing all this coding you will inevitably create errors, commonly referred to as *bugs*. There are three types of errors:

- ✔ **Syntax errors** occur when you write invalid code that the computer doesn't understand. For example, in CSS, you write `color: blue;` to change the font color of text. If you wrote `font-color: blue;` instead, you'd generate a syntax error because `font-color` is an invalid property.

- ✔ **Semantic errors** occur when you write valid code that has an unintended effect. For example, trying to divide a number by zero is a semantic error in JavaScript.

✔ **Logic or design errors** occur when you write valid code that has the intended effect, but the code produces the wrong result. For example, in JavaScript, converting miles to feet using `var miles = 4000 * feet` is a logic error. Although the code is written correctly and does what the programmer wants it to do, it still produces the wrong answer because a mile consists of 5,280 feet, not 4,000.

Some programming languages such as HTML or CSS code work even in the presence of syntax errors. However, in other programming languages, such as JavaScript, code with syntax errors won't run.

The best way to find and eliminate bugs is to first check your code syntax and then check the logic. Review your code line by line, and if you still can't find the error, ask another person to take a look at your code, or post it on an online community forum such as `http://stackoverflow.com`.

Just Ship It

When you start coding, you will likely be reluctant to show others your creations, whether it's your first basic website or something more complex Reid Hoffman, the founder of LinkedIn, famously said, "If you are not embarrassed by the first version of your product, you've launched too late." Hoffman was commenting on this desire to keep trying to perfect what you have built, and says instead to release (or "ship") your code to public view even if you feel embarrassed. Regardless of the size of your website or app, it is better to receive feedback early and learn from your mistakes than to continue heading in the wrong direction.

Also, remember that the highly trafficked, highly polished websites you use today started from humble beginning and simple prototypes. Google's first home page, for example, had only a fraction of the functionality or style of its home page today, as you can see in Figure 9-6.

Figure 9-6: Google's original home page in 1998.

Collect Feedback

After you finish coding the first version of your website or app, collect feedback on your code and on the final product. Even if everything is working and your website looks great, that doesn't mean your code was written correctly or that your site solves a problem. For example, YouTube initially started as a video-dating site but changed to a general video-sharing website based on user feedback.

The best way to obtain this information is to collect quantitative and qualitative data on your code and the product. For example, measuring the places where visitors click on a website and how long they stay on each web page gives you quantitative information, which helps you diagnose and improve low performing pages. You can collect qualitative information by surveying users, either by emailing them survey questions or by watching people in-person use your website and then asking questions.

Often this data will surprise you — users may find confusing the features you thought were obvious and easily understood, and vice versa. Similarly, if possible, have someone examine your code, in a process called a *code review,* to ensure that you didn't overlook any major problems.

Iterate on Your Code

After you've collected feedback, the next step is to *iterate* on that feedback: Keep coding until the major issues in your feedback have been addressed and you have improved both the code and the product. Keep in mind that it's usually best to confirm the usefulness of your product first, before spending time improving the code.

This process — building a product with a minimum set of essential features, collecting feedback on the product, and then iterating on that feedback — is sometimes referred to as a *lean startup methodology.* These days, changing software is as simple as modifying a few lines of code in real time. This contrasts with the way products used to be coded, which involved longer development cycles, less upfront feedback, and documentation for any software change in the product.

Just like with document drafts, save the old versions of your code. You might realize that an older version is better, or you might want to debug the current code by using an older version.

Share Your Successes and Failures

While coding, you may have come across documentation you found confusing or just plain wrong. Maybe you found a great resource or a tool that worked especially well for a product you were building. Or perhaps the no one used the features you coded, and you had to give up the project.

In all these situations, the best thing you can do for yourself and the larger community is to blog about your successes and failures. Blogging benefits you because it shows others the issues you're thinking about and trying to solve. Similarly, blogging benefits others who used Google to search for and read about your experiences, just as you used Google to search for ideas and solve problems. Many nontechnical entrepreneurs, such as Dennis Crowley of Foursquare and Kevin Systrom of Instagram, taught themselves enough coding to build small, working prototypes and successful products, and then shared that journey with others.

Writing about your failures is important too. An honest account of what you learned will generate support from others and may reach a wider audience than those who initially used your product. For example, the CEO of Earbits, a music-streaming service for independent artists, wrote a blog post about shutting down the service after four and a half years and their failure to find a working business model. Within three days, his post became so popular than an investor stepped in to allow the company to operate indefinitely. See the original blog posts at `blog.earbits.com/online_radio/earbits-will-be-shutting-down-june-16th`.

You can blog for free and share your experiences using blogging sites such as WordPress (`www.wordpress.com`), Blogger (`www.blogger.com`), or Tumblr (`www.tumblr.com`).

Chapter 10

Going to Boot Camp

. . . .

In This Chapter

▶ Learning about the coding boot camp experience

▶ Seeing the daily and weekly boot camp curriculum

▶ Deciding which boot camp is right for you

. . . .

> *What we face may look insurmountable. But I learned something from all those years of training . . . we are always stronger than we know.*
>
> —*Arnold Schwarzenegger*

*T*he words *boot camp* historically referred to the intense three to four months of training given to new recruits in the armed forces. These programs are famous for their grueling physical tests, direct instruction, and intense motivation. Coding boot camps are not nearly as intense as the military version, but the goal is similar — to train a person with little or no technical skills in a short period of time to be a professional.

This chapter describes coding boot camps, helps you decide whether the boot camp experience is for you, and fills you in on what to do before attending and after graduating.

Discovering Coding Boot Camps

Coding boot camps are classes designed to turn students with little to no programming experience into employable junior-level developers in about three months. Students come from different backgrounds, including grocery store clerks, coffee baristas, IT support engineers, marketers, and financial research analysts.

The experience ranges from 8 to 13 weeks. In-person coding boot camps usually take place in a dedicated facility. Each week, students spend 70 to 80 hours learning, with instructors teaching classes from 9 to 6 during the weekdays. Students complete homework assignments and projects in the evenings and on weekends. The instruction is usually interactive: A concept or method is explained, and then students work together to complete an example to implement the concept or method. Working in groups of two, as shown in Figure 10-1, is often referred to as *pair programming*.

Figure 10-1: Students in a coding boot camp work together to code a program.

Credit: Claudine Gossett via Dev Bootcamp

Coding boot camps were founded in early 2012 in San Francisco, and the concept has since exploded, with over 40 coding boot camps appearing in New York, Chicago, Boston, Detroit, Miami, Los Angeles, Omaha, and other cities both big and small. Coding boot camps collectively trained almost 6,000 graduates in 2014, which is significant considering that US colleges grant approximately 50,000 computer science degrees per year.

Unlike US colleges, coding boot camps are not accredited and do not have a standardized curriculum. As such, boot camps differ in quality, outcomes, instructors, and attendees. Later sections describe how to filter and choose the right boot camp for you.

Compared to traditional online learning, the retention and graduation rates for coding boot camps are high. Some online courses have seen hundreds of thousands of student enrollees, but on average across online classes of different sizes only 5 to 10 percent of enrolled students complete a course. By contrast, approximately 80 to 90 percent of enrolled students finish an in-person coding boot camp, and of those, 85 to 95 percent find employment that uses their newly learned programming skills. A few major factors help contribute to these outcomes, including personalized attention from an instructor and support from your peers when you get stuck.

These graduation and employment results, dedicated classroom spaces, and high-quality teachers come at a cost. The average cost to attend a coding boot camp is $10,000, and the price can go as high as $15,000. (A few camps are free.) In addition to tuition, you also need to pay for living in the city where the boot camp is located. Limited financing options exist, such as loans from alternative lenders, discounts for underrepresented groups in the tech industry, and grants from federal, state, and city agencies. Still, most participants pay for coding boot camps out of pocket.

In popular locations such as San Francisco or New York, rent, utilities, food, and transportation can add another $6,500 to the cost of a 10-week boot camp. This figure assumes monthly costs of $1,500 for rent, $700 for food, $200 for utilities, and $200 for transportation.

One item you'll need is a laptop. A laptop will make it easy for you to work in class and continue your work at home. MacBook Pro and Air laptops are popular among boot camp attendees and in startup professional environments because they are easy to set up, render graphics in high detail, and run a version of Unix, for which many coding utilities are written. However, Apple laptops are expensive, with retail prices of $2,000 or more. Alternatively, you can use any laptop running Linux, with prices starting as low as $200. Finally, you can use a laptop running Microsoft Windows, but you will need to spend more time setting up your computer. For details on the various options, see the section in Chapter 9 on spending money to learn coding.

Some boot camps earn a referral fee when they introduce you to an employer and the employer hires you. The demand for people who can code exceeds the supply of qualified coders, so companies are willing to pay others to find talented candidates. Traditional recruiters earn approximately 15 percent of the full-time annual salary for a successfully hired candidate, so the referral fee earned by the boot camp can range from $7,000 to $15,000. In some cases, the boot camp will pass a portion of the referral fee on to you as a hiring bonus.

Boot camps that earn a referral fee can have different incentives than you. In theory, a boot camp might be influenced to steer you toward a lower-quality employer paying a referral fee instead of a higher-quality employer that is not paying a referral fee. To manage this conflict, always make sure you know whether the boot camp will receive an incentive fee if you accept an offer, and make sure you apply to a broad range of companies so you can consider multiple options before making a decision.

Filtering Boot Camps by Topic and Quality

Boot camps come in different sizes and also vary in the following dimensions:

- **Topic:** Boot camps teach specific topics and usually teach one main programming language. The major topics are web development, mobile app development, and data science, and for each topic a different programming language is emphasized.

- **Quality:** Generally the instructor's previous experience, the quality of the facility, and the graduate job placement rate contribute to the quality of the experience you will have during and after attending a boot camp.

- **Type:** Most boot camps charge an upfront fee, but some are sponsored by companies or government agencies as part of workforce development grants. A few coding camps are free.

- **Delivery:** Most boot camps are organized around in-person classes, which make it easy for instructors to provide setup and debugging help when you get stuck. A few online options, such as `thinkful.com` and `bloc.io`, provide support through screen sharing and live video chats. You can read more about these online options in Chapter 9 in the section on adding mentor support.

Coding boot camps usually teach web development, data science, and mobile app development. Of the three topics, web development is the easiest and most commonly taught.

Web development can be accomplished with Ruby, Python, PHP, and many other languages, but almost 60 percent of boot camps that teach web development teach Ruby and the Rails framework, in addition to HTML and CSS. Ruby is popular, in part, because it is a simple language to teach, well documented, and common among startups, which hire many boot camp graduates.

By contrast, data science boot camps primarily teach Python because it has more supporting libraries and applications designed for data analysis.

Finally, boot camps that teach mobile app development, which is the hardest of the three topics, are primarily geared toward iOS development and teach Objective-C.

Given the price tag of boot camps, make sure you are signing up for a high-quality experience, which you can assess in a few ways. First, boot camp instructors are either good engineers, with years of coding experience in the language being taught, or good teachers, with previous experience teaching beginners. If you're lucky, your instructor will be strong in both engineering and teaching. Second, see how long the boot camp you are considering has been open. Boot camps are popping up at a fast pace, and newer boot camps may still be working out the kinks with logistics, curriculum, and attracting employers to hire graduates. Finally, ask the boot camp what the job placement rate is for students who graduate the program; the rate should be 80 percent or higher.

You can verify a boot camp's job placement rate by using LinkedIn to find recent graduates and seeing the roles and companies where they're working. Top boot camps place graduates in junior developer or quality assurance testing roles at well-funded startups and Fortune 500 companies such as Yahoo! and PayPal. Additionally, many boot camp graduates write reviews on Quora, blog about their experiences, and have extensive online profiles with links to their email address and Twitter username, so feel free to reach out and ask for a candid review of the program.

The high price of coding boot camps might scare you off, but their recent success has created some opportunities to attend for free. Federal agencies, encouraged by technology education initiatives promoted by President Obama, have released grants to coding boot camps to lower the cost of attending for underrepresented and rural populations.

Similarly, some cities, such as New York, have used workforce development grants to sponsor boot camp classes for citizens who have not attended college and earn less than $50,000. Additionally, boot camps themselves lower the cost of attendance. Some boot camps have an initial highly selective application process but are free to attend; employee referral fees and corporate sponsorships fund these boot camps. Other boot camps offer $500 to $2,000 tuition discounts for women and minorities.

The boot camps in Table 10-1, which are sorted by topic, are some of the more established and well regarded in the United States. If one of these is not available in your city, use this data as a benchmark to evaluate other boot camps you may be considering.

Table 10-1	Reputable Boot Camps in the US		
Boot Camp and Website	*Cities*	*Cost*	*Topics*
General Assembly generalassemb.ly	Atlanta, Austin, Boston, Chicago, Los Angeles, New York, San Francisco, Seattle, Washington DC	$11,500	Web development
Dev Bootcamp devbootcamp.com	Chicago, New York, San Francisco	$12,700 – $13,950	Web development
Launch Academy launchacademy.com	Boston	$12,500	Web development
Hack Reactor hackreactor.com	San Francisco	$17,780	Web development
Flatiron School flatiron school.com	New York	$10,000 – $12,000	Web development Mobile apps
Iron Yard theironyard.com	Atlanta, Austin, Charleston, Greenville, Houston, Indianapolis, Las Vegas, Little Rock, Nashville, Orlando, Tampa, Washington DC	$12,000	Web development Mobile apps
Zipfian zipfianacademy.com	San Francisco	$16,000	Data

Boot Camp and Website	Cities	Cost	Topics
Metis thisismetis.com	New York	$14,000	Web development Data
Recurse Center recurse.com	New York	Free	Self-directed

Of the companies listed in Table 10-1, General Assembly has the most locations and graduates the most students. The only full-time coding course the company offers is web development, but there are part-time courses for both data and mobile development. The most expensive web development program is Hack Reactor, which justifies its higher cost because it offers 50 percent more formal instruction than other programs, with classes six days a week for 11 hours a day.

The dominant boot camp in the south is Iron Yard, with locations in North and South Carolina, Texas, Arkansas, Georgia, Nevada, Tennessee, and Florida. The company, along with Flatiron School, also offers courses in mobile app development for Apple devices. Although mobile device use is rising quickly, boot camps have yet to embrace teaching mobile app development, in part because of the increased difficulty of learning mobile programming languages.

Two companies, Zipfian and Metis, each teach a data science boot camp. Metis is a subsidiary of Kaplan, an established education company known for its test preparation products. In addition to learning to code, these programs also emphasize data science theory by teaching topics such as big data processing, machine learning algorithms, and natural language analysis.

The Recurse Center, formerly known as Hacker School, has a different model than the other boot camps listed. There is no fee to attend, nor is there a set curriculum. Students apply to attend and are screened for their interest in learning; those who are accepted form their own self-directed learning plan. You might pursue learning web development, creating a programming language, or coding a game. Fellow students and resident mentors help support you and answer questions throughout the program, which culminates with a project. Companies sponsor the program and pay a referral fee if they hire a graduate, though there is no obligation for any graduate to accept a job. Similar programs in data science that charge no tuition include Insight Data Science, available at `insightdatascience.com` and the Data Incubator, available at `www.thedataincubator.com`.

The acceptance rate for programs with no attendance fee is less than 5 percent — many students apply, and the programs select students most likely to succeed after completing the curriculum. Give yourself an edge in your application by highlighting the reasons why you want to learn to code and why you will be a successful graduate.

Understanding the Coding Boot Camp Curriculum

Boot camp courses run every week day for ten to twelve weeks. Boot camps vary in the structure of their curriculum, so find out the specifics for the boot camps you're considering. A daily boot camp schedule should include time for the following:

- **Live instruction:** An instructor should explain basic concepts and highlight areas where students typically get stuck, helping save you time when troubleshooting.

- **Application:** Learning by doing is often the best way to make concepts stick. In-class time to complete exercises and challenges cements concepts so you can keep practicing on your own after class is over.

- **Pair programming:** Learning with someone else will help you resolve problems more quickly and see how others approach the same problem. Additionally, as you work together, and see how someone else solves problems you'll create and add to a mental checklist of things to check when problems arise.

- **Office hours:** Sometimes you and your pair programming partner will not be able to solve an issue on your own, or maybe you don't understand a particular concept. Office hours give you the personalized one-on-one help to get up to speed and keep pace with the rest of the group.

- **Industry speakers:** As a career switcher, you should soak up as much as possible from others in the industry. Look for talks from industry veterans and successful boot camp graduates on challenges and rewards of the job, cultures at various companies, and the latest technology developments. See Figure 10-2.

Figure 10-2:
Vice
President
Biden visits
Step It Up
America, a
boot camp
in Michigan.

Following is a sample web development boot camp daily schedule. When coding boot camps say you will eat, breathe, and sleep code you'll see that they aren't kidding!

Time	*Description*
8:30 am–9:45 am	The day officially starts. The instructors share what you will learn today and cover two to three programming concepts.
10:00 am–12:00 pm	With another student, you complete challenges that test your understanding of the programming concepts. You might write a program from scratch or fix an incorrectly written program.
12:00 pm–1:00 pm	Break for lunch! Occasionally, a boot camp alum or an industry veteran might join the group and talk about breaking into the industry or the latest tech trends.
1:00 pm–2:30 pm	Instructors teach more concepts that you will apply in the challenges and to your final project.
2:45 pm–5:00 pm	With another student, you continue working on challenges and projects.

Time	*Description*
5:00 pm–5:30 pm	Class pauses to recap what was taught today and to address major questions or issues that came up. The day is officially over, but most people stay to keep working.
5:30 pm–6:00 pm	Instructors have office hours daily and at various times during the week to answer your questions.
6:00 pm–7:00 pm	Break during dinner to catch up with other boot campers about tech news and products.
7:00 pm–8:30 pm	Time for camp-organized events, such as a career panel or a resume workshop, or community-organized events, such as a MeetUp or company-sponsored hackathon.
8:30 pm–10:00 pm	Students go home, finish incomplete challenges and exercises, and rest up for tomorrow.

You'll repeat a rough version of this daily schedule for 10 to 12 weeks. Toward the end of program, less time will be spent on instruction, and more of your day will be allocated to completing your final project.

From the start to finish of the course, you should learn these core skills:

- ✔ **Languages and frameworks:** A variety of programming languages are used to make a professional looking websites, including HTML, CSS, JavaScript, jQuery, and Ruby. In addition, frameworks and libraries such as Bootstrap for HTML and CSS, Rails for Ruby, and Backbone.js for JavaScript make programming faster and easier for you.

- ✔ **Databases:** Permanently storing, retrieving, and updating data is necessary for almost every web application. As a bonus, look for courses that cover both relational SQL databases and nonrelational NoSQL databases.

- ✔ **Version control:** You'll almost always write code in teams when you work at a company. Version control software such as Git allows multiple people to write code on the same program at the same time without problems.

- ✔ **Specialization:** In a class of 20 to 40 students, getting time to learn on your own will help differentiate you from everyone else. Learning a popular API or framework, with support from your peers and instructors, can help you stand out.

- ✔ **Capstone project:** Employers screen candidates by assessing the final project a student builds toward the end of the boot camp. Choose a project that you find meaningful, and make sure there is enough time in the schedule, usually two to four weeks, to code something technically challenging so other developers will be interested in how you put it together. See Figure 10-3.

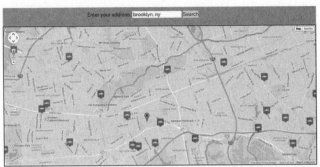

Figure 10-3:
This app
identifies
the closest
car wash
from your
current
location.

Credit: Zachary Fine

The following is a sample week-by-week web development boot camp schedule focused on Ruby and Rails. Many boot camps assign pre-work, and assume that when you arrive you'll already be familiar with basic HTML, CSS, JavaScript, and Ruby on Rails.

Week	*Description*
1	Git and Github basics are covered so you can publish code that you write. You also start learning basic Ruby. Finally, the first evening will have an installfest to resolve any software installation issues on your system.
2	You start with advanced Ruby topics such as loops, classes, and objects.
3	You begin using SQL to query and modify information stored in databases.
4	You use the Rails framework and HTML to create dynamic websites. The model-view-controller concept is used to separate different parts of your application.
5	You learn advanced HTML and CSS so you can style and lay out your application with precision.
6	You cover advanced Rails concepts such as authentication so you can create user accounts. You also learn advanced JavaScript and jQuery to make your web pages interactive.
7	You integrate external data from Twitter or Google Maps using their APIs. You also learn an advanced JavaScript framework such as Backbone.js.

Week	Description
8	You start your project, either in a group or by yourself. You also cover theoretical concepts, such as Big O notation, which describes the complexity of an algorithm.
9	You continue working on your project, working through missing data and broken external programs. You begin interview preparations with sessions on resume reviews and networking tips.
10	It is crunch time — you work hard to finish your project. You also practice answering programming challenges with your classmates and present your finished project to employers.

A lot of material is covered in these ten weeks. You will get stuck at some point — avoid getting discouraged and keep your motivation high by asking for help when needed from your peers and instructors.

Choosing the Right Boot Camp for You

With so many available boot camp options even after you've filtered by topic and quality, and the significant expense to attend most of them, take the time to think about which boot camp is the right choice for you. Keep the following in mind at as you weigh your options:

- ✔ **Your personality:** Boot camps provide many opportunities for you to work with others and learn from an instructor. Still, the bulk of time spent learning in a boot camp will be on your own. Honestly assess whether you have a self-driven, problem-solving personality, which will help you keep learning when the material becomes tough.

- ✔ **Your obligations:** Attending a boot camp will leave you with little free time. Before you start, you should be free from as many personal obligations as possible. For example, avoid working a full- or part-time job, cancel vacations that conflict with the boot camp, and let your friends and loved ones know that for three months your availability will less than normal.

- ✔ **Boot camp's location:** Boot camps are located in multiple cities. Ideally, choose a city where you feel comfortable and where you will want to work after graduation. You don't have to attend a boot camp in your current city, especially if the city is small, has limited opportunities for work at technology companies, or you are ready to leave and try another city. In addition, while graduates do pursue jobs nationally, boot camps have the strongest relationship with local employers.

✔ **People at boot camp:** You'll spend a lot of time with boot camp instructors, staff, and fellow students. Different instructors have different teaching styles, which you may or may not like. Similarly, boot camps attract different types of students, and you should confirm that you feel comfortable with the general student mix.

If possible, attend an event at the boot camp or take a tour of the facility. There is no substitute for seeing the facility and meeting the instructors in-person.

Helping win jobs offers with Eddie Washington

Eddie Washington works on the career development team for General Assembly, one of the largest coding boot camps in the world. He helps graduates of General Assembly's web development boot camp find positions at startups and Fortune 500 companies. We discussed successful strategies and common mistakes he has seen from working with hundreds of boot camp graduates.

✔ *What is the typical profile of someone who takes the web development boot camp?*

Typically, these are job seekers, who are more serious than people trying out coding as a hobby or part-time interest. These students have three to six years of work experience and come from a variety of fields like law, finance, science, and consulting. There are a small minority of people learning to code to work on their own startups.

✔ *For students trying to transition careers and get a new job, what strategies are the most successful?*

First, graduates really need to put themselves out there. Connect with people on LinkedIn, ask people to have coffee chats, participate in meetups, find people at companies where you are interested in working, and most importantly apply to 5 to 10 roles per week. Boot camps also help by creating online resume books, holding

smaller meetups for select companies, and having a large science fair for all graduates of a boot camp class meet with employers and share their background and portfolio projects.

✔ *Could you name some companies that have hired your graduates?*

Companies we've worked with include TD Ameritrade, Publisher's Clearinghouse, American Express, The Wall Street Journal, Conde Nast, JP Morgan Chase, 2U, and Sailthru. There's a mix of publicly traded companies, private companies, and startups.

✔ *What common mistakes do boot camp students make?*

The number one thing is imposter syndrome. Despite learning the skills, people sometimes feel like imposters in the industry — like they don't know enough to get a job, even though they've done the work. Another mistake is to stop coding after the boot camp is over — you always want to be working on your portfolio, adding projects and keeping your skills sharp. Finally, sometimes students think that companies are looking for people who have memorized the syntax and commands. Companies are really looking for people who have a curiosity for new technologies and a passion for building programs.

Applying to a Coding Boot Camp

Boot camps require that prospective students complete an application, and accept anywhere from 5 to 20 percent of applicants. The application helps the boot camp identify those most likely to succeed. Additionally, boot camps are evaluated on their job placement rate, and select candidates with profiles that will be interesting to potential employers. Here is a sampling of the questions asked on the application, and advice on how best to answer:

✔ *Why are you applying to this boot camp?*

Whether you're applying to one or multiple boot camps, show in your applications that you've done your homework and have a reason for applying to each specific program. Perhaps you've spoken to an alumnus, read reviews online, or attended a sample class and enjoyed learning from the teacher.

Almost every boot camp has in-person or live video info sessions covering the boot camp curriculum, alumni, and application. Attend at least a few to get a sense of the boot camp and what your expectations should be.

✔ *What is your previous coding experience?*

Don't fret if you don't have formal coding experience. The real question here is if you previously tried to learn to code, especially because many free resources are available online. It's worth trying to code before applying because boot camps assign prework — online courses you must complete before you join. If you've completed some online coding courses or, better yet, built a website (no matter how simple), include the course name or website address in your application.

Codecademy.com is one of several free resources with online courses that many boot camps assign as prework. For additional resources, see the section in Chapter 9 on learning from online websites.

✔ *Why do you want to become a programmer?*

You might want to become a programmer for many different reasons. Perhaps you want to advance your career, build an app that solves a problem you're experiencing, or become a maker instead of a manager. Whatever your reason, it should be meaningful and serve as motivation during the highs and lows of your boot camp experience. Poor reasons to learn to code include "wanting to become rich" (the average coder's salary is $70,000), or "because coding is easy" (becoming job ready can take at least 700 hours).

✔ *Describe a time when you solved a complex problem in a structured, step-by-step way.*

Many problems you'll face when coding will seem impossible to solve. If you try solutions at random or haphazardly, reaching a resolution will take much longer. The key to solving any complex problem is to list every step that might be at fault, and then methodically test each step. For example, if you turn on a light switch and the light bulb doesn't turn on, you know the problem must either be the light switch, the wiring to the light socket, the light socket itself, or the light bulb. You can find the problem by testing or replacing each part, usually starting with the light bulb. Debugging a program follows a similar process. If you haven't debugged a program, describe any complex process or problem and the systematic approach you used to find the answer.

✔ *Describe your previous educational and professional experiences.*

Neither a college degree nor a current job is necessary to join a coding boot camp, though both show the ability to follow through with a commitment. For education, list anything that might show your aptitude and ability to learn. If you did not receive a college degree, include completed courses. For professional experiences, a history of consistent employment and increasing responsibility are positive signals of your future ability to be a good employee.

✔ *Write a program that counts the numbers from 3 to 117. But for multiples of 3, add 3 instead of 1, and for multiples of 5, add 5 instead of 1. For numbers that are multiples of both 3 and 5, add 15 instead of 1.*

Boot camp applications can include a programming challenge, like the preceding question from the Zipfian Academy application, which requires you to write code. You can usually write the answer in any programming language — understanding your logic is the most important part of the question. This specific question is a variation of a popular programming challenge called Fizzbuzz and can be solved by using a programming loop and testing each number for its divisibility by 3, 5, and 15.

✔ *List your LinkedIn profile.*

After you start looking for a coding job, your LinkedIn profile is a critical piece of your application. Get your profile in shape now and update your profile to include an accurate employment history, descriptions of each employer and role, and the leadership positions or effect you had. See Figure 10-4.

Some boot camps will ask if you're an international applicant in need of a visa. The overwhelming majority of boot camps are not officially recognized educational institutions. Although previous students may have successfully applied for visas, it is unlikely that the boot camp will be able to give you a great deal of assistance with the visa process.

Figure 10-4:
Update your profile to include complete employer history and descriptions.

Preparing to Attend a Coding Boot Camp

Congratulations — you've been accepted to a coding boot camp. Before you officially join, you'll need to complete the *prework,* which is work the boot camp assigns you to complete before you arrive, and pay for your education.

Completing the prework

When learning a foreign language, much of the initial work is learning the syntax and vocabulary. Learning to code is no different, except mistakes in syntax or commands can result in your code not running at all. Coding boot camps assign you prework to expose you to programming languages and tools so you become more comfortable with how they operate. Depending on how quickly you progress, the prework can take 50 to 100 hours to complete.

You can view the complete prework for the Flatiron School's web development and iOS development courses by visiting prework.flatironschool.com.

The following topics are typically included in prework. I've included resources for you to learn more:

- ✔ **HTML and CSS:** These markup languages display and style content on web pages. Practice for free without installing any software by using the Codecademy web course (shown in Figure 10-5), which is available at `www.codecademy.com/tracks/web`.

Figure 10-5: Complete prework by using the Codec- ademy website.

- ✔ **JavaScript and jQuery:** Both add interactivity and allow you to take user input, store variables, and change elements on web pages. Learn more by using Codecademy's JavaScript course, at `www.codecademy.com/tracks/javascript`, and jQuery course, at `www.codecademy.com/tracks/jquery`.

- ✔ **Command line:** Operate your computer and run programs without using your mouse. Many programs are written only for the command line, also called *bash,* so learning how to use the command line is not optional. Try your hand at the command line with an interactive shell tutorial available at `learnshell.org`. You might also want to read Zed Shaw's *Learn the Command Line the Hard Way,* available at `cli.learncode thehardway.org/book`.

- ✔ **Git:** Git allows you to save multiple versions of your code and work with others. Code School has an online Git tutorial at `www.codeschool.com/courses/try-git`.

- ✔ **SQL databases:** Every web application uses a database to store, modify, and retrieve data. Learn SQL, the language used to access databases, with an interactive SQL course at `sqlzoo.net/wiki/SQL_Tutorial`.

- ✔ **Ruby and Rails:** Ruby is a programming language, and Rails is a framework to make coding Ruby web applications easier. You can learn Ruby with Codecademy's Ruby course, at `www.codecademy.com/tracks/ruby`, and Rails with Code School's Rails for Zombies course, at `railsforzombies.org`.

- ✔ **Design:** Much of a developer's work is translating a designer's vision into code. Understand the visual principles that guide how websites are designed by signing up for email lessons curated by design professionals and available on Hack Design at `hackdesign.org`.

As you complete these coding exercises, start brainstorming on what coding project you would want to build as your capstone project to show employers. As your coding ability increases, so too will the ideas you have for your project.

Financing your education

The cost of a coding boot camp averages $10,000 and can be as high as $18,000. Paying the fee up-front is the cheapest option, but you may not have the savings on hand to afford the entire sum at once. Several options exist that allow students to pay the fees in installments:

- ✔ **Boot camp financing plans:** Boot camps offer various financing plans, including installment plans, which spread the cost evenly over 12 to 24 months, and deferment plans, which delay up to 50 percent of the payment up to six months after the boot camp has finished. The additional cost for installment and deferment plans can range from zero to an additional 15 percent of the total cost.

- ✔ **Traditional bank lenders:** Apply for a personal loan from a traditional bank. Interest rates will vary based on your credit history. You can view quotes across a variety of lenders by using LendingTree, at `www.lendingtree.com/quotes/personal-loans.html`.

- ✔ **Alternative lenders:** In addition to your credit score, alternative online lenders use factors such as educational history, income, savings, and job history to reduce the cost of loans underwritten by traditional banks and to pass the savings to consumers through lower interest rates. See Figure 10-6. You can receive a quote by visiting lenders such as `affirm.com` and `meetearnest.com`.

- ✔ **Investor-backed loans:** These platforms allow lenders to invest in specific people and educational or business goals. You receive a loan at a fixed interest rate based on multiple factors, similar to alternative lenders. Receive a quote by visiting platforms such as `upstart.com` and `pave.com`.

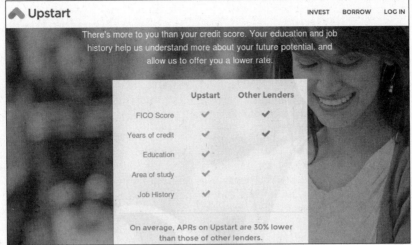

Figure 10-6:
Alternative
lenders use
data beyond
credit
scores to
determine
interest
rates.

✔ **Crowdfunding:** Solicit pledges from your friends, family, and social networks to fund your tuition with a crowdfunding campaign. Backers are charged only if the sum of all pledges exceeds your goal, in this case your tuition. Websites such as `crowdtilt.com` enable you to promote your campaign and collect payments for a 5 percent fee of total funds raised.

✔ **Government grants:** Workforce training, economic development, and education grants are given directly to coding boot camps to reduce the cost for certain groups. However, individuals cannot directly apply for Pell or Stafford loans because coding boot camps are currently not considered a qualified education institution.

Finding a Job after a Coding Boot Camp

At the end of your boot camp experience, you should have greater confidence, increased abilities, and a larger portfolio than when you started. You will have completed a difficult journey and may be tempted to take a break. However, your work is not over yet! You'll need to network with employers, convince them of your newly learned skills, and go through the interview process to secure a job offer.

Getting hired like Cassidy Pignatello

As an undergraduate student, Cassidy studied audio and radio and began his career in radio production. He switched to digital advertising operations, working at the *Wall Street Journal,* LinkedIn, and Hearst Digital Media to manage ads seen by millions of users.

After three and a half years, Cassidy decided to make the switch and become a developer. Without previous professional web development experience, he applied to and attended The Flatiron School. During the boot camp, he built two apps for his portfolio — a Friend of the Day app, which made it easy for you to text a friend based on people in your Google Contacts, and Flatiron General Store, an e-commerce website with user accounts and checkout functionality that made it easy to buy and sell products.

After conducting a job search, Cassidy secured a position as a front-end software engineer at Yahoo! You can view Cassidy's GitHub profile at `https://github.com/cassidypignatello` and his blog at `http://cassidypignatello.github.io/`.

Hiring managers are turning to coding boot camps in increasing numbers. Startups are especially receptive to hiring boot camp graduates because the existing team is small, the need for talent is great, the formal procedures are few, and hiring an additional coder would have a great effect. The recruiting process becomes more challenging as the size of the company increases. Bigger companies have more established hiring processes, and some recruiters still use traditional screens, which shortlist applicants based on college, major, and GPA.

Whether you're recruiting for a position in a large or small company, the basic recruiting strategies remain the same: Network to build as many personal relationships as possible, and put enough time into your final portfolio project to show off what you can do after a few months of intense preparation. The goal is to convince just one recruiter or hiring manager that you have the aptitude and the attitude to continue learning on the job at a fast pace. Your boot camp will help you by reviewing your resumes, helping you practice interview skills, and organizing events with employers, but you'll need to do most of the work involved in setting up interviews and winning the job offer.

Chapter 11

Exploring Undergraduate and Graduate Degrees

. . . .

In This Chapter

▶ Learning to code with a bachelor's or master's degree

▶ Coding outside class in clubs and hackathons

▶ Securing an internship to learn with a job

. . . .

When I was in college, I wanted to be involved in things that would change the world.

—*Elon Musk*

Going to college to learn how to code is probably the most traditional and expensive path you can take. A bachelor's degree, designed to take four years, is rooted in the tradition of the English university system and was made popular by the GI Bill after World War II. More recently, the two-year associate degree has become more popular. It costs less than a bachelor's degree, but many are designed as a way to eventually transfer to a four-year bachelor degree program.

But when it comes to computer programmers, you likely know more people who didn't graduate from college than did. Entrepreneurs such a Bill Gates, Steve Jobs, Mark Zuckerberg, and Larry Ellison dropped out of college to create technology companies worth billions of dollars. Still, the world's biggest technology companies continue to hire mainly college graduates.

Whether you're thinking about going to college, are already in college, or attended college and want another degree, this chapter is for you. I explore learning to code in college or graduate school, and then building your credibility with an internship.

Getting a College Degree

The recent media attention on coding, with movies such as *The Social Network* and TV shows such as *Silicon Valley*, might make it seem like everyone in college is learning how to program. Although computer science (CS) graduates earn some of the highest salaries in the US (see Figure 11-1), less than 3 percent of students major in computer science, and less than 1 percent of AP exams taken in high school are in computer science.

Figure 11-1: Bachelor's degrees awarded in CS over the last 40 years, courtesy of NPR.

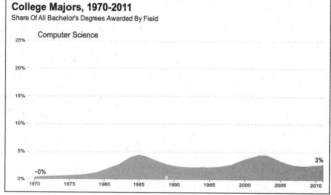

Source: Digest of Educational Statistics; credit: Quoctrung Bui/NPR

The supply of students is low but improving relative to the jobs that are available. Companies such as Apple, Microsoft, Yahoo!, Facebook, and Twitter recruit computer science engineers from schools such as Carnegie Mellon, MIT, and Stanford. It's not just the companies you read about in the news that are hiring either. CS graduates are in high demand — the Bureau of Labor Statistics estimates that by 2020 there will be 1.4 million computing jobs but only 400,000 trained computer science students to fill those jobs.

Yet far more important to employers than the name of the school you went to is what you did while you were in school. Employers will ask how you challenged yourself with your course load, and the applications you built and why.

College computer science curriculum

College CS courses offer a sweeping survey of entire computer systems from the hardware used to allocate memory to the high-level software that runs programs and the theories used to write that software. As a result, you gain a great sense for why computer systems behave as they do, which gives you the foundation to advance a technology or a programming language when the need arises.

This approach differs dramatically from the learning you'd typically do by yourself or in a boot camp, where the focus is only on software development in a specific language such as Python or Ruby. Given the typical 12-week duration of a boot camp, there isn't much time for anything else.

The core CS curriculum across universities is similar. Table 11-1 compares select core curriculum classes required as part of the Computer Science degree at Stanford and Penn State — a private university on the West Coast and a public university on the East Coast, respectively. Both have introductory classes to acquaint you with programming topics, math classes that cover probability, hardware classes for low-level programming and memory storage, software classes for designing algorithms, and higher level classes that cover advanced topics such as artificial intelligence and networking.

Until recently, universities generally did not teach web programming courses. As web programming has increased in popularity, this has begun to change — for example, Stanford offers a web programming class (CS 142) that teaches HTML, CSS, and Ruby on Rails, and Penn State has a similar class that teaches web programming with Java.

Table 11-1   CS Select Core Curriculum at Stanford and Penn State

Course name	*Course description*	*Stanford*	*Penn State*
Programming Abstractions	Intro to programming using C++ with sorting and searching	CS 106B	CMPSC 121
Programming with Web Applications	Intro to graphics, virtual machines, and programming concepts using Java	N/A	CMPSC 221
Math Foundations of Computing	Topics include proofs, logic, induction, sets, and functions	CS 103	CMPSC 360
Probability	Probability and statistics relevant to computer science	CS 109	STAT 318
Algorithms	Algorithm types (e.g., random) and complexity	CS 161	CMPSC 465
Hardware systems	Machine registers, assembly language, and compilation	CS 107	CMPSC 311

(continued)

Table 11-1 *(continued)*

Course name	Course description	Stanford	Penn State
Computer systems	Storage and file management, networking, and distributed systems	CS 110	N/A
Operating systems	Designing and managing operating and system tasks	CS 140	CMPSC 473
Computer and network security	Principles of building and breaking secure systems	CS 155	CMPSC 443
Intro to Artificial Intelligence	AI concepts such as searching, planning, and learning	CS 121	CMPSC 448
Intro to Databases	Database design and using SQL and NoSQL systems	CS 145	CMPSC 431W

Technical versus practical education

As you look at the courses offered in the Stanford and Penn State CS programs, you'll notice that the overwhelming majority speak to the theory of computer science and aren't always used every day. For example, as a person interested in software development, you likely aren't going to use much if any of your hardware systems courses. Note that some classes will be very relevant — algorithms and databases are two topics frequently used in web programming.

However, understanding the theory is useful. For example, database systems were initially created assuming that storage was expensive and the amount of data that needed to be stored would grow linearly. The reality turned out to be different — the cost of hardware plummeted and hard drives became bigger and cheaper, while people generated more data at a faster pace than ever before. Computer scientists, with a solid understanding of databases, took advantage of cheap hardware and create distributed databases, which store data across multiple computers instead of a single one.

Whether or not you should learn programming in college comes down to your goal. If you want to one day be in a position to change the industry or work on cutting-edge technology, the theory you learn studying computer science is without substitute or comparison. There are few other places where you can engage with a professional, in this case a professor, of a high caliber to push the limits of fundamental understanding. Also, specific programming languages and technologies are constantly changing, while the underlying concepts and theories stay the same. Python and Ruby, for example, are only twenty years old.

On the other hand, if your goal is to use these concepts to make a living in the industry instead of trying to change the industry, you could learn to code in a less expensive and less time-intensive way than obtaining a computer science degree.

Doing extracurricular activities

Many students complement their coursework by applying what they've learned in a tangible way. Your coursework will include project work, but projects assigned in class may not have changed in a few years to make it easier for the instructor to provide support and grade your work. Also, with so many technologies constantly popping up, using your coding skills outside the classroom will help build confidence and skill.

One option is to code side projects, which are personal coding projects that perform some small basic utility and can be built in a short amount of time, over a weekend to a few months at most. For example, not many people know that before Mark Zuckerberg built Facebook, he had coded many side projects, including an instant messaging client for his dad's dental practice, an MP3 player that suggested the next song to listen to, and a tool that helped students choose their semester schedule based on which classes their friends were enrolling in. In another example, three students at Tufts University wanted an easy way to find the cheapest place to buy all their textbooks. They created a site called GetchaBooks, which lets students select the classes they would be taking in a semester and then retrieved the full list of books needed and the total prices across many stores to find the cheapest price. Although the site is no longer actively developed, all the code is open sourced and can be viewed either at getchabooks.com or github.com/getchabooks/getchabooks.

In addition to coding on your own, coding and discussing technology topics with others can be more engaging. On-campus clubs are usually formed by students and cater to almost every interest. You can find clubs on robotics, financial technologies such as bitcoin, technology investing from the venture capital stage to the public equities stage, and more.

 The Dorm Room Fund is a student-run venture capital firm with locations in San Francisco, Boston, New York, and Philadelphia that invests in student-run companies. Backed by First Round Capital, the goal is to nurture and support young technology companies, teach students how to evaluate and invest in technology companies, and find the next billion dollar company on a college campus.

The most intense extracurricular pursuit for a student is participating in hackathons. A *hackathon* is a one-day to weekend-long event with the goal of brainstorming, designing, and building a small useful app. Hackathons are most popular among students, who often stay up all night coding their apps, while the hosts are often technology companies. However, some of the largest hackathons, such as CalHacks, which is hosted by UC Berkeley, and PennApps, which is hosted by the University of Pennsylvania (see Figure 11-2), are organized by students and attended by thousands of students from schools around the country.

Credit: Andrew Mager via Flickr

Figure 11-2:
Students
show a
mentor
their mobile
applica-
tion at
PennApps.

Two-year versus four-year school

You may not be able to afford the time, expense, or commitment demanded by a four-year degree. Even though some college offer financial aid, not earning money for four years or earning a far reduced wage may not be feasible, especially if you have to support yourself or family members.

One alternative to the Bachelor of Arts (BA) degree is the Associate of Arts (AA) degree, which is typically granted by community colleges or technical schools. You can complete an AA degree in two years. In addition to taking less time, tuition and fees, according to the College Board, are on average $3,200 per year, compared to $9,000 per year at public four-year institutions. Courses are also offered during evenings and on weekends, so students can work while attending school. When evaluating an institution that grants the AA degree, review the instructors teaching the courses and make sure they are experienced practitioners in the field. Additionally, see the types of jobs recent graduates went on to do and the employers they worked for to make sure that both match with your goals.

A close relative of the AA degree is a certificate granted by a school of continuing education. Certificates are non-credit offerings completed within a year. They usually cost less than $10,000 but don't result in a degree. To get the most bang for your buck, get your certificate from a school with a good regional or even national reputation. For example, NYU has a Certificate in Web Development that teaches web development basics with HTML, CSS, and JavaScript along with more advanced topics such as PHP, a popular programming language for the web, and SQL, a language used to query databases. See Figure 11-3. Learning these topics in a structured way from an instructor can help jumpstart your learning so you can teach yourself additional topics on your own.

Curriculum		
▾ Required Course—Option 1		
1 of the course is required.		
Course	Title	Price
INFO1-CE9742	Web Development Intensive	$3995
▾ Required Courses—Options 2 and 3		
2 of these courses are required.		
Course	Title	Price
INFO1-CE9740	Webpage Development with HTML	$1595
INFO1-CE9764	Front End Web Development	$1045
INFO1-CE9794	Web Architecture and Infrastructure	$990
INFO1-CE9755	JavaScript	$1095
▾ Electives—Option 2		
2 of these courses are required.		
Course	Title	Price
INFO1-CE9224	Introduction to PHP Programming, Part I	$1045
INFO1-CE9367	MySQL with PHP	$1250
INFO1-CE9807	Web Programming with PHP	$1045

Figure 11-3: NYU's Certificate in Web Development offers classes in SQL and PHP.

When enrolling in a certificate program, keep in mind that instructor quality can be highly variable. Make sure you talk to current students or find some student reviews before signing up for either the certificate program or courses that the certificate requires.

Enrolling in an Advanced Degree Program

The options for learning how to code never seem to end, and advanced degrees typically appeal to a particular group of people. While not necessary for either learning to code or obtaining a coding job, an advanced degree can help accelerate your learning and differentiate you from other job candidates. The two types of advanced degree programs follow:

- **Master's degree:** A technical degree that allows you to explore and specialize in a particular area of computer science such as artificial intelligence, security, database systems, or machine learning. Based on the course load, the degree typically takes one or two years of full-time, in-person instruction to complete. Upon completion, the degree can be a way for a student who pursued a non-technical major to transition into the field and pursue a coding job. Alternatively, some students use the master's degree experience as a way to gauge their interest in or improve their candidacy for a PhD program.

A growing number of part-time online master's degree programs are available. For example, Stanford and Johns Hopkins both offer a master's degree in Computer Science with a concentration in one of ten topics as part of an online part-time degree that takes on average three to five years to complete. Similarly, Northwestern University offers a master's degree in Predictive Analytics, an online part-time program in big data that teaches students SQL, NoSQL, Python, and R.

- **Doctorate degree:** A program typically for people interested in conducting research into a specialized topic. PhD candidates can take six to eight years to earn their degree, so it's not the most timely way to learn how to code. PhD graduates, especially those with cutting-edge research topics, differentiate themselves in the market and generally work on the toughest problems in computer science. For example, Google's core search algorithm is technically challenging in a number of ways — it takes your search request, compares it against billions of indexed web pages, and returns a result in a less than a second. Teams of PhD computer scientists work to write algorithms that predict what you're going to search for, index more data (such as from social networks), and return results to you five to ten milliseconds faster than before.

Students who enroll and drop out of PhD programs early have often done enough coursework to earn a master's degree, usually at no cost to the student because PhD programs are typically funded by the school.

Graduate school computer science curriculum

The master's degree school curriculum for computer science usually consists of 10 to 12 computer science and math classes. You start with a few foundational classes, and then specialize by focusing on a specific computer science topic. The PhD curriculum follows the same path, except after completing the coursework, you propose a previously unexplored topic to further research, spend three to five years conducting original research, and then present and defend your results before other professors appointed to evaluate your work.

Table 11-2 is a sample curriculum to earn a master's degree in CS with a concentration in Machine Learning from Columbia University. Multiple courses can be used to meet the degree requirements, and the courses offered vary by semester.

Table 11-2	Columbia University MS in Computer Science	
Course Number	*Course Name*	*Course Description*
W4118	Operating Systems I	Design and implementation of operating systems including topics such as process management and synchronization
W4231	Analysis of Algorithms I	Design and analysis of efficient algorithms including sorting and searching
W4705	Natural Language Processing	Natural language extraction, summarization, and analysis of emotional speech
W4252	Computational Learning Theory	Computational and statistical possibilities and limitations of learning
W4771	Machine Learning	Machine learning with classification, regression, and inference models
W4111	Intro to Databases	Understanding of how to design and build relational databases
W4246	Algorithms for Data Science	Methods for organizing, sorting, and searching data
W4772	Advanced Machine Learning	Advanced machine learning tools with applications in perception and behavior modeling
E6232	Analysis of Algorithms II	Graduate course on design and analysis of efficient approximation algorithms for optimization problems
E6998	Advanced Topic in Machine Learning	Graduate course covers current research on Bayesian networks, inference, Markov models, and regression

The curriculum, which in this case consists of ten classes, begins with three foundational classes, and then quickly focuses on an area of concentration. Concentrations vary across programs, but generally include the following:

- ✔ **Security:** Assigning user permissions and preventing unauthorized access, such as preventing users from accessing your credit card details on an e-commerce site.

- ✔ **Machine learning:** Finding pattern in data, and making future predictions, such as predicting what movie you should watch next based on the movies you have already seen and liked.

- ✔ **Network systems:** Protocols, principles, and algorithms for how computers communicate with each other, such as setting up wireless networks that work well for hundreds of thousands of users.

- ✔ **Computer vision:** Duplicating the ability of the human eye to process and analyze images, such as counting the number of people who enter or exit a store based on a program analyzing a live video feed.

- ✔ **Natural language processing:** Automating the analysis of text and speech, such as using voice commands to convert speech to text.

Performing research

Students are encouraged in master's degree programs and required in PhD programs to conduct original research. Research topics vary from the theoretical, such as estimating how long an algorithm will take to find a solution, to the practical, such optimizing a delivery route given a set of points.

Sometimes this academic research is commercialized to create products and companies worth hundreds of millions to billions of dollars. For example, in 2003, Farecast created an algorithm that analyzed 12,000 airline ticket prices. Later, it could analyze billions of ticket prices in real-time, and predict whether the price of your airline ticket would increase, decrease, or stay the same. Microsoft purchased the technology for $100 million and incorporated it into its Bing search engine.

In another example, Shazam was based on an academic paper that analyzed how to identify an audio recording based on a short low-quality sample, usually an audio recording from a mobile phone. Today, Shazam lets a user record a short snippet of a song, identifies the song title, and offers the song for purchase. The company has raised over $100 million in funding for operations and is privately valued at over $1 billion. Both products were based on published research papers that identified a problem that could be addressed with technology, and presented a technology solution that solved existing constraints with high accuracy.

Your own research may not lead to the creation of a billion dollar company, but it should advance, even incrementally, a solution for a computer science problem or help eliminate an existing constraint.

Interning to Build Credibility

Your classroom work helps create a theoretical foundation but can be divorced from the real world. Actual real-world problems often have inaccurate or incomplete data and a lack of obvious solutions. One way to bridge the gap from the classroom to the real world is to take on an internship.

Internships are ten- to twelve-week engagements, usually over the summer, with an employer on a discrete project. The experience is meant to help an intern assess whether the company and the role are a good fit for permanent employment, and for the company to assess the intern's abilities.

The competition for interns is just as strong as it is for full-time employees, so interns can expect to be paid. Top tech companies pay interns between $6,000 and $8,000 per month, with Palantir, LinkedIn, and Twitter topping the list. After the internship is finished, companies offer successful interns anywhere from $5,000 to $100,000 signing bonuses to return to the firm to work full-time.

Types of internship programs

Companies structure their internship program differently, but the following configurations are more common than others:

- ✔ **Summer internship:** The majority of internships happen during the summer. Because of the work involved in organizing an intern class, larger companies usually have a formal process with application deadlines and fixed dates when interviews for the internship are conducted. After offers are extended, companies ideally screen projects given to interns to make sure the work is interesting and substantive. There are also a significant number of social events so that full-time employees and interns can meet in an environment outside work.

✔ **School-year internship:** Some internships take place during the school year, from September to May. These programs are usually smaller, hiring is on an as-needed basis, and the entire process is less formalized. Usually, the intern does more work to find divisions who need extra help, networks with managers of those divisions, and then finally interviews for and accepts an internship position. You can get a more realistic view of what working at the company is like because there likely aren't many other interns working with you, and you might be able to integrate more closely with the team.

✔ **Fellowship:** Many students get the itch to try a longer professional experience before graduation. These experiences, called fellowship programs, last six to twelve months and give a person enough time to work on a project to make substantive contribution. For undergraduates, the work confirms an existing interest or creates an interest in a new area of technology. For graduate students, the work can highlight the difference between theory and practice, inform an area of research, or help them break into a new industry.

Positions for internships are often more selective than positions for full-time jobs, so apply early and for more than one internship position. If you don't receive an internship, try again for a full-time position. Companies have large hiring needs and one purpose for hiring summer interns is to ensure that the interns have a great time at the company so when they return to campus they tell other students, who then feel more comfortable applying.

Securing an internship

Much of the advice in Part IV for obtaining a full-time job applies to securing an internship offer as well. There are a few strategies to keep in mind when pursuing an internship.

Choose products and companies you are passionate about. As an intern, you join a company for three months at most, and much of that time is spent meeting new people, understanding the company, and fitting into existing processes. As a passionate power user of the product, your excitement will naturally show, and your ideas will give the company a sense for what you want to work on and provide a fresh and valuable perspective to the team, which likely feels that they have already explored every possible idea. Be able to describe how you use the product and what additional features would help increase your engagement or retention.

For any product that has a public profile, link to your profile so team members can easily see how frequently you use the product.

How Bob Ren learned to code

Between classes, clubs, hackathons, and internships, the possibilities seem endless for students in college or graduate school to learn how to code. Here is how Bob Ren, a college senior, stitched together his learning experiences while in school.

Bob attended the University of Illinois at Urbana-Champaign. After his first two years, he decided to take a break from school and gain some real-world experience at a technology company. He applied to and joined the fellowship program at Codecademy, a startup in New York. As a Codecademy fellow, Bob worked at the startup for one year as a full-time employee, was paid $80,000, and contributed to product development as an engineer. While at Codecademy, Bob contributed to a number of projects and wrote code to redesign the main website, add language support for Spanish and French, and develop an open source platform called EventHub, which allows companies to understand various actions that visitors perform on a website.

While at Codecademy, Bob also kept busy outside work. A few months into his fellowship, he attended the Techcrunch Disrupt hackathon, and created a common application for startups based on issues he faced applying for jobs at startups. Like the common application for college, the app was designed so students could enter their information once and apply to multiple startups at the same time. TechCrunch, the startup blog and event organizer, wrote about the project at `techcrunch.com/2013/04/28/startup_common_application_hackathon`.

After the Disrupt Hackathon, Bob continued coding and built the following, either by himself or with a team:

- **LivingLanguage:** A Chrome extension that translates random words on any web page into a foreign language you want to learn. The app won first place at the Facebook Summer Hackathon in 2013.

- **SnapMeNow:** Like Snapchat for your computer, this web app uses your computer's camera to create images that self-destruct after up to 10 seconds. Bob released the app on Reddit, where is was barely noticed. After ten months, however, the app was reposted to HackerNews and ProductHunt, went viral with hundreds of thousands of people using the product, and was covered by media outlets such as MTV and BuzzFeed.

- **ClassTranscribe:** An open source project that uses crowdsourcing to quickly and accurately transcribe college lectures. After the lectures are transcribed, students can search for keywords in the lectures to better understand concepts presented in class. The app is available at `http://classtranscribe.com/`.

After you've chosen a few companies, start looking for current students who have worked at the company as well as school alumni who currently work at the company. Reach out by email and schedule short phone calls or a coffee chat no longer than thirty minutes to try and build a connection. Current students can share information about their experience, tell you which groups have the greatest need, and share some of the company culture such as what the company values. Alumni will be able to share much of the same information, but they can also send a recommendation to HR on your behalf or may be able to hire you.

There is a balance between the response rate, ability to help, and seniority of a person you reach out to. Try to reach for the most senior alumni you can find at a company, because a quick email from them to HR will guarantee an interview, but recognize that they may not always have the time to respond. Alternatively, more junior employees will likely have more time to chat with you but likely do not have as much influence over interview or hiring decisions.

Finally, include a mix of startups and more established companies in your search process. Given the number of interviews they do, established companies can be formulaic in their interview and hiring decisions, often looking for candidates from specific schools with a minimum GPA. If you aren't attending a top school or have below a 3.0 (out of 4.0) GPA, you should still apply to the larger companies and include an explanation for your lower GPA if one applies. Another option is to apply to startups, which will likely care more about the products you've built than your grade in Chemistry. The tradeoff is that startups likely have less time and people to help train you and a smaller selection of projects for you to choose from. After you join a company and finish a brief orientation period, you'll often need to start coding right away and contributing to the product.

Be careful of startups formed by a nontechnical founder that have not yet built a product. Sometimes these companies are looking for cheap labor to help build the first version — the experience can involve many hours, unreasonable deadlines, and low to no compensation, especially if you're paid in equity. As an example, you can see a sample of recruiting pitches for coders that nontechnical founders sent to the University of Pennsylvania CS mailing list at whartoniteseekscodemonkey.tumblr.com.

Chapter 12

Training on the Job

I hated every minute of training, but I said, 'Don't quit. Suffer now and live the rest of your life as a champion.'

—*Muhammad Ali*

As an employee, whether you're a marketer, a sales person, or a designer, you likely find that technology dominates more and more of your conversations with your boss, coworkers, and clients. Perhaps your boss wants to know which customer segments the company should target with online advertising, and you need to analyze millions of customer records to provide an answer. Or maybe a client wants to add or change a feature and will double the contract if the process can be done in six weeks, and you need to know whether it's possible. More tangibly, you might find yourself performing mundane and repetitive tasks that you know a computer could do.

You have probably found that an ability to code could help you perform your current job more efficiently. Companies are also noticing the value of having nontechnical employees learn to code, and offering various on-site training options and support. This chapter shows you how to learn to code on the job and ways to incorporate what you've learned into your job.

Taking a Work Project to the Next Level

As a busy professional with a full work schedule, you need a tangible project to work toward and keep you motivated while you learn how to code. Think of all the tasks you perform during the week — how many could be automated if you had the right tools and skills?

The following sample tasks can be done more efficiently with some coding and could help you think of a goal of your own:

- **Spreadsheet consolidation:** You have fifteen team members who submit timesheets to you using spreadsheets, and you create a consolidated weekly report by manually cutting and pasting entries from each spreadsheet.

- **Content updates:** You cut and paste the latest press stories every week into a content management system to update the company's website.

- **Data retrieval:** You work for a financial services company, and monitor acquisitions and sales made by ten private equity firms. Every day you visit each firm's website to look for updates.

- **Quality assurance:** You test updates made to the company's website by clicking the same set of links to make sure they work as expected.

- **Prototyping designs:** You create website designs, but it's difficult to explain to clients the user experience and interactions through static illustrations.

Whatever task you choose, make sure that you can describe how to complete it from start to finish. For example, the steps to complete the data retrieval task might be listed as follows:

1. Visit the first firm's website, and download the list of companies on the acquisitions page.

2. Permanently store the list. If the acquisition list has previously been retrieved, compare the list downloaded today with yesterday's version, and note any additions or deletions.

3. Display the additions or deletions.

4. Repeat Steps 1–3 for the next firm, until all the firm websites have been visited.

5. Repeat Steps 1–4 daily.

You may be part of a technical process, such as a designer who hands off mockups to a developer to create. Instead of automating your existing work, you could try to complete work the technical team normally does after you. For example, if you do customer or sales support, you regularly receive customer and client feedback and file support tickets for issues that require an engineer. The number of support tickets always exceeds the number of engineers, so choose a low-priority non-mission-critical issue to fix.

Don't worry about choosing a task that seems too simple. Fixing an issue on a live site currently in use is always more complex than it initially appears. However, try to choose a work-related task so you can ask for help from coworkers.

Learning on the Job and After Work

After you've selected a task, you need to learn some coding to be able to fix the issue. Given that you're already working, going back to school or taking a hiatus from work to learn full-time is likely not feasible. Your next best option is to learn coding on the job, ideally with your company's support. Companies are increasingly supporting employees who want to expand their technical skillset by providing resources to help them learn and by incentivizing those who learn tangible skills.

Wistia code school

Companies are starting to recognize the demand for coding education and the benefits of having more employees who can code. Wistia, a video-hosting and analytics company, hosts a code school so that nontechnical employees can learn how to code. Employees work as customer champions, or customer support agents, and are paired with a developer who conducts an hourly mentoring session every week for five to six months.

Normally, people learning to code usually practice their skills on personal projects. One advantage Wistia employees have is that the programming skills they learn are used to solve real problems that customers are experiencing. Solving coding issues, no matter how small, for a live website is difficult because the fix will immediately affect customers using the website.

As employees learn more, they still refer complex issues to the technical staff but are able to handle the easier technical problems themselves, resulting in quicker resolution times.

Training on the job

You are likely familiar with the compliance and leadership training available at your company, especially in medium- to large-sized firms. However, you may have never looked for the technical training options available to you. Here are some tips to get started learning on the job:

- ✔ **Virtual training resources:** Corporate training libraries such as Safari, Skillsoft, Lynda, and Pluralsight are popular among companies, and are a good place to start learning programming fundamentals. See Figure 12-1. Each provider has a mix of text and video content, which you can read and view on-demand. Additionally, look for company generated wikis and other training resources that describe internal programming tools and procedures.

- ✔ **In-person training programs:** Company employees often teach orientation training courses to introduce new engineers to basic concepts and the way to code in the company. Additionally, outside vendors may occasionally conduct specific training courses on more advanced programming topics and languages. Ask whether you can view the list of training topics typically made available to engineers, and then attend introductory training sessions.

Let your supervisor know that learning to code is a development goal, and include it in any reviews. Your supervisor can help you access training programs not traditionally offered to nontechnical employees. Additionally, letting as many coworkers as possible know about your goals will increase your accountability and motivation.

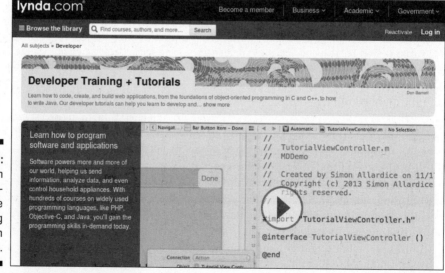

Figure 12-1:
Lynda.com
is a popu-
lar online
training
tool used in
companies.

✔ **Support from company developers:** Your company likely has developers who already assist you with the technical side of your projects. Whether you've chosen a project to improve the efficiency of your own workflow or are trying to complete work a developer would typically do, make sure to recruit a developer, usually one you already have a relationship with, so you have a resource to help you answer questions when you get stuck.

Your coworkers, especially on technical teams, are just as busy as you are. Before asking for help, try finding the answer by reviewing internal materials, using a search engine, or posting a question on a question-and-answer site such as Stack Overflow. Include where you looked because developers might use the same resources to answer questions.

Learning after work

Your company may be too small to have on-site technical training, or your office may not have any developers. Don't fret! You can take classes after work to learn how to code. Look for classes that meet twice a week in the evenings, and set aside time to do coursework during the weekend.

Companies often partially or fully reimburse the cost for employees who successfully complete a job-related course. Think of a few tangible ways that learning to code would help you do your job better, or take on a new project and then make the pitch to your manager. If you receive approval, make sure to keep up with the coursework so you're ready to contribute at work after the class is over.

A few places teach in-person coding classes designed for working professionals. Because a live instructor is teaching and assisting you, many charge a fee.

Lower cost and free options are usually taught exclusively online, though completion rates for in-person classes are usually higher than online classes. Online coding resources are listed in Chapter 9.

Here are some places where you can learn to code from a live instructor:

✔ **General Assembly:** Teaches part time, in-person classes across a range of subjects, and has a presence in major cities in the US and internationally. Topics include front-end, back-end, data science, and mobile development. Classes typically meet twice a week for three hours over 12 weeks. General Assembly is one of the largest companies teaching coding classes. You can view their classes at `www.generalassemb.ly`.

- **Local boot camps:** As coding has become more popular, coding boot camps have sprung up in many cities around the world. Many of these boot camps offer part-time programs that don't require you to quit your job. You can search boot camps by subject, location, and cost by using Course Report, available at www.coursereport.com, and CourseHorse, available at www.coursehorse.com.

Before signing up, make sure you review the instructor, the physical location, and the cost, which should be no more than $4,000 for a part-time program with 70 hours of instruction. Course Report profiles 10 part-time boot camps at www.coursereport.com/blog/learn-web-development-at-these-10-part-time-bootcamps.

- **College courses:** Traditionally, college computer science courses were theoretical, but colleges have recently started offering more applied web development and data science courses. Check your local university or community college's continuing education departments to see what's offered. For example, the City College of New York offers an Intro to Web Development class with 16 hours of instruction for $280.

- **Library classes:** Public libraries offer desktop productivity and other computer classes, and have recently started offering web development classes as well. For example, the New York Public Library has a free, 10-week program called Project_<code>, in which you build a website for a small business.

Coding on the job with Kelsey Manning

Kelsey Manning worked in media during and immediately after graduating from college. At Notre Dame, she was a sports editor for the school newspaper and wrote blog posts for various outlets. In addition to writing, she also did marketing and publicity for a PR agency and then Hachette, a book publisher. Hachette needed a developer to design responsive web pages, ones that display correctly on desktop and mobile devices, and hired Kelsey for the job.

Without any previous coding experience, Kelsey had to learn to code on the job to complete her work. During her first few weeks, she had to redesign real pages being used on the website. She tackled the problem by first taking online classes at Codecademy, and solving as many

problems as she could on her own by searching with Google. When she hit a wall, she would ask coworkers how to solve her problem. She also kept learning and supplemented her learning with in-person coding classes taught locally in New York.

Kelsey's journey has been far from easy, but it appears to have paid off. You probably will have more time to learn with less pressure than she did, but I hope her story gives you confidence that it's possible to learn to code while working a full-time job. You can read more about Kelsey's journey at www.levo.com/articles/skills/learning-to-code-on-the-job.

Freelancing to Build Confidence and Skills

You've taken training classes at work, found a coding mentor, and solved your first problem by using code. Congratulations! So where do you go from here? Like a foreign language, if you stop coding you'll forget what you've learned. The most important thing is to keep coding and building your confidence and skills.

Here are a few ideas for you to practice coding in the workplace:

- ✓ **Clone a website:** Unlike programs that may have code you can't access, company websites allow you to see and save text and images. You may not be able to recreate all the functionality, but choose a specific company's web page and try creating a copy of the layout, images, and text. This process will help you practice your HTML, CSS, and JavaScript skills.

- ✓ **Build a mobile app:** People purchase more mobile devices and spend more time on them than desktops and laptops. Still, some companies have been slow to adapt, and don't have a mobile presence. Create a mobile website using HTML and CSS, or a native application using Swift for the iPhone or Java for Android devices.

- ✓ **Code a small workplace utility app:** There are many tasks that everyone at your company and in your office performs. Your coworkers come to the office around the same time, eat lunch at the same places, and leave work using the same modes of transportation. They also share the same frustrations, some of which might be solved with a simple program. Try building an app that solves a small workplace annoyance — no one knows what would appeal to your coworkers better than you. For example, build a website that sends an email to those who opt-in whenever there is a traffic jam on the highway that everyone uses to leave work. Similarly, you could build an app that sends an alert if any of the restaurants close to work fails a health inspection. The goal here is to learn a new technology to solve a problem, and get real feedback from other users.

After you've practiced and built a few things, publish your code on a hosting service such as GitHub and create a portfolio website pulling everything you've built into one place. You'll be able to share and others will be able to find your work, and the progression in your coding skills will be visible for anyone to see. Chapter 13 has more tips and examples on what makes for a good portfolio website.

If you are stuck and can't think of anything to build, try freeCodeCamp, available at www.freecodecamp.com. The website, shown in Figure 12-2, connects working professionals with non-profits who need a website or app built. After you complete the challenges, you'll start working on a vetted non-profit project. Current project include an animal adoption database for Latin America through the non-profit People Saving Animals, and a charity fund-raiser website for the Save a Child's Heart Foundation.

Figure 12-2:
freeCo-
deCamp
connects
profession-
als who code
together for
non-profits.

Transitioning to a New Role

Like any skill, coding can take a lifetime to master, but after you learn a little you may find that you want to move into a technology-based role. The first step is to do a self-assessment and evaluate what you like and dislike about your current role, and how that matches with the technology role you want. You'll likely also need input from others; networking and chatting with developers you trust will help give you a balanced view of the job. If you decide to take the leap, you have the big advantage of being inside a company, so you'll know what they need before a job posting is ever written.

Assessing your current role

You've worked hard to get to where you are — perhaps you just landed a job in a competitive industry or have been working and advancing in your role for a few years. In either case, if you're thinking about switching to a coding job, you should do a self-assessment and decide whether a new role would be a better fit for you.

Think about what you like and dislike about your current job. For some people, the issue is office politics or poor team dynamics, but these are present in every role that involves working with other people, and switching to a coding job carries the risk of seeing the same issues. On the other hand, if you are ready to learn a new topic or have limited advancement opportunities, switching roles could be a good idea.

After evaluating your current job, think about what you think you would like or dislike about a coding job. For some, tech jobs seem attractive because companies overnight can become worth billions of dollars and employee salaries are reportedly in the millions. It is true that companies such as Facebook and Twitter are worth billions of dollars, and engineers at these companies are well compensated, but these are the exceptions not the rule. According to the federal Bureau of Labor Statistics, web developers and computer programmers make on average between $65,000 and $75,000, which is higher than many jobs but will not make you a millionaire overnight.

Networking with developers

One major benefit you have over other job seekers is that you probably work with developers who hold the position you're trying to obtain. Seek out some of these developers, either from people you already work with or in a department that you think is interesting.

After you connect with a few people, ask them how they spend their days, what they enjoy and what they would change about their job, and for any advice they have for you on how to make the transition. These types of conversations happen less frequently than you might think, so don't be shy about reaching out — you might be surprised to find that some developers are happy to chat with you because they are wondering how to transition into a nontechnical or business role.

The biggest constraint any company faces when hiring externally is not finding people who are technically capable of doing the job but finding people who will fit in with the company and the team culturally. As a current employee, you've already passed one culture screen, and you're in a good position to learn about how you might fit in with the existing developer culture at the company. After you build relationships with developers, maintain them and keep them updated on your goals. At some point, they'll likely be asked how serious you are and whether you'd be a good fit.

Identifying roles that match your interest and skills

Technical roles are just as numerous and varied as nontechnical roles. The positions include data analysts who analyze big data, traffic analysts who monitor website traffic and patterns, web developers who create website front ends and back ends, app developers who create mobile web apps and native apps for mobile devices, and quality assurance testers who test for and help solve bugs in new releases.

Apply for roles in which you have a strong interest. If you like working with statistics and math, a data analyst or traffic analytics role might suit you best. Or if you're a visual person and like creating experiences others can see, consider a front-end developer role.

No matter the role, you should aim for a junior title and be committed to learning a lot on the job. Don't be afraid of starting over. For example, if you've been in marketing for four years and are interested in being a web developer, you will likely start as a junior developer. Your previous job experience will help you be a better team member and manager, which could help you advance more quickly, but you'll need to show that you're able to complete basic technical tasks first. Also, no matter the role, you'll be spending a lot of time learning on the job, and will be relying on your coworkers to teach you, so choose your role and team carefully.

Part IV

Launching Your Career Path

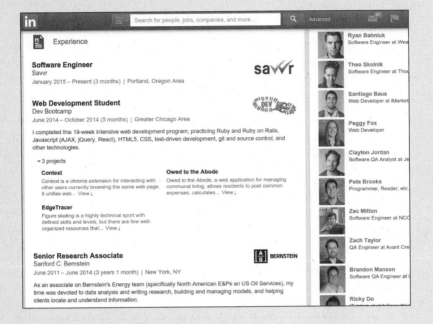

Check out www.dummies.com/extras/gettingacodingjob for tips on setting up an informational interview.

In this part . . .

- ✔ Create your portfolio site
- ✔ Network to find opportunities
- ✔ Discover winning interviewing techniques
- ✔ Interview for and land the job

Chapter 13

Building Your Portfolio Site

You've probably seen an artist or art student carrying a portfolio. The word means several things. One meaning of *portfolio* is the oversize container that holds the works. The second meaning of the word *portfolio* is all the designs or artwork someone has created and wants to show other people. This type of portfolio can include drawn or painted artworks, sketches, cels from animation, blueprints, and descriptions of the pieces that it contains.

For our purposes, I use the word *portfolio* in yet another way: an online representation of the breadth and depth of your work. I call the printed pieces that you've seen artists carry around a *print portfolio*. If you're a designer, you may have one of these yourself.

Many artists, art students, and designers put a great deal of work into curating their print portfolio. They keep it under lock and key when they're not using it, and go to great lengths to protect it if they're taking it with them somewhere and rain threatens. And when they create a piece that they're especially happy with, they'll set it aside and say, "That one goes in the portfolio."

The focus in this chapter is on something that has largely replaced the print portfolio for many developers: the online portfolio site. Your online portfolio site should contain your best work as well as represent the breadth of what you've done.

In this chapter, you see what a strong but not too complicated portfolio site looks like.

Introducing Sarah Rudder's Portfolio Site

Sarah Rudder is a young visual designer of the first water, as the Brits say — meaning that she's at the top of her game. She has a wide range of abilities, combining visual design and coding skills and a lot of relevant experience.

Sarah's background and experience are an excellent example of how a web developer can start with skills in design and grow into an all-around web-development badass, all before turning 30.

Sarah's career so far

Sarah's career and the online presence she's developed based on it are good examples for anyone with a design-based career in web development to look at and emulate in his or her own career path.

Sarah was an honors student at California State University, Fresno, graduating in 2008. She studied mass communication and journalism. While still at CSU Fresno, Sarah worked as an assistant to a photographer, helping with both photography and marketing. Her work included photo editing, the use of filters, and touch-up — basic skills for a designer.

Also while still in school, Sarah worked as a production assistant at the local city magazine, *Fresno*. She did graphic design and page layout, with lots of work in the Adobe suite of design tools, using Photoshop, Illustrator, and InDesign.

After graduation, Sarah worked as a graphic designer for Logos Bible Software in Bellingham, Washington for more than four years. She helped create a new brand identity for that company, and she implemented it in site content, email marketing pieces, web-based ads in Flash (remember, this was way back in 2010), and even in videos she helped produce. Sarah was also developer-relations coordinator for the company. She worked in PHP, AJAX, and the Big Three of modern web development: HTML5, CSS3, and JavaScript.

Sarah then returned to the Bay Area, where she took contract positions and worked as a freelancer for two and a half years.

Recently, Sarah took a position as a web developer for Asana, a company that makes communication tools for teams to use. Its slogan is "Teamwork without email." Web development is crucial to the product itself, not just to the company's website that describes what it makes and how to buy it.

You can see Sarah's LinkedIn site in Figure 13-1. You can also visit it yourself at www.linkedin.com/in/sarahrudder.

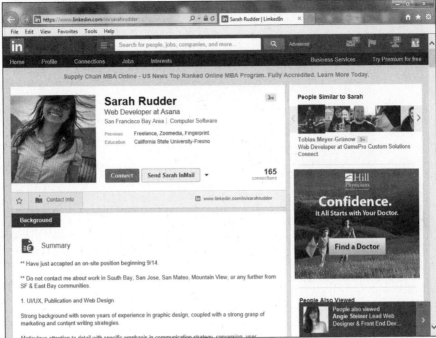

Figure 13-1:
Sarah's LinkedIn page shows a burgeoning web development career.

Sarah's LinkedIn page is a good example of how to handle periods of contracting and freelancing in your portfolio. She gave each of the longer contracts (between 6 and 12 months) a brief, separate entry in her online resume, and then combined smaller jobs into a period of contracting about a year and a half long. For these smaller jobs, she just listed the client names, without any detail about what she did for each.

Sarah's portfolio site, above the fold

For an example of a good portfolio site, check out Sarah's site at www.sarahrudder.com. The home page is shown in Figure 13-2. Sarah has chosen to put everything on a single page.

Single-page websites have become popular as a way to quickly get across a focused idea or set of information, without inflicting the complexities of creating and maintaining navigation between pages on the site's owner, nor inflicting the complexities of finding things located at different spots on the website on users. The user just has to scroll up and down, and everything in the single-page website is revealed.

Figure 13-2:
Sarah's
portfolio
site packs a
lot into one
page.

Using a single-page website doesn't excuse you from the need to do web design, though. Like any good web developer, Sarah knows that a well-designed site makes a visual statement.

This means that the home page of the site (which is the entire site in this case) and, in particular, the area above the fold are important in setting expectations for the site as a whole. People look at the web on all sorts of devices these days, but generally, *above the fold* refers to content in the top 350 to 400 pixels of a web page.

Take a look at what Sarah has put above the fold on her portfolio site:

- ✔ **Her name:** Her name, in all caps. The upper-left corner of a web page is where the user's eyes go first and return to again and again. So that's where you should put your brand — or, in this case, your name.

- ✔ **Links:** Sarah's page contains icons that link to her LinkedIn page, Dribble (a site that hosts designers' images), Twitter, and email. Including these links helps Sarah keep her portfolio page simple because users have other places to go for additional information.

"Above the fold" in the news

The phrase *above the fold* comes from the newspaper world. This might seem obvious to people over 40, but perhaps not so much to younger people. The fold is the strong physical horizontal fold that results when you fold a newspaper in half.

When people pick up a newspaper, they naturally scan the top half of the front page to see what's important. They then unfold the newspaper, which reveals the bottom half of the front page, and then open it, exposing more and more content. A smaller version of the same phenomenon occurs for the internal sections of a newspaper — the sports section, local section, and so on. Above the fold matters.

If you're a writer, and you get a story on the front page, you definitely want your story to have *play above the fold*. That makes it one of about half a dozen things that the newspaper's editors have seen fit to highlight that day.

Photographers also want their front-page photos above the fold, especially in the "hero" spot, a few columns wide, and taking up perhaps as much as a quarter of the space on the top half of the front page.

You have to unfold a newspaper to open it, so *above the fold* means less for internal pages. But it's still a thing; people notice content above the fold more than content below it.

Keep physical dynamics like these in mind as you do web development. The user's attention is a precious thing; keeping concepts like *above the fold* and *below the fold* in mind will help you make better use of it.

Although Sarah did not, many developers include on their portfolio site a link to GitHub, a website that publicly shows the code you have written. GitHub is an effective way for anyone to review, modify, or improve the code for your programs, and for others to see the overall progression of your coding ability.

- ✔ **Photo:** Sarah has a high-resolution photo across the top of her page — much like the big photos that Facebook has added to its pages. Note also that the photo, while friendly, obscures enough of Sarah's features that you wouldn't recognize her in public from it.

- ✔ **Statement:** It's good to have some brief statement summing up what you're offering. Sarah's career is varied enough that this is not easy. So she says, "Hi. I'm Sarah and I love to make." This statement covers all her many different skills and is also a subtle reference to *maker* culture, associated with Burning Man, 3D printing, and other cool stuff.

- ✔ **Descriptive header:** This initial header describes what Sarah does, at a high level: "Website Design & Development." People looking at the page, and perhaps hoping to get help with a project, can easily make an initial decision as to whether to keep looking.

The power of links

One of the weird things about the web is that it is truly just a collection of individual web pages. The only reason we call a collection of pages a *website* is because they share a main domain name, a look and feel, and a navigational structure.

When these conventions are broken — for instance, when a link that looks like part of the navigational structure pops up an email message instead — it can be quite disturbing. The Sarah Rudder site shows how you can make a small site — even a single-page site — feel much bigger by using links cleverly.

The first link that the site provides, in the small collection of links in the upper-right corner, is to LinkedIn. Now lots of people link to their LinkedIn page in emails or on personal websites. But this link is different. When a portfolio site and LinkedIn are connected, each provides vital support to the other.

Your LinkedIn profile gives vital background information about the who, what, when, where, and why of the work shown in your portfolio. Your portfolio illustrates how you carried out the assignments alluded to in your online resume.

The Dribble link also extends Sarah's portfolio site. It gives her a way to highlight specific works and comments others have made on them.

Minimalism is a big part of good design on the web. For consumer products; compare an early iPhone to a then-current BlackBerry, with its built-in keyboard. All Apple products have minimalism in their gene pool. It's certainly possible to take minimalism too far; the recent trend toward single-page sites, for instance, is probably being overdone. But the Sarah Rudder site uses minimalism, plus links, effectively.

✔ **List of key skills:** Sarah then lists her key areas — basically, things for which someone might want to hire her: UX and visual design; semantic HTML, CSS, JavaScript, and PHP; custom themes for WordPress; mobile and responsive sites; wireframing and prototyping; and content strategy. Sarah probably could have added other things here. A list like this usually contains not just the kind of work you've done but also the kind of work you'd like to do.

The part of Sarah's home page that's above the fold conveys many powerful messages, and even offers a fair amount of functionality, with just a few words, icons, and a single large image. Visitors can definitely figure out immediately if they want to scroll down and learn more, or go somewhere else — and that's one of the key things that all web developers try to accomplish with their page.

The rest of Sarah's page — and site

I can describe the rest of Sarah's home page and the entire site at the same time because the entire site is only one page. Figure 13-3 shows another screenshot of the home page, from farther down on the page. However, the entire home page is about a dozen screens deep. To scroll down through all of it yourself, go to www.sarahrudder.com.

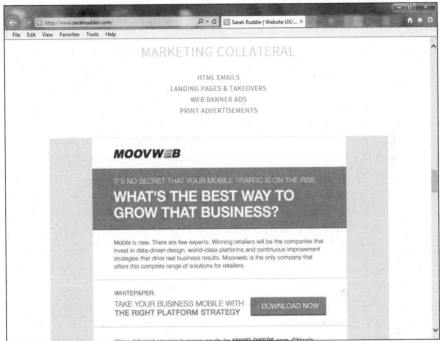

Figure 13-3:
The Sarah Rudder site packs a lot of information into one page.

Here's what you'll find on the rest of the page:

- ✔ **Cepheid site:** This is a medical products site, and the Sarah Rudder websites shows both an extended screenshot and an iPhone screenshot of the site (cleverly overlaid onto a picture of an iPhone).

- ✔ **Natera site:** Also shown are three pages from the site for Natera, a genetics testing company.

- ✔ **"HTML, CSS, WordPress, & .Net" subheader:** This subheader is followed by thumbnails for Faithlife Bible, Faithlife Women, and Vyrso, a site for Christian-themed ebooks.

- ✔ **"Marketing Collateral" major header:** The specific skills listed under this header are HTML emails, landing pages and takeovers; web banner ads; and print advertisements. Following this is an HTML email with a lot of content, carefully laid out. Again, potential clients can quickly see whether Sarah has the skills they need.

> ✔ **"HTML Email Design & Code" subheader and "Content Design" header:** These areas provide additional depth on the remainder of the skills that Sarah is promoting on her portfolio site.

> ✔ **"The Story So Far major header:** In just seven paragraphs, Sarah tells a few pieces of her life story, along with a brief description of her philosophy for web development.

These pages clearly show Sarah's graphic design expertise but also feel light and open. In addition, she uses color and photographs effectively.

By providing so many examples, Sarah also helps those who want a designer with expertise in a certain kind of content. Someone creating a medical-oriented site, for instance, would see lots of examples from that field here, while someone creating a sports-oriented site, not so much. Sarah doesn't make any broad claims about what she is or isn't good at; she lets her work speak for itself.

Sarah's work leaves a strong overall impression: If you had a medium-sized web project, you'd certainly feel assured that Sarah was someone who could lead the project or, if you already had a lead in mind, be a big contributor.

And of the extent of the examples provided, you get the impression also that Sarah might be a good person to bring on board if you needed something similar to her previous work done quickly, yet with polish.

Always look on the bright side of life

Sarah may have made a subtle mistake on her portfolio site. She uses a light bright orange for some text — for her first name, and for the headers on her site. When this orange is against a dark background, it's easy to read. But when it's against a light background, as it is in two places on the home page and above the fold, it's hard to read. Perhaps Sarah designed her site on a conventional monitor, which is usually up to the job of showing deep, rich colors.

The orange-on-white text shows up fine on a conventional monitor, tolerably well on a MacBook screen and an iPhone — and not very well at all on a Windows laptop. Windows laptops are made by different manufacturers and vary widely in their color range, how well they maintain their initial color range over time, and in other aspects as well. Always consider a wide range of potential target machines when making design choices, especially important ones such as text contrast with its background color. And test your results on a wide range of machines.

WARNING!

Showing an entire home page on your site implies that you were the lead person for creating or extensively revising the site. If not, make your role clear. If you played a supporting role in creating a site, go ahead and show it on your portfolio site but provide an explanation: "Provided UX services for a team of 12 that created the Vickenlooper website," for example.

Introducing Matt Rudder's Portfolio Site

Sarah Rudder's portfolio site has a funny line about working with teams of developers: "I got along so well with the developers that I married one."

The words "I married one" are a link to the site of Sarah's husband, Matt Rudder. Matt's portfolio site is shown in Figure 13-4. You can visit the site at `mattrudder.com`.

Matt's a software developer, so, unlike his wife Sarah, Matt can't just show graphics that he created and let the site visitor figure out that he created them. Instead, he shows product logos and describes his contribution to each project.

Figure 13-4:
Matt Rudder's site uses a multipage layout and gives a description for each project.

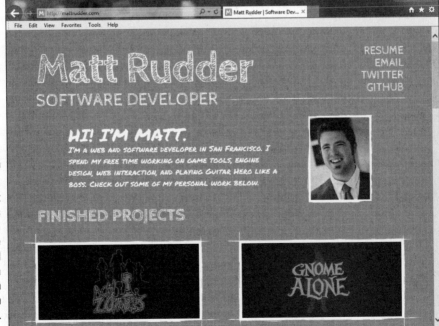

Here are some highlights of Matt's site:

- **"Finished Projects," "In Progress," and "Research" headings:** Matt divides his projects up into three groups, showing that he's capable of a wide range of work.

- **GitHub links:** GitHub is the most popular online repository for code. Matt provides links to all his projects.

  Sometimes developers can't post their projects on GitHub because the code is confidential or proprietary.

- **Resume link:** Matt provides a link to his resume, in PDF format. Matt also has a LinkedIn page.

Note that Matt's site is attractive, interesting, and not very wordy. Yet it's full of relevant technical terms for web development work, including C++, Direct3D, ActionScript, JavaScript, and HTML5. Someone holding a job requisition in his hands could quickly see whether Matt had at least some of the specific skills needed for the position he was trying to fill.

Matt's resume is shown in Figure 13-5. You can access it at `mattrudder.com/media/Matt-Rudder-Resume.pdf`.

You can compare Matt's PDF resume to his LinkedIn page, shown in Figure 13-6. Visit his LinkedIn page at `www.linkedin.com/in/mattrudder`.

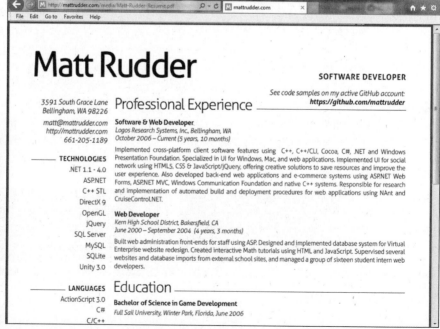

Figure 13-5: Matt Rudder's resume is chock-full of the names of software tools he uses for development.

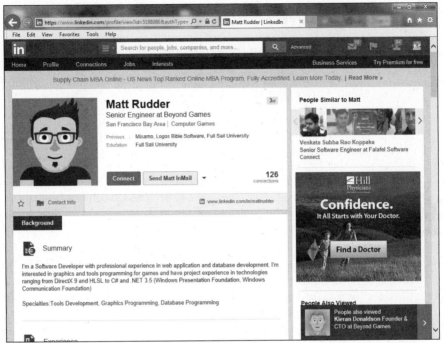

Figure 13-6:
Matt Rudder
LinkedIn
profile com-
plements his
resume.

Matt's resume is full of technical terms, even more so than the home page of his portfolio. It includes a link to his GitHub repository and uses an innovative format to list key technologies and programming languages down the left side of the resume.

Matt's resume fits on one side of one page of paper. If you have more than five years of experience and are switching careers, it's acceptable to use two pages to highlight leadership experiences in your previous career and show technical ability in your current projects.

By using this model, Matt provides a brief chronological resume and a list of selected projects without making entirely clear when some of the project work happened. This leaves the question hanging, likely to be answered in a phone screen or job interview.

Whereas Matt's highly technical resume would be appealing to those "in the know," many HR people and other stakeholders — such as a less-technical interviewer and in some cases also the hiring manager — might have a hard time with it. The technical slant of the resume is increased by the choice he makes of putting it all in one page — there's no room for explanatory text or for using bullet points to separate different elements of the description. Consider adding some explanation, and using bullet points, if you use a lot of technical terms in your resume.

Creating Your Own Portfolio Site

The portfolio sites for the Rudders are great examples of what you want in a portfolio site of your own. Attractive, interesting, easy to digest, and demonstrating that you're plugged into the web development world as a fully capable professional.

You need a portfolio site because the nature of how we get work has changed. Often, potential employers are researching you online well before you're even aware of it.

One problem with some projects is that they're confidential — for an internally facing website or work in progress. To solve this problem, put the project on your website but with no identifying details. Refer to similar sites and describe your role.

A portfolio site does several things that put you well ahead of most jobseekers:

- ✓ **Brings your resume to life:** People use chronological resumes because they answer many key questions, but they're terrible for helping people understand what you really did in a job. A portfolio site demonstrates your skills and ties them to live projects that people can check out.

- ✓ **Distinguishes you from people without one:** If a recruiter has several possible candidates for a job, and one has a portfolio site and others don't, guess who's more likely to get called first?

- ✓ **Saves you from wasting time:** Recruiters are picky, and they may be looking for someone who is almost like you but not quite. You don't want them to call you if you're not a fit. And, having seen your site, the recruiter will probably come straight back to you when there is a fit.

- ✓ **Solves the confidentiality problem:** If you fill in your portfolio site with "like this one" entries for internally facing, confidential work, you've filled gaps in what your experience looks like to recruiters.

- ✓ **Solves the "too much hassle" problem:** When a job posting or a recruiter call includes a request for work samples, it often seems like too much trouble. If you create your portfolio site up front, it's easy to apply for all positions that fit your interests.

- ✓ **Solves the "narrowness" problem:** Resumes tend to put people in a box — graphics person or coder, writer or artist. LinkedIn makes this worse because you can't customize it to fit a job requisition before recruiters, unbeknownst to you, look at it with that requisition in front of them. Portfolio sites show the full range of your abilities.

> ✔ **Helps with the "getting started" problem:** You can't get experience
> without getting a job, but you can't get a job until you have experience.
> A portfolio site lets you put student work, pro bono work, and consult-
> ing work front and center, inviting the viewer to see what you can do.

Creating a portfolio site is the single biggest thing that most people in web
development can do to boost their careers. Some employers may not seriously consider you unless you have your own web presence. You may well
find that a resume gets you an interview, but a portfolio site gets you the
job. Get going on starting your portfolio site — or improving your existing
one today!

Chapter 14

Networking for Opportunities

· ·

In This Chapter

▶ Using real-world networking

▶ Networking online

▶ Creating a stellar resume

▶ Using LinkedIn

· ·

So you're ready to look for work. You've determined that coding would be a good fit for you (Part I), found different ways you can learn to code (Part III), and created a portfolio site (Chapter 13). How do you proceed?

The natural temptation for a web developer is to use an online job site to look for something suitable. However, as I explain in this chapter, online job sites are useful but perhaps the least effective way to get a job. To put it briefly, you're better off when people are contacting you (such as executive recruiters); when people know you (such as former colleagues and others in your network); or when you simply get a promotion or internal transfer.

In this chapter, I explain all these ways of getting a job, with tips and tricks for maximizing your chances.

Networking in the Real World

One effective way to network in the real world is simply to do a good job in your current role. Get things done on time; show respect to your colleagues and help them get their own tasks done; introduce new ideas and new technologies at appropriate times; and keep the overall project's goals, not just your own goals, in mind as you do your work.

This approach helps generate a friendly and productive atmosphere across your team. Team members steadily become extremely productive reference sources for each other. Whenever one of the team members gets a new job — in your current company or at a new company — the first thing she wants to do is to hire her favorite members from a previous team. If you play your cards right, this could mean you.

Networking has developed a bad reputation in many circles as an empty exercise of people who barely know each other rushing to exchange business cards and pushing each other for contacts and job recommendations. Don't do this. However, do make ongoing efforts to stay connected to, and on a positive basis with, people with whom you work closely or who do similar work to you, both in and outside your company.

Figure 14-1 shows networking tips from CIO, a media company that caters to IT leaders. Although the article is titled "12 Tips for Shy People," these tips are good, top-level ones for anyone. You can find them at `j.mp/cionetworkingtips`.

People with a technical mindset tend to assume that you have to know someone well to be an effective networking contact for them. But studies show that looser connections can be even more effective in job searches. Definitely strive to make strong connections with your core project colleagues, but remember that it's also worth the extra effort to reach out to — and make a good impression on — more distant connections.

Figure 14-1:
CIO has many good introductory networking tips.

Home > Careers/Staffing > Relationship Building/Networking

FEATURE

How to Network: 12 Tips for Shy People

Schmoozing is a trial for shy people, but armed with these common-sense tips they can increase their networking mojo.

By Meredith Levinson | Follow
CIO | Dec 11, 2007 7:00 AM PT

MORE LIKE THIS ::

Career Counselor

Selling Yourself Without Selling Out

The Executive Woman's Guide to Self-Promotion

on IDG Answers ➜
I'm considering a slight career change to IT security - what do I need to...

INSIDER

5 Common WI-FI Attacks – and How to Defend

Networking is the key to success in business, says Keith Ferrazzi, business coach and author of *Never Eat Alone*, a book about the power of relationship building and networking. It helps you find jobs, recruit talent, win new customers and discover investors who'll support your ideas.

OTHER NETWORKING STORIES

Learning How to Network

How to Make the Most of Those Holiday Networking Sessions

But networking is a trial for shy people—geeks especially. They view it as insincere at best, manipulative at worst. They eschew networking for a variety of reasons including lack of confidence, fear of rejection and a sense of unworthiness.

Nobody knows the future but we can get you

Here are some effective networking *targets* from closest to you to further away:

- ✓ **Your core team:** Everyone you work with on a daily basis should have good things to say about you.

- ✓ **Other teams that your team works with:** You and your team will have a reputation for being easy to work with or not, creative or not, focused on meeting deadlines or not. Strive to establish a good reputation for yourself and for your team as a whole.

- ✓ **People right across your department:** For instance, in departmental meetings or on internal discussion boards, make the effort to make useful, constructive, incisive comments every now and again. By doing so, you show that you are at the top of your game and are willing to make an effort to contribute to larger discussions.

- ✓ **People with your same job description or technical focus:** Use professional group meetings and online gathering places for people in your profession or who use specific technologies as a place to constructively work out new ideas and offer opinions.

- ✓ **Professional conferences:** Seeing and being seen at professional conferences is a boost to your networking efforts. And snagging a speaking slot or a seat on a panel every so often should be a big boost to your career.

Networking in your current company

Effective networking begins in your current job and at your current company. The core effort that makes networking work doesn't fall under the traditional definition of networking: doing a great job in your current role.

The next step, though, starts to move into the definition of networking: finding ways to let people know that the good work is happening. Casual mentions by you, followed by positive comments from coworkers or your manager, can accomplish this.

You can take specific steps to network in your company:

- ✓ **Say hello:** Learn to say hello to people on a casual basis. This habit can do a lot to make the workplace more comfortable.

- ✓ **Ask others about their work:** Find out what other people do and what problems they're facing. Starting a conversation can give you opportunities to help and can inspire others to ask you the same in return.

- ✓ **Speak up in meetings:** Make helpful comments and share your opinion in meetings.

✔ **Use internal and customer service bulletin boards:** More and more companies have internal bulletin boards so employees can network as well as customer-facing bulletin boards for solving customer problems. Contribute on these platforms.

✔ **Join non-job-related company groups:** Most companies have voluntary teams for pursuing broad goals and for building skills, such as an internal Toastmasters club to share efforts at learning public speaking. These groups are great networking venues.

✔ **Get mentors:** A mentor is a senior person who takes an interest in your career and gives you inside tips and other advice. As someone interested in coding, consider having two mentors: one technical, for helping you build up your skills, and one organizational, for helping you look for new jobs or a promotion in your current company.

In-company networking is key to all your networking efforts. People outside your company will view people in your company as credible sources about you. People inside your company, but not on your work team, view people on your work team as credible sources about you. Build your network, and your credibility, from the inside out.

Networking outside your company

As mentioned, the traditional view of networking is a sad effort where people meet at a semi-social event and try to use that connection to get each other to employ their networks to get themselves a new job. And this can seem most desperate outside your company, where you probably don't know many people.

Love the one you're with

The best way to get a great new job is to be good at and widely recognized in your current job. It's common for people to try to solve being unsatisfied, unproductive, and unhappy in their current job by looking for a new job. Finding for a new job is one solution, but it can come with its own problems.

When things are going poorly in your current job, you're less confident, less likely to get strong recommendations, less likely to be developing with new technologies, and therefore less likely to put forth a strong resume or interview well.

All this turns around when you're doing well in your current job. Doing well also makes you more likely to be headhunted — contacted by executive recruiters — and contacted by managers at your current company for new opportunities.

So, ironically, the single best strategy for getting a great new job is to do well at your current job. Until you can be with the one you love — that exciting, high-paying new job with great benefits, where you use all the latest technologies — do your best to love the one you're with.

Three touches to sell

One of the things that's hardest for technically oriented people to understand is the confusing way that selling works — especially when the product is you.

First, people are inherently sales-resistant, so they often have to hear something several times before it even begins to break through.

Second, one source is rarely enough to convince people. They like to hear news — good or bad — from several sources before they believe it. This issue is separate from the repetition issue; hearing something from the same source three times doesn't cover the "variety of sources" concern.

Third, the usual marketer's beginning guess for number of repetitions — the number of times that someone has to hear something before he or she begins to believe it — is three.

So, for people to understand that you're a top contributor, they should hear this three times, from two or three different sources.

For instance, you can gently let people know that you accomplished some goal (one repetition); give a talk or write a paper, so that the conference or meeting or publication appears as an endorser of your expertise (second repetition); and count on coworkers or your manager to say good things about you to others (third repetition).

More is better, of course, so don't limit yourself to three repetitions. But targeting three is a good first step.

When networking outside your company, take a low-key approach. Don't appear desperate by trying too hard.

Create an elevator pitch; your name, job title, and a couple of well-known people with whom you work. Also mention the key technologies you use.

Then use the pitch. Look for people with whom you can follow up due to shared job or technical interests. Connect with them through a brief email and on LinkedIn, described later in the section "Following the Rules for LinkedIn."

Educational settings are great opportunities for networking, with fellow students and instructors as well. Use your elevator pitch when needed, but also take the opportunity to go deeper. The long and in-depth conversations you can arrange to have, such as before or after class over coffee, can form relationships that help you, and your new friends, throughout your careers. And start building bonds with career services people; these connections can be helpful well beyond your first job out of college.

Be active in alumni groups too. They offer the kinds of broad connections that can be helpful in finding new opportunities.

Meetup.com groups, code-a-thons, and mentoring for young people are additional opportunities to network, and also offer the chance to make new friendships that are personally as well as professionally meaningful to boot.

Building Your Online Network

One of the great conundrums of modern life is how one's online life interacts with one's real life, where you see and interact with people in person. At best, the two realms support each other. You have a lively, interesting real life, supported by lively and interesting interactions online.

If you're better known, better respected, and having more fun in your online life than in your real life, that's not a bad thing. You want to be having a positive experience in both realms, so if you're rocking it online, that's one down and one to go.

As a coder, however, your technical interests and breadth of interest can make it easier to be a big shot online than in person. If this happens, how can you bring that strong persona into your real-world life?

Use these tips to help you build a strong network in both worlds, online and off:

- ✔ **Go for a two-fer:** Try to be well known and well regarded in both your online and real-world lives. Don't settle for one or the other.

- ✔ **Match your online technical focus with your working life:** If you work with Python every day but blog about Ruby, your personas aren't supporting each other. Try to spend your online time and your real-world time on the same topics. Either change your online focus or move to a different job that matches your current online focus.

- ✔ **Overlap your online friends and your work friends:** Ask your work colleagues where they hang out online. Try hanging out there too. You can do good mutual reputation building if your online and work lives overlap.

- ✔ **Prioritize work:** When in doubt, put more energy into your work than into your online life. (And much more than into nonproductive online pursuits such as dating sites and online games.) Work can and should be rewarding in many ways, and you can help yourself make it so by putting work first.

- ✔ **Reduce screen time:** Studies show that sitting — a necessity for logging screen time — is actively harmful to your health. All coders need to move around more. So cutting screen time in favor of moving around — and even getting outside — will be better for you, even for your career, over time.

Sites such as Hacker News (news.ycombinator.com) and https://stackoverflow.com are frequently visited by developers. You can build your reputation on these sites by answering questions, submitting links to interesting articles, and commenting on contributions made by others.

Creating a Winning Resume

The last few years have seen a lot of attention on resumes. Some people advocate for a *functional resume* — a list of skills and skill areas, with occasional mentions of dates and employers. Others tell you that your resume has to be a single page.

However, the operative standard for a printed resume, or a resume in Word or PDF format, seems to be an old-fashioned, chronological resume, two pages long, with a summary statement at the top (optional) and educational background at the bottom (required).

If you are short on experience, consider fitting your resume on one page, and putting your educational accomplishments at the top.

For an online resume, you simply transfer the printed resume to an online format. For an online resume you no longer have to worry about keeping it to exactly two pages, but otherwise, the format for an online resume is exactly the same.

In the following sections, you learn how to create a strong chronological resume, ready to print — and then how to use it to create a strong presence on LinkedIn.

Making a print resume stand out

Your print resume needs to be a minor work of art.

Yes, the world has changed. It's highly likely that your "print" resume will rarely be printed. Instead, it will be viewed onscreen. But it's still important that it looks great so that it is easy to scan and read.

Follow these rules to make your print resume stand out:

✔ **Format it carefully and consistently:** Your resume should look polished and professional even before anyone reads it. If you need to, find a sample resume online, and then type your own information into the format. Also, your resume should be consistent — for example, if you use bullet point descriptions or bold font for company names, make sure all descriptions are bulleted and all company names are in bold font.

Being a 10xer

The concept of a *10x* employee has recently gained widespread popularity. If you can be seen as a 10xer in any role, your chances of moving to the top of the salary and opportunity pyramid skyrocket.

The idea behind 10xers was widely popularized in the famous programming book *The Mythical Man-Month* by Frederick P. Brooks (Addison-Wesley). In this classic, Brooks labels as a lie the idea that a stalled programming project can be kick-started simply by throwing more people at it — especially by throwing more mediocre people at it.

Brooks says that adding people causes an exponential increase in the time everyone spends communicating instead of getting things accomplished. The best communication, according to Brooks, is inside the heads of the most talented individuals, who were ten times more productive than the least. Next most effective is informal communication in a small, experienced, talented team.

More recently, it's been observed over and over that adding just one highly talented software developer, designer, or writer to a troubled project can put it back on track almost overnight. This highly talented individual races through backlogs of project tasks and succinctly communicates his or her needs and helpful new ideas to relieved colleagues.

Being a 10xer is a more intense version of the idea that being happy in your current job is the best way to ease the way into a new one. If you can be a happy, super-productive employee — a 10xer — you're likely to find getting your next great job very easy indeed.

Don't overdo the formatting in your resume. Companies often use automated software to scan your resume, and this software can experience issues processing resumes that have text in headers or footers and tables, images, or logos.

✔ **Proofread it carefully:** Your resume has to be perfect. Everyone knows this — or, at least, everyone believes it — so errors on your resume are seen as evidence of extreme carelessness and cluelessness. Make sure there are no errors.

✔ **Then, proofread it again:** You can't proofread your resume too many times. Also get others to proofread it for you. Even if there are no actual spelling errors, out-of-date information can come across as an error too.

✔ **List jobs in reverse chronological order:** Start with the most recent, and go back in time. Include the company name, month, and year of the start and finish dates, the city, and several lines about what you did in the job. Each job description can have four to six bullet points, with each bullet point no more than two lines long and fewer bullets for roles earlier in your career.

✔ **Include buzzwords:** It's crucial that you include key buzzwords in the resume text. HTML5, CSS, JavaScript, Python, Ruby on Rails, SQL, Backbone.js — these are just some of the buzzwords you want to be sure to include, wherever they apply.

✔ **Include a skills section:** Consider listing current skills in a separate section at the top. That makes it a lot easier for an HR person to quickly scan your resume to see if it's worth further consideration for jobs that require specific skills.

✔ **Include accomplishments:** List important accomplishments that you achieved on your own or as part of a team. Include what you did, and highlight leadership, teamwork, and technical ability.

✔ **Include helpful dollar figures:** Words like "$5 million project" can be helpful; "I saved the company $2,123.92" are not. Put in significant dollar figures in round numbers where you think they might help, and then check with a trusted friend about whether they actually do.

✔ **Make sure your key attributes are reflected:** If you exemplify an attribute, make sure your resume reflects this. For example, if you're detail oriented, put this in the Summary section — and then make sure that your accomplishments reflect a person who's detail oriented. "Created a large SQL database that worked flawlessly in just two months, saving $5 million in inventory costs" is a statement that says *detail oriented* without having to use the actual words.

✔ **Don't automatically list all jobs:** In the older sections of your resume, you can cut off your job list at a certain point, rather than go all the way back to the start of your career. Many people list only about ten years' worth of jobs to keep the resume length reasonable, reduce the presence of outdated technologies on their resume, and reduce the possibility for ageism in the hiring process.

For better or worse, anyone reading your resume will tend to guess that you were about 22 when you got your bachelor's degree, if any. There's no easy way to avoid this assumption.

✔ **Try for one page, use two pages if needed:** People like a resume that fits on one single sheet of paper, front and back, chock-full of information — but without using extra-small type or narrow margins. If you're new in your career, though, don't strain to fill the space. Don't go over one page unless you have a lot of accomplishments.

✔ **Print it:** Print your resume periodically. Make sure it looks great printed, and proofread the printed copy. You can more easily spot errors on the page than on the screen.

✔ **Tweak it:** For each specific job, create a new version of your resume with the relevant buzzwords from the job description — especially at the top of the resume.

✔ **Get advice:** Do the best job you can on your resume, and then get an experienced professional or friend to weigh in. In addition, your university career services office may be able to help.

If you don't have access to career support on your own or through university alumni, use a site such as www.evisors.com to hire a professional to do a review for you for less than $100.

You're likely to use your resume again and again during your career. It's worth taking care to create and maintain a strong resume.

Following the rules for LinkedIn

LinkedIn has several different functions. It can be a simple resume-hosting service. Or you can add recommendations and comments, making your resume the centerpiece of a little online community focused on you.

You can also join various groups and networks on LinkedIn, building up your reputation. For technical people such as web development pros, a certain degree of cool is attached to being low-key. Using LinkedIn as a simple resume-hosting service might be for the best.

Figure 14-2 shows the LinkedIn profile of a career-changer, Helin Shiah, who switched from finance to web development by going through a code school called Dev Bootcamp. Note how her tech experience includes references to live projects she built that cover a range of technologies. You can see Shiah's LinkedIn profile at www.linkedin.com/in/helinshiah.

Keep these thoughts in mind when using LinkedIn:

✔ **Make the summary count:** A recruiter should be able to tell whether you're a good candidate just from the summary. Write your summary carefully and be thorough.

✔ **Keep your overall resume inclusive:** When you apply for a specific job online, you can tailor your resume to the job description. On LinkedIn, you need to cover all the bases — a single resume has to attract all kinds of employers.

✔ **Go short:** Keep descriptions short. It's harder to read online than in print, so a smaller amount of detail goes a long way on LinkedIn.

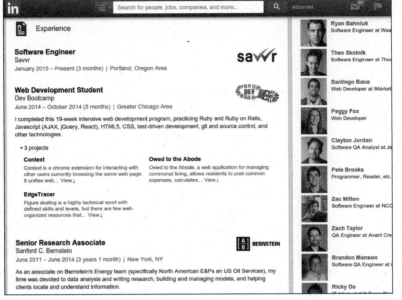

Figure 14-2:
Shiah links
to her
LinkedIn
profile on
her resume
and blog.

- ✔ **Go long:** You don't need to trim your list of jobs to keep within a page limit.

- ✔ **Give recommendations:** Give LinkedIn recommendations to the people you know best or who recommend you.

- ✔ **Include some personal info:** List some interests outside work. What you do outside work, especially for your community, helps people see beyond the online profile.

- ✔ **If you're free to travel, say so:** Many employers want to know that you're free to travel at least some of the time. If you can travel at all, add "free to travel as required" to your resume. You can back out if the travel demands of a job are too much. If you're not free to travel, just don't mention it.

- ✔ **Update the Skills section:** Put your strongest skills in the Skills section. You can include up to 25, but it's best to include only those you feel most confident in. That way, you get a follow-up from recruiters who use keyword search to filter resumes on only your best skills, avoiding a disappointing waste of time all around.

As with your printed resume, your LinkedIn profile may get a lot of attention during your career. Take the time to make it strong and useful.

Chapter 15

Interviewing and Becoming a Star

· ·

In This Chapter

▶ Getting the interview

▶ Surviving the interview

▶ Becoming a star employee

· ·

S o you attained enough education and have built a portfolio site. You've had a few jobs — or you're working on getting your first job. Coworkers (or fellow students) say good things about you. And you're starting to get some interest for an upcoming job in web development. How do you nail it down? I describe the process in this chapter.

Then comes a time when you get the job — or you want to think a bit about the job you're already in. How do you do the job well enough to be seen as a star, one of those 10x employees who can make or save a project? This chapter answers those questions from a web-development point of view, telling you what's special about this process for graphics-based, coding-based, and mixed roles. With this information in hand, you'll be ready to boost your career, in the short term and permanently.

Getting the Interview

One of the hardest and most important journeys you'll ever undertake is the journey from sitting at your computer, looking at a job listing, to sitting in a potential employer's office, undergoing an interview.

For coders, this journey is easier than it is for many other people. Coders continue to be in strong demand. And the use of many different, specific technologies in the field means that your chances of getting a given job can be pretty good if you have experience with the right technologies and a solid overall background

Most people are generally familiar with the process of applying for a job. Here are a few highlights of the process, specifically for web developers:

- ✔ **The presubmission phone call:** Before you send your information for a job, give a call, if at all possible. Ask any key questions you have, plus the core question for any such process: Where is the company in the hiring process? Often you'll find that the process is completed, nearly completed, or some other status that may leave you deciding not to apply for the position. If the hiring process is still open, ask about key tools and technologies.

- ✔ **The cover letter:** Always find a way to write a cover letter, even if you have to paste it along with your resume into a job application form that only accepts resumes or in the body of an email. In your cover letter, take the three or so top requirements from the position description (as you judge them) and tie them to your experience. Also describe your availability — looking for work; employed but looking; not actively looking but attracted by this specific job description (or a personal recommendation), and so on. Be straightforward and to the point, rather than funny or cute. Proofread your cover letter to perfection.

- ✔ **The resume:** You should have a somewhat generic resume saved on your hard drive or in the cloud. For a specific job, take your generic resume and customize it to fit the position. For instance, if specific technologies or tools are required, identify the jobs where you used each one, and make sure that the technology or tool name is mentioned, with appropriate prominence, in the description for each job where you used it.

Get and keep the reviewer's attention by rearranging the sections in your resume so your strongest qualifications or accomplishments related to the job are listed first.

- ✔ **The follow-up phone call (immediately):** After you apply, follow up with a phone call. This one simple step measurably increases your chances of getting the job. Ask if your information has been received. Then ask what's most important about the position and offer to resubmit your information with those points highlighted, which will make your application stand out.

- ✔ **The follow-up phone call (two to three days later, and then weekly):** After you apply and follow up with a phone call, call again a few days later. See how the process is going and ask if it's likely that you'll move forward. If not, ask the person to whom you're speaking to consider you for future positions.

If you follow these suggestions, your chances of getting an interview will improve.

The Career Center site on the website for the state of California, shown in Figure 15-1, has advice on writing a cover letter. Like most such advice, it's a bit too formal and complicated for most web development jobs. Your cover note will often be just a short email, with a resume attached in Word format. But even a short cover note should contain the gist of the content described on the Career Center site. Visit it at www.calcareercenter.org/Home/Content?contentID=133.

Employers can fixate on finding people who are familiar with the top one or two technologies or tools used in the company. Ideally, for the employer, the desired technology and tool keywords appear in most or all of your recent jobs or projects. Not much else matters; you might be a nice person, learn fast, and so on, but if you don't have the specific technology or tool experience desired, you will often not be contacted.

For some reason, many companies — especially larger ones — will put up a restrictive job posting, wait months, get no candidates they can hire, and then bemoan the result. The thought of lowering the years of experience required, asking for experience with similar rather than exact matches to technologies and tool experience needed, or allowing partial work from home, for instance, doesn't seem to occur to them.

Figure 15-1: Career Center site covers job-searching basics, including cover letters.

I. get. stuff. done.

You sometimes encounter people in the workplace who are proud to say, with a long pause between words, "I. get. stuff. done." (*Stuff* might not be the exact word they use.)

When you think of the interview process, it's good to think of the people in the hiring process as mostly having this attitude. People go to the trouble to get budget approval for new headcount, open a job requisition, write or revise the job description, and so on because they're overwhelmed. The hiring process makes them more overwhelmed. And your arrival won't help right away because it might take you a few months to get up to speed. This up-front cost of hiring someone is especially true in web development, where ambitions are high but budgets, not so much. Companies are insistent on finding someone with experience with specific technologies and tools because it can shorten the time it takes the new employee to become productive.

So the people conducting the hiring usually find the process not a lot of fun as well as unproductive in the short term. When you think of people who you encounter in hiring, think of them as having the attitude of wanting to "get stuff done." The easiest "done" is to find some reason to say "no" to you; avoiding that is a crucial goal for you in each step of the process.

During interviews, you might finally talk to some people who take the time to start to get to know you and to think creatively about whether you're a good fit. Let the interviewers lead on that. Keep your answers during interviews of all sorts short, simple, and positive. This approach allows the interviewers to get through their routine questions quickly — and either finish quickly, which will make them feel more relaxed, or engage with you on more interesting aspects of the potential job or the hiring company, which will give you a chance to show what you know.

The trend of companies using narrow search criteria and requiring many years of experience is part of the reason why networking is so powerful; when someone is a trusted friend and former colleague, the strict requirements of the job posting are often relaxed.

Surviving Interviews

Job interviews can be stressful. Your performance has a large influence on whether you get the job — assuming, that is, that the company is truly ready to hire. If they aren't, the job interview won't help much.

This section shares some coding-specific tips on the interview process.

The phone screen

A phone screen is a usually brief phone call between you and someone representing the company doing the hiring. This representative can be the hiring manager, an internal or external recruiter, or anyone else involved in the process.

The key word to remember in the term *phone screen* is *screen,* They're really trying to weed out candidates. If you're interested in the job, try to get screened in, not screened out.

The person doing the phone screen is often a lower-level employee or contractor with only modest understanding of what's needed for the position he or she is asking after. The interview's lack of context can be a big problem for coding jobs; despite your knowledge of technical tools and programming languages, the interviewer might be looking for candidates with experience using a specific technical tool and could screen you out if you don't have that experience. By contrast, your manager may be comfortable with your experience using similar tools and could be more than willing to give you time to train yourself for a specific tool.

Unfortunately, the one thing phone screeners don't want to hear is a manager telling them, "You sent through people who don't fit the job requisition." The response means they've missed the point of the exercise. Coding uses many similar languages, frameworks, and tools, and it's easy to screen out capable people by using overly specific criteria.

So be brief and positive when talking to a phone screener. If you don't have a given requirement, give a similar alternative. "No, I don't have a bachelor's degree, but I do have an associate's degree and five years of experience." Or, "No, I have two years of Python experience, not three, but I do have Python experience and I also know SQL and Hadoop." The screeners will usually pass on such comments to their bosses, if the comment is clear and simple enough to write down easily.

It's good practice to follow up after a phone screen by calling the next day to ask if you're still in the pool. You might well rise to the top of the pile as a result. You might also be given the chance to correct any negative information, an opportunity that can be invaluable.

Before you interview

Live interviews are fraught with potential pitfalls. You should do some research first. Here are a few coding-specific tips:

- ✔ **Network with other developers:** Find out from other developers currently at the company what the interview process is like and about working there generally. The interview may differ depending on whether you are interviewing for a data, web development, or other coding job.

- ✔ **Find out if there are any "famous" interview techniques:** Some tech companies are famous for posing complex problems, using a fixed set of questions, asking a particular unusual question, planting a hostile interviewer, and so on. Using a search engine enter the company's name and the word *interviews*, and use the other approaches mentioned here to find out if there are any such tricks up this company's sleeve.

Some tech companies are famous for giving hostile, lengthy, or tricky interviews. You need to find out if this is true before you interview — not only to be sure you can handle the tricky part, but also because the people interviewing you will think you didn't do your homework if you didn't find this out in advance. Be prepared.

- ✔ **Be ready for behavioral questions:** Many companies now ask questions in the format, "Tell us about a time when you . . .." They then insert words such as *succeeded, failed,* or *overcame an obstacle.* Unfortunately, these questions are at least as much a test of your verbal dexterity in an anxiety-producing situation as anything. Consider writing down some of these questions beforehand and identifying three or four accomplishments you're proud of and challenges you've overcome, so you're ready for these kinds of questions.

- ✔ **Look at the company's website:** If it sucks, stay away from the interview, unless you're being invited to help replace it. A crappy website is a warning sign of a potentially frustrating and professionally limiting coding experience. But if the website is at least decent, dive into it. Figure out what technologies are being used. Note both good and bad points, but use your discretion when speaking about the bad parts of your interview unless the website is really awful.

- ✔ **Check out Glassdoor:** Glassdoor (www.glassdoor.com) has a lot of good company-specific information, especially for big, technology-oriented companies. Use this information to learn about the place you're considering working, such as typical salaries and employee satisfaction (or dissatisfaction). Glassdoor can help prepare you for what your interviewers will think that you might think of their company, which is confusing but an important for navigating the interview successfully.

When you use Glassdoor, you may find that a few horror stories or snarky comments about the CEO stick in your mind. Do not go into the interview ready to challenge your interviewers about this. Use the negative information when choosing whether to accept a job offer, not to make yourself a hostile witness during the interview.

✔ **Check out your interviewers on LinkedIn:** The hiring company will check you out on LinkedIn, so return the favor. Use what you see on LinkedIn to identify items in your background that will be interesting or relevant to your interviewers.

✔ **Hit the boards:** Check out coding discussion boards such as HackerNews (news.ycombinator.com) or Quora (www.quora.com) for your area and see what you can learn. Asking for information in an open message board can be a bit dicey, but a message like, "Hey, a friend" — you're a friend of yourself, right? — "is thinking of taking a job at Company X. Does anyone have any info" can be productive.

✔ **Use your e-resources:** Use email and Facebook in a similar way to crowd-source information and insights.

Companies and their employees get sensitive about negative remarks posted on Glassdoor, Yelp, other online messaging systems, in emails, and so on. Find as many of these as you can, but be careful about mentioning them. If you do, ask in a neutral tone; don't badger your interviewers.

Acing the interview

When it's time to go to the actual, live interview — probably several interviews with different people — it's easy to be nervous.

Don't be. Interviews are first and foremost about showing your interpersonal skills. For web development jobs, interpersonal skills are considered less important than for many other jobs. Yes, they matter, but they're not the single most important factor as they are, for instance, in a sales or customer support role. So relax.

Technical people pride themselves on dealing with things logically and rationally, and even on being able to handle a fairly high amount of conflict in support of doing the best possible job on a project. The focus on technical problem solving means that interpersonal skills are not likely to be put under the same scrutiny as technical skills.

Your technical skills will largely be assessed from your resume and any work samples you've shared. You may be asked technical questions during your interview, but all you can do is answer those honestly and hope your experience meets the needs of the company.

It's also important to realize that many decisions about whether you're going to get a job have little to do with how well you interview. Many interviews are a waste of time; the company knows that you're not quite what it wants, and uses the interview to confirm it. Or it knows that it wants you, and uses the interview to confirm that instead. Sometimes, the company isn't even sure if it has an opening, or the opening disappears after the interviews but before the time to make an offer.

Figure 15-2 shows an interview with an IT specialist who works for the Library of Congress. The questions and answers are a good proxy for a low-key job interview. Use this interview to practice for job interviewing. You can find it at `blogs.loc.gov/law/2012/06/an-interview-with-patrick-ouellette-information-technology-specialist/`.

There are only a limited number of times when an interview makes a "yes or no" difference as to whether you get a job, and rarely does the evaluation of an interview hinge on a single question. As long as you're friendly, positive, and honest, you're likely to do well in an interview.

Figure 15-2:
This interview reads a lot like a job interview.

Companies sometimes make ridiculous requests of candidates — to do several interviews spread out across different days, to add sessions after an interviewer cancels, and so on. Graciously refuse excessive requests; offer a phone meeting instead, if needed, but don't keep making trips back to a place that can't organize an interview.

Here are a few coding-specific tips:

- ✔ **Practice, practice, practice:** We all like to think we can be heroes under stress, but people are usually worse under stress than they are when they're calm. Have a friend conduct three practice interviews with you. You'll work through a lot of stuttering, hesitation, indecision, and brain freezing that you might otherwise suffer through during the interview.

- ✔ **Feel free to be direct:** Web developers are famous, or sometimes even infamous, for sharing their opinions freely. Don't go overboard in an interview, but don't shy away from expressing yourself clearly.

- ✔ **Introduce yourself at the beginning of each interview:** Be ready to repeat your basic information to each individual or group that you meet with.

- ✔ **Have, or come up with, a couple of questions for each interviewer:** Pivoting from defense (answering) to offense (asking), politely, takes a lot of the pressure off you — and off the interviewer, too. It makes the interview less of an interrogation and more of a discussion.

- ✔ **Have extra questions for your potential manager:** The most important interviewer is usually the person who will be your manager if you get the job. Even if this person is your last interviewer and you're exhausted, or the first and you're anxious, have a few questions written down for him or her in particular.

- ✔ **Speak slowly and pause between sentences:** It's helpful to slow down your speaking during interviews. When taking a coding test as part of an interview, where you're intermixing graphical, technical, usability, and interpersonal concerns at the same time, speaking slowly is especially valuable. You will look thoughtful, not nervous. And no one can leave an interview remembering the stupid thing you didn't say because you gave yourself the opportunity not to say it.

- ✔ **Follow up afterward with a thank-you email:** Address it to the person who set up the interview. Add or reaffirm a couple of key points, shore up any weak spots in your answers, and make your availability and interest in the position clear.

The military is famous for its heroes, people who show courage under fire. But the most important military adage relating to heroism is, "You're only as good as your training." Soldiers train over and over so they have "muscle memory" when under stress. You can do the same for yourself by having just a few practice sessions for your interview.

Becoming a Star Employee

People in all fields often look at a new job as a kind of silver bullet. A new opportunity will make them more money, introduce them to better coworkers, let them work on the latest technologies, and on and on.

However, a new job can sometimes be like that line in the song from the famous rock group The Who: "Here comes the new boss, same as the old boss."

The main influence on whether you are happy in any given situation is you. You'll find lots of actual and potential difficulties at work, but over time, you have the biggest say in how things work for you.

Your attitude is especially important when it comes to becoming a 10xer — a star employee, as previously mentioned. Star employees aren't people who will become a star in their job — they are people who are already a star in their current job.

So when you get a new job, set out to become a star employee. And if you've been in your current job for a while, figure out how to become a star employee there, as much as possible.

Figure 15-3 shows testimonials from customers of 10x Management, a firm that acts as a talent agency for top web development and other technical talent. You want to hear these kinds of testimonials with regards to your own work.

If you're starting to look to greener pastures in your career, consider spending one year becoming as much of a star as you can manage in your current job. You're likely to become much more employable in the process.

It's true that people often develop an opinion of you quickly in a new job. If you've already been at a job for a while, you may be able to change people's opinions only so much. Moving from average or good employee to star employee might take either several years in your current job or, more likely, at least one job change. But there's no time like the present to start.

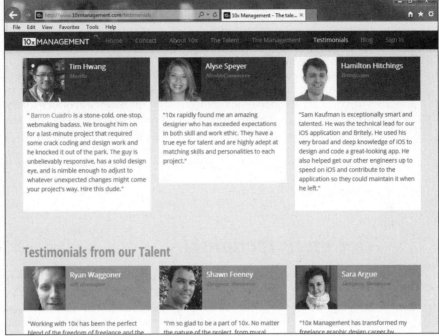

Figure 15-3:
10x Management customers love working with top talent, and vice versa.

The three keys to becoming a star employee as a coder are be stellar at your core skill; get more technical; and learn to communicate better and earlier.

Be stellar at your core skill

College admission to a top school is one of the most competitive arenas on Earth. In this competition, you can divide applicants into two groups: all-rounders and angular students.

All-rounders are omnicompetent, good at a whole bunch of things, such as math, English, sports, and student government. Top colleges are full of all-rounders, but here's the secret: A lot of all-rounders get told "no" by top colleges.

Angular students, on the other hand, are good at one thing. An angular student is one of the best in the entire applicant pool at, say, chess, or calculus, or lacrosse, or writing short stories. Top colleges are also — and, perhaps, increasingly — full of angular students as well. But perhaps fewer angular students who truly excel in a niche, no matter how small it is, get told "no" by top colleges.

Just like in college admissions, all-rounders and angular applicants are going for the top coding jobs. Lots of people are good at core coding skills such as web development using HTML5, CSS, and JavaScript, or data analysis using Python, R, and SQL. Being one of these people is lucrative.

But if you're truly expert — widely recognized or visibly outstanding — in some specific programming aspect (say, you give lectures on how to structure stylesheets in a hierarchy, or you teach introductory Python), you're going to stand out further. You will find fewer jobs that are a good fit, but you'll get a high percentage of the jobs for which you apply.

So, for the highest rewards, become stellar at the aspect of your work that you love most. You'll have more fun and be more likely to have top pay and respect as well.

Get more technical

Most coders know a few programming languages for performing bread-and-butter tasks. But top coders stay up-to-date by learning the latest languages. Those who don't keep learning the latest techniques and languages find themselves left behind eventually, whether after six month or sixteen years.

No matter the job, you'll have a lot of opportunity to keep learning. For instance, JavaScript is the core skill for most graphics-based web developers. If you can be strong in basic JavaScript, which still usually requires only revising scripts you get elsewhere, you can be a threat out there in the web development job market. Going beyond basic JavaScript, it can be useful to know some of the latest JavaScript frameworks such as Angular, Ember, or React. These frameworks make it possible to create even more complex web pages and experiences and are in demand by certain companies.

Going beyond JavaScript, knowing Python or SQL, among others, can be useful. These languages get you thinking about how your website interacts with the databases that drive more and more of what happens on the web and in mobile apps as well.

After you gain technical skills, find ways to get recognition for them. Courses, certificate programs, and projects where you're the lead for coding work are all ways to get this recognition.

Then assess where you want to grow. You may want to be the best front-end developer you know who also knows how to handle database access — or the best Python programmer you know who's also skilled at graphics.

Communicate better and earlier

The biggest single frustration that managers at all levels have with coders is that managers don't know most of what they need to know. They don't know what a website is going to look like when the project is signed off. They don't know whether all the promised features will be there. They don't know whether the schedule will be met or how big the schedule overshoot will be. And they don't know whether the site will be relatively bug-free, especially in the vital area of data security.

The odd thing is, if developers on a project felt that they could be honest, they could probably answer many of these questions much earlier in the game. Management might not like the answer, but everyone would benefit from the information getting out there sooner rather than later.

So perhaps the biggest skill in development has nothing directly to do with development. It has to do with communication — understanding the scope of a project or part of a project; assessing progress toward goals; calculating realistic finish dates, likely feature sets, and so on; and then communicating the information to others, especially management.

The main difficulties with communication have to do with having the courage to be the bearer of bad news and earning the respect of others so that they'll accept it from you. If you're highly skilled and willing and able to work hard, you can sometimes single-handedly make the news less bad by filling gaps in the project yourself. But it's more important to assess, and communicate about, the gaps in a project than to try to fill them all yourself.

As you work on your projects, don't just think of technical and artistic challenges. Think of business goals and where the technical and artistic challenges stack up against those. Assess where your project is against those goals, and start sharing your opinion with others.

Part V
The Part of Tens

Check out www.dummies.com/extras/gettingacodingjob for ten hackathons where you can practice your skills.

In this part . . .

- ✔ Understand what interview questions really mean
- ✔ Review job search strategies for coding jobs
- ✔ Learn some common coding myths

Chapter 16

Ten Interview Questions Decoded

In This Chapter

▶ Can you walk me through your resume?

▶ What recent project have you worked on?

▶ Why do you want to work here?

▶ What feature would you add to or remove from product X?

▶ What team conflict have you resolved?

▶ What is your ideal company and job?

▶ What is your superpower?

▶ Which three adjectives would your friends use to describe you?

▶ What do you know to be true that most people disagree with or find surprising?

▶ What questions do you have for me?

---

*Y*ou learned to code. You built your portfolio. You submitted your prototypes to Hacker News, Product Hunt, and Reddit, and people rewarded you with upvotes. All that work helped you secure some phone and in-person interviews from companies that want to learn more about you.

Interview questions generally fall into two categories: technical questions and culture and fit questions. A technical question is one where you are asked to design or solve a technical challenge. A culture and fit question assesses whether you would fit in and work well with the current team of employees.

The questions listed in this chapter are some of the most common culture and fit questions. For each question, the interviewer is asking you one thing but listening for something else. Read on to understand what the interviewer is assessing while you answer the question.

Can You Walk Me through Your Resume?

Ideally, the question "Can you walk me through your resume?" is unnecessary if your interviewer has read your resume before meeting you, did a Google search on your name, read your recent tweets and blog posts, and even checked out some of the projects in your portfolio. In reality, an interviewer may come to the interview prepared but is just as likely to instead be unprepared, breathlessly running from meeting to meeting.

Even if your interviewer knows who you are, this question is meant to

- ✔ Build rapport between you and the interviewer
- ✔ Help you get ready to talk (a lot!) and become comfortable by speaking about a topic you know intimately — you!
- ✔ Give you the opportunity to highlight the best parts of your past

Many interviewees hear this question and launch into a long and detailed biography. Practice until you can answer this question in less than one minute, which will allow interviewers to continue the conversation by diving into the areas they find most interesting. You can also use this question to share a little more about what you learned from each experience. Perhaps you previously worked in marketing but felt more satisfaction creating a product than just pitching it, or you worked on a game and found the process less fun than you thought it would be.

Use your resume to include details about leadership, teamwork, or impact from your previous projects. Examples of impact include details on the revenue generated, time saved, users who signed up, or the size of your team. These "breadcrumbs" make it easy for interviewers to ask more questions about a particular project.

What Recent Project Have Your Worked On?

By now you have likely worked on a few projects, so you have some options to discuss when asked, "What recent project have you worked on?" Every project has two pieces — the story behind the project's creation, and the technical decisions made when coding the project. While your interviewer will be mostly interested in the technical side of the project, a good story will make your project more memorable.

Your design choices carry more weight if you have some expertise pertaining to the problem that the app solves. For example, maybe you created a bike route mapping app because you used to be on the bicycle team, or you launched a cheap flight tickets app because you love flying and have visited over 40 countries. Unless your interviewer is also a bicyclist or travel enthusiast, he or she will take your word that these are the most important features to build.

The interviewer is assessing a few areas with this question, including:

- ✔ **Build versus buy**: A coding project is a combination of many parts. For each part, you need to prioritize what you will build versus what you will buy or incorporate from someone else. For example, if you are building a restaurant reservation app, it may be faster to use Google, Yelp, or Foursquare to get a list of restaurants rather than trying to gather the data yourself.

- ✔ **Community knowledge**: Every day, coders release tools, libraries, and APIs that make it easier to program. You would likely only know about them if you spent some time following the community. For example, suppose that you follow the latest in mobile mapping for your bike route mapping app, and you found a mapping library with greater speed and accuracy than other industry solutions. Showing the interviewer that you know something about even a small technical area will translate into you coding more efficiently when you are on the job.

- ✔ **Technical efficiency:** For the parts of the app you did build, be ready to talk about the algorithms you created and potential alternative solutions you could have used. Programs are written against a set of constraints, and the interviewer might challenge how you think by making you respond to stronger constraints. For example, your cheap flight tickets app may query as many airlines as possible in two minutes to find the lowest price, but how would your app design change if you had only twenty seconds to query airlines for the lowest price?

Coding is never a perfect process: There is a goal outlined in a specification, the code you write to achieve that goal, the obstacles you face along the way, and the final product. The interviewer will want to see how you handled each of these parts because you will follow the same journey when you join a company as a developer.

Why Do You Want to Work Here?

When asked, "Why do you want to work here?" most interviewers are not looking for the answer, "Because you'll have me!"

When you started your job search, you probably used a few filters to start your search and then narrow the list. You may have chosen companies in an industry you like or those located in a specific city. Industry and geography are fine reasons to mention, but try to go deeper if possible.

The interviewer is looking to see whether you have researched to find a little more information than what is available on the company home page or blog. Here are some potential responses for you to explore:

- **Mission:** Alignment with the company's mission is always a good reason to want to work at a company. For example, if you're applying to a company that builds a workout app, it's good to mention your interest in physical fitness.

  However, so many people use the company's mission as the reason for applying that it can sometimes be hard for an interviewer to separate those who are genuine from those who are faking it. For this reason, make sure to recall past experiences that show genuine interest. In the case of applying to the workout app company, perhaps you could mention your time on the basketball team, the recent half-marathon you ran, or your blog post on doing the 7-minute workout for a month. If your hobbies and activities naturally tie in to the work a company does, don't be afraid to mention them.

- **Role:** Before interviewing, have enough conversation with employees so you have a good idea of the three to four projects you might work on if you were hired, and then express interest in the work and the role. At smaller companies, you'll likely have a broad role on whatever you work on; at larger companies, your role might be narrower but your company might set the standard for the industry. Gaining more responsibility or learning from a major industry player are both great reasons to work at a specific company.

- **Employee connection:** Referring to conversations and relationships you've had with current employees acts as a positive reference for you, and shows your interviewer that you've taken time to better understand the company and its culture. You can't know someone at every company you're applying to, but when you do know someone it can be a great boost.

  Don't make your connection to an employee larger than it actually is. Your interviewer is almost sure to ask the coworker about you, and nothing sinks a candidate faster than the coworker saying, "I don't really know him that well."

- **Long-time user:** Every technology product has users, and power users of a product often make great employees because they know exactly what works well and what needs improvement. While other candidates might ask about features that have already been built or were retired, you'll know all about the product's history. Use your knowledge to ask how where the product is going, and how that direction fits with what the team has learned from past product decisions.

For just about any tech product, it is easy to verify when you joined and how frequently you use the product. Make sure you don't claim to be a power user if you used the product for only a week more than a year ago.

What Feature Would You Add to or Remove from Product X?

Developers and their time are in short supply, so teams constantly debate about what to build next. To see how you could contribute to the discussion, your interviewer might ask you about a product you use frequently, and one feature you would add or remove. Usually the product is external to the company, so you should feel comfortable giving honest feedback.

When answering this question, ground your thoughts in facts of some kind, and debate a product's merits in a constructive way. It's typically fair game to rely on larger market trends, features in competitors' products, feedback from users, and your own experience. After you know *why* you would add or remove a product feature, the other question to answer is *how*. Consider how the technical work would need to be accomplished, how that affects the current product, and whether the addition or removal is feasible.

For example, my favorite app is Google Maps, and the feature I would add is integration of public bike sharing when the bike option is selected during route planning. This feature could increase usage of the app because bike share riders take tens of millions of bike trips annually, public bike ridership is expected to increase as cities increase the number of available bikes, and a competitor, Citymapper, already has an app that includes public bikes as part of its route planning. On the technical side, there are some serious considerations to consider. Knowing a bike kiosk location isn't enough — I also need to know whether any bikes are at the location. Even when bike data is available, it is usually delayed by 15 to 30 minutes, providing outdated and inaccurate data in high volume areas. Finally, I need to know whether including this feature and pulling this data would slow down the overall speed of the Google Maps app.

As you can see, many considerations both help and hurt my case, all of which makes for a good discussion with the interviewer.

What Team Conflict Have You Resolved?

In the past, coding was largely a solo activity. Many of the most famous programs and programming languages were created by one or two people. Today, however, software development is a team-based activity. Tools such as Git, SVN, and Mercurial allow coworkers to work on the same piece of code. Companies need to ensure that you can work well with the existing team and deal with inevitable conflicts.

Team conflicts occur for so many reasons, such as miscommunication, office politics, changing technical requirements, competitive pressure, or underperforming teammates. When asked, "What team conflict have you resolved?", choose one that involves serious stakes, with people you know well, and where you played an active role to reach a resolution. This approach will allow you to easily answer any follow-up questions.

Interviews are short enough that you won't have time to go into every detail, so use the SOAR framework to keep your thoughts concise:

- ✔ **Situation:** Briefly describe any relevant context to understanding your story — the participants, your relationship with them, the goal everyone is working toward, and the result of success or failure.

- ✔ **Obstacle:** Conflicts can arise between people or when working with limited resources, such as time or money. Highlight all the areas that made achieving the ultimate goal difficult.

- ✔ **Action:** Focus on the specific action you took, which usually involves repairing relations between people or improving a process. It's best if the action didn't succeed on the first try; otherwise, the obstacle probably wasn't that difficult.

- ✔ **Resolution:** Describe the effect of solving this issue, and try to frame it in terms of time saved or money generated. For example, did your solution have no perceived effect, or were you able to create $1 million in additional revenue?

Practice until you can describe all these pieces in less than two minutes. If you're doing a good job telling the story, expect the interviewer to ask you many questions that really dig into what happened.

You likely don't have stories about team conflicts in a technical context. That's okay. You can use any previous experience; what matters most is your contribution and the quality of the story.

What Is Your Ideal Company and Job?

The question "What is your ideal company and job?" is as much about finding out what you are looking for as it is for the company to see if it can provide it. On first blush, you may not have strong preferences, but give it some thought because anything you flag upfront as important to you can become a negotiating point later.

If you do have preferences, show your future employer that you understand the resulting implications. For example, you may hear companies raving about their open office space and flat organizational structure. The flip side is that it can be too noisy to get any work done, and the lack of clear decision makers can stall execution of important decisions. Paint a picture of your own trajectory, and be clear about the direction you want to take your career.

Here are some factors to consider when thinking about your ideal company and job:

- ✓ **Company size:** Perhaps you previously worked at a big company, and now you want to bring your expertise to a smaller shop where you will have more influence. Alternatively, maybe you come from a small company and now want the influence of a larger player. Even large companies have small teams, so have a sense for what size is best for you.

- ✓ **Travel:** Developers don't usually travel much unless they're located in a different city than the company office. Some tech firms have no problems with remote workers, while for other companies remote workers never feel like part of the team. If you must work remotely, one compromise is to offer to travel to the home office once every four to six weeks if the company will pay for it.

- ✓ **Remote work:** Some products require intense collaboration or have a culture where everyone works in the office. Other companies have employees who regularly work from home two or more days a week. A liberal remote work policy can be beneficial if you have a long commute or kids to take care of occasionally at home.

- ✓ **Organizational structure:** Smaller companies usually can have a more undefined organizational structures in which you don't report directly to a boss and your team provides feedback on your performance. For example, Valve Corp, a 400-person, $4 billion company, has no bosses or upper-level management and bonuses are determined by team consensus. One way to test which type of company you're interviewing with is to ask who your direct manager would be.

✔ **Role:** Think about what you want in the role. Perhaps you want to work with or further develop specific technologies. Technology aside, maybe you want strong mentorship or the chance to manage a team. Being honest in the interview will help set expectations and give your employer the chance to create a good experience for everyone involved.

✔ **Evaluations and reviews:** Make sure you understand how you will be evaluated and reviewed. You may want specific targets, or some room to explore and set your own targets. Even if how you will be evaluated isn't clear yet, find out how the company generally evaluates employees.

If possible, investigate these factors before the interview so you know upfront whether any of your preferences differ greatly from how the company usually operates.

What Is Your Superpower?

The question, "What is your superpower?" tries to bring out what makes you special. Variations to this question include the airport test, which asks: If your flight was delayed, would your interviewer want to be stuck with you at the airport? Similarly, Zappos, the online shoe company, asks in interviews how weird you are on a scale of 1 to 10.

Answer this question by speaking to an area of strength that you haven't talked about before. You superpower might be attending thirty conferences a year but never needing to pay, always getting the exit row on an airplane, being an internationally ranked poker player, or having 200,000 Twitter followers.

Think about what makes you unique and interesting. Then after you answer, ask your interviewer about his or her superpower.

Which Three Strengths and Weaknesses Would Your Friends Use to Describe You?

Neil Roseman, the former VP of Technology at Amazon, and Michelle Peluso, the CEO of Gilt, have both said that they like asking "Which three adjectives would friends use to describe you?" because it forces candidates to give a more balanced view of themselves. Another variation of this question is to ask a candidate for three strengths and weaknesses.

Overall, this question can be tough to answer and trip up even the strongest interviewers. Although it can be painful, the first tip is to show that you have the self-awareness to know that you aren't perfect. Choose some adjectives that describe you positively, and some that expose a weakness.

When talking about a weakness, choose one that is authentic to you, but won't raise any red flags. For example, saying that you have anger management issues is probably too revealing. Some honest example weaknesses I have heard described by junior interviewees include not contributing enough in team meetings, micromanaging or excessively worrying about tasks you've delegated, or not having enough organization or a process for tasks.

For any weakness you choose, have some concrete steps you are taking to work on the issue, which is really what the interviewer is looking for. Finally, for both in areas of strength and weakness, be prepared to talk about specific examples that show the adjective in action.

What Do You Know to Be True that Most People Disagree With or Find Surprising?

The question, "What do you know to be true that most people disagree with or find surprising?" is a favorite of PayPal cofounder Peter Thiel. The purpose of the question is to see whether you can generate insights, and speak out and share them. Useful answers are based on facts, rather than personal opinions, and help start a conversation.

Although the question is open, avoid topics that deal with religion, race, or sex. You or your interviewer may have strong feelings, and there won't be enough time in an interview to resolve them.

For example, one interesting fact is that trains and subways in the US rely on monitoring instead of penalties to ensure people are paying for a ticket. In New York, riders take almost 2 billion rides on the subway each year, and a ticket is checked for every ride. A less costly administrative approach that could result in the same number of ticket purchases might be to randomly check a fraction of riders exiting the subway; those without tickets pay a hefty fine.

Such a system might or might not work for many reasons, leaving you with plenty to discuss with the interviewer.

What Questions Do You Have for Me?

You've done a great job answering all of the interviewer's questions, and with a few minutes left the interviewer asks, "What questions do you have for me?" The thought here is that some questions may have come up during the interview. However, the interviewer is also seeing whether you'll take the opportunity to dig in to learn more about a job where you potentially will be spending many if not most of your waking hours.

As the interviewee, don't use this time to ask for information that you can easily find on the company website or from a recruiter or HR professional. Do use this time to ask personal questions, especially now that both you and the interviewer know each other. Potential questions to ask include:

- What has been your favorite project or team so far?
- If you had to leave this job tomorrow, what would you do and why?
- No job is perfect, so what would you change about your current job?
- What is one stretch goal you have this year that if accomplished would make the year a resounding success?

The answers to these questions could help you spot some of the better performing internal teams, the interviewer's true job ambitions, and parts of the job you may not love.

Chapter 17

Ten Job Search Strategies

Finding a job in any industry has always required time and effort. However, the strategies used to find a job have changed. The way your parents went job hunting or even the way you did a few years ago is likely outdated today. It has never been easier to publish information about yourself, and successful candidates are writing more about themselves more frequently than ever before.

The strategies listed in this chapter go beyond sending a resume and cover letter to a job site or an email address and hoping for the best. No strategy is a silver bullet, but one or a combination of these could help you get noticed for your next job.

Publish Your Code

As someone who has just learned how to code, you may feel embarrassed or self-conscious about your programs. Maybe you designed a website for a small business and the code is messy, with pages not appearing correctly on certain browsers. Or perhaps you wrote a data analytics program with many temporary variables and not as well documented as it could be. Resist the urge to keep your files on your hard drive, and instead publish your code to GitHub (or Bitbucket) for others to use and share.

Following are a few reasons why you should post your code:

- **Show off your skills.** Instead of asking about your previous job or where you went to school, employers ask what you've built recently and check your Github account.

- **Work with others.** The latest project you are working on might be too difficult to finish by yourself. The easiest way to invite others to help with your work and keep your project going is to publicly post it.

- **Elevate your profile.** Other coders might reuse your code in their own projects, especially if your code is open source. For example, Bootstrap was created by two Twitter developers to make creating the front-end for websites easier. Shortly after they posted the project to Github, it became the most popular project on the site.

GitHub already hosts appointment reminders apps, code editors, and cat photo web scrapers, so whatever you've built will have plenty of company.

Blog Regularly

Coding involves setup, installation, and debugging. Perhaps you spent two hours trying to add credit card purchases to your website, despite following the credit card processor installation instructions to the letter. Or maybe you tried but failed to add user logins with Facebook or Twitter.

If you followed instructions but the service, integration, API, or app doesn't work, you may have found a bug or you may be doing something wrong but don't know it yet. Documenting your experience helps others who are having the same issue, and also shows potential employers how you solved a real problem. Employers want to understand your thought process — because you could soon find yourself troubleshooting their servers at 2 in the morning, and keeping calm under pressure and methodically working towards a solution are important traits to have. Additionally, employers value employees who stay abreast of the latest changes in the industry and incorporate them into their work.

You don't need to document only when things go wrong — you can also blog about when things go as planned. Many companies encourage individual engineers to blog about how they solved technical challenges. For example,

Netflix engineers have written on the company blog (`techblog.netflix.com`) about the algorithms to personalize the video titles shown to you. This might sound easy at first, but remember that each personalized page will look different depending on the member and the size of the device being used to access Netflix.

Don't feel as though everything you write must be novel or some crazy solution no one has ever seen before. Jennifer Dewalt is a designer who decided to learn to code by building 180 apps in 180 days and documenting the experience on her blog (`www.jenniferdewalt.com`). Her blog posts went viral, resulting in an invitation to speak at the TED conference and a job with Wit.ai, a Facebook subsidiary.

Learn New Technologies

Programming languages are tools and are constantly being improved. Every week a programmer makes a library faster or creates an easier way to code a common task. Less frequently, programmers release a new programming language. It's hard to know ahead of time which of these new libraries, languages, or frameworks will become popular, but when something catches on, it can spread quickly. For example, Rails, the popular web-programming framework, was released in mid 2004, and by late 2006 Apple announced it would be included standard as part of the Mac operating system.

Many developers commit to learning something new to stay current despite all this change. Learning a new language or library shows employers that you're willing to put in the effort to improve your skills. Companies often have custom code written in a language no one knows — a relic from a former employee. Someone on the team has to figure out what the code does and how to maintain it.

After you've learned the basics, here are some cutting-edge libraries, languages, and frameworks to add to your list to learn:

- ✔ **React:** A JavaScript library developed by Facebook for creating user interfaces that are constantly being refreshed with new information, such as the Facebook news feed.

- ✔ **SASS:** A language that helps you quickly and easily create CSS files, which control a website's appearance.

- ✔ **Swift:** A mobile programming language created by Apple, released in 2014, and meant to replace Objective-C, the traditional language used to code iOS apps. Swift is new but rapidly increasing in popularity.

> ✔ **Sinatra:** Unrelated to the famous singer, this lightweight Ruby framework is meant for simple websites. It is not as well known as Rails, a popular Ruby framework, but is still used by companies such as Apple, LinkedIn, and the BBC.

Update and Refresh Your Resume

Many job seekers are advised to use active verbs, avoid too many acronyms, and include your latest employer when writing a resume. Although these tips are important, it's far more important to make sure that you include lots of description for each position.

Whether using an internal resume database or an external resource such as LinkedIn, recruiters and HR professionals use keywords to search and sift through candidates. For example, if a company uses Python to create software and a recruiter needs to find more engineers, the first search is likely for developers who know Python. If you don't list Python anywhere in your profile, your resume might never be seen.

Because you're just starting to learn programming, use side projects to show your experience with a programming language. After your project is live and running, include on your resume and on LinkedIn a short description of the project, the languages used, and your contribution.

If you're unsure of a phrase in your resume, or you're debating between two ways to say the same thing, use Google for each phrase and choose the one that is more popular.

Review Your Public Information

There is no shortage of public information about you. In addition to what you post on the Internet, there is also information others post about you. Personal websites such as a blog or a home page, and social networks including LinkedIn, Facebook, Twitter, Instagram, and Pinterest all paint a portrait of who you are.

Prospective employers can find information about you manually by using a search engine, such as Google. Or they can use a service such as Rapportive and FullContact to find and link all your online profiles to one email address. Now it's easier than ever for employers to find almost everything about you with just a few clicks.

Many personal websites and social networks used to be just for your friends. However, recent privacy changes mean that unless you specifically exclude people, almost anyone can view your content — and employers do pay attention. Almost 80 percent of employers research candidates and look beyond just the resume, so here are common themes to avoid in your online personas:

✔ **Alcohol:** Many people take pictures during social events, but if every picture on Facebook or Twitter shows you holding an alcoholic beverage, it will definitely send the wrong message. Pictures are a great way to show your interests, so make sure to show some diversity.

✔ **Profanity or violence:** Avoid profane language in status messages or comments. While you may be talking to a good friend or responding to a sports game, a prospective employer will not have the time or desire to understand the context.

Check code you've submitted to any code repositories such as GitHub or Bitbucket for inappropriate variable names or language.

✔ **Inappropriate attire:** Photos should show you wearing clothes you could wear in an office. Email providers such as Gmail automatically associate your profile picture with emails you send, so form a good first impression when contacting prospective employers.

Avoid swimwear photos in your profile photo, and increase the privacy setting of any beach or pool photo albums so that the general public cannot view them.

Attend Hackathons

Hackathons are events where developers gather to work on an idea from start to finish over a short time frame, typically 24 hours or a weekend. See Figure 17-1. Hackathon are usually organized by a school, a company, or an independent group, such as a Meetup interest group.

TechCrunch, a technology blog, hosts a popular hackathon called Disrupt, where companies have been founded and gone on to become fully funded companies. For example, GroupMe was created at TechCrunch Disrupt, and was eventually acquired by Skype for $85 million. Another popular hackathon, PennApps, is hosted by the University of Pennsylvania. TechCrunch Disrupt and PennApps have each had over 1,000 participants at their latest hackathons.

Figure 17-1:
HackNY
hackathon
brings
students
together
to work on
NYC start-
ups' APIs.

Photo courtesy of HackNY.org and @matylda on Flickr

Developers typically attend hackathons to meet other people, learn a new technology, or win a prize, which are given to the top app as decided by attendees or a panel of judges. Prizes can include free products, up to $5,000 in cash, and credits for hosting services. In addition, hackathons sponsored by companies have information sessions on how to use their APIs, with company developers on site to troubleshoot problems you might have.

For companies, these events are a chance to spark new ideas for existing products. For example, hackathons at Facebook have resulted in the Like button, photo filters, and tagging people in comments. If you are a developer, even one who has just started learning, hackathons can be a low-pressure way to meet representatives from companies, build another project to add to your portfolio, and generally show your passion for coding and building applications.

To search for upcoming hackathons in your area, visit these sites: `hackathon.io`, `hackerleague.org`, or `eventbrite.com`.

Teach Yourself a Popular API

Companies build and promote APIs to help expand use of their products by making private programs and code available for public use. For example, Uber has an API to allow anyone to integrate car service into an app. Developers have created or proposed apps that tell users how far to walk to avoid surge pricing, and how to integrate air fare bookings with car service to and from your hotel.

Companies have a fixed number of employees who work as developers on their core products. APIs leverage external developers' time and ideas to create interesting products the company just doesn't have time to build or support. Learning an API shows that you are interested in the core technology and have ideas for new product directions.

Additionally, learning a popular API is useful not only to the company that makes it but also to everyone who uses it. For example, Google has a Maps API used by many companies to plot points on a map and show directions. In addition to the Google Maps API, here are some other popular APIs for you to learn:

- **Facebook:** The Facebook Login API is one of the most popular in the world, allowing users to skip creating an account and use their existing Facebook credentials to log into your website or app.

- **Stripe:** Accepting online credit card payments is a common development task that used to be difficult, requiring bank registration and approvals. The Stripe API simplifies the payments process, and makes it much easier to accept payments from domestic and international customers.

- **Twilio:** Sometimes your users need to connect with a human before completing an action or a transaction. The Twilio API allows programs to send and receive SMS and voice calls between users.

- **Foursquare:** Any app connecting users to local services has to look up the businesses providing those services. Foursquare is a crowd-sourced database that allows you to find address and review information for almost any business or place in the world.

Build and Release Something People Want

Many companies ask about the apps you've built recently, in addition to or sometimes instead of requesting a resume. The best way to show that you know how to build an app that can handle real users is to do it. And if your app becomes popular, it will attract potential employers.

Deciding what to build can be difficult. Instead of brainstorming ideas you think will be popular, build something you would use and can build in a weekend. Here are some ideas that have been built into apps:

- ✔ **IsUp.me** (`www.isup.me`): You can enter the URL of a website you cannot access, and see whether the website is down or whether you are experiencing problems with your Internet connection.

- ✔ **NomadList** (`https://nomadlist.com`): Displays a ranking of fifty best cities for remote workers based on weather, Internet availability, cost of living, and safety, as shown in Figure 17-2.

- ✔ **FollowUpThen** (`www.followupthen.com`): When sending an email, you can add a cc or bcc email address (for example, `3days@followupthen.com`) to receive a reminder to follow up.

While you can't predict what will become popular, some of the simplest websites can gain traction quickly. In the case of NomadList, over the span of two weeks the site received 110,000 users, 2,000 tweets, and coverage in over 20 media outlets. The site developer also wrote a blog post detailing how he created NomadList, making it easy for anyone, including prospective employers, to learn more.

After you build your website or app, post it on HackerNews, available at `news.ycombinator.com`, or Product Hunt, available at `www.producthunt.com`. These two websites have large audiences that frequently sign up and try new websites and apps.

Figure 17-2:
NomadList ranks cities for remote workers across multiple criteria.

Consult to Fix a Painful Problem

People repeatedly face many painful problems. As coder, you can often consult on a part-time basis to assist with these problems and gain useful experience. You'll be paid to learn, and sometimes these smaller tasks can lead to a permanent job.

In web development, businesses use WordPress to quickly and easily create a web presence. However, many users creating a site for the first time experience problems customizing the look and feel of the site — perhaps images don't align properly, text input fields are not big enough, or the site appears correctly on desktops but renders incorrectly on mobile devices. These tasks all likely require CSS modifications, which are often just out of reach for the nontechnical user.

For data analysis, gathering and cleaning data is often one of the most time-consuming tasks in the entire process. For example, the nontechnical user compiling a list of sales leads often has to look up businesses contact information from an online directory and manually copy and paste this information into a spreadsheet. After copying, the data has to be standardized, especially if multiple databases were used. These initial steps can be automated with a script in Python or Ruby, and much of the information scraped and standardized automatically.

Both these tasks are not glamorous, but they do provide a good opportunity to practice your coding skills. You can usually find short projects like these offered for $50 to $500 on the following contractor websites:

- ✔ **oDesk (www.odesk.com):** Sign up to be a contractor, bid on jobs that people have posted, and take coding certification tests to show your knowledge.

- ✔ **Freelancer (www.freelancer.com):** Similar to oDesk, Freelancer matches clients with short-term assistance. You can participate in contests with others where a prize is awarded to a winner, or work on a project basis for a fixed price or an hourly fee.

- ✔ **CodersClan (www.codersclan.net):** Designed for quick, small coding tasks, the average CodersClan challenge was solved in 30 minutes and received a $50 reward.

Do a Trial Engagement

The two biggest questions an employer has about you are "Can you do the work?" and "Will you fit in with the team?" The interview process can help evaluate and answer the first question but not the second.

One way to lower the risk for yourself and a potential employer is to offer to do a trial engagement with the company. These test drives are usually two to six weeks and are more common among startups, where teams are small and attrition is a concern. Although the engagement is temporary, you should not expect to work for free, though the rates may be lower than if the company hired a consultant. For example, at Automattic, the creators of the blogging platform WordPress, all hires go through a trial period and are paid $25 an hour.

The key to a successful trial engagement is to have a discrete task to work on that can be evaluated at the end of the trial. Because of the short time frame, choose projects that are not too complex and depend on input from six or fewer people. Additionally, you should make sure to set up milestones throughout the trial period and regularly check in with one point person, so you receive feedback frequently and can correct the project's direction if necessary.

Remember that while the company is evaluating you, you should evaluate the company. Try to get a sense of the following:

- **Team:** To make sure you mesh well with the team, spend some time getting to know people outside work. You should be able to get a general sense of whether people are happy and whether any major concerns are under the surface.

- **Company trajectory:** During the interview, you likely heard the best version of the company story. Now that you have more access, try to understand how the company is doing overall, and whether any major events over the next year could affect the company, such as a renewal of a big client account or major fundraising for the company.

- **Advancement:** The interview likely gave you a good sense for the role you would be doing. Now try to understand how others around you have advanced, what made them successful, and what the path for advancement looks like.

Before beginning a trial period, you most likely will have to sign an independent contractor form. Make sure your contract does not have a non-compete clause. If it does, check that the clause is limited to a few weeks or months at most. In case things do not work out with the current employer, you should be able to seek work with other employers in the industry.

In addition to reaching out to companies directly, you can also use an IT recruiting firm to help match you to a company. In return for a successful placement, these companies receive a fee, usually 15 to 20 percent of a candidate's total annual salary.

Chapter 18

Ten Coding Myths

The tech profession is filled with myths and rumors. It can be hard to separate fact from fiction, especially given the reports of eye-popping salaries and prices for company acquisitions in the news. After you cut through the hype, the tech industry is like any other, with demand for talent far exceeding supply.

The following are ten myths about coding that just aren't true. These myths mainly apply to people learning to code for the first time. Read on to separate myth from reality.

You Must Be Good at Math

Developers who are building cutting-edge games, data scientists trying to create the next big machine-learning algorithm, or engineers working in the financial services industry likely need some proficiency in physics, statistics, or financial math. However, many developers, such as those building e-commerce applications or typical web pages, do not need much more math than basic addition and subtraction, and high school algebra.

A good deal of math operates and powers applications, but there often isn't a need to understand everything that is happening. Computer languages and programs are designed to manage complexity by requiring that you understand the inputs and outputs — but not what happens in between, a concept called *abstraction*. For example, when driving a car, you don't need to understand how the internal combustion engine works or the physics behind converting the energy from the piston to the wheels. To drive a car you need to understand how to operate the accelerator, the brake, and the clutch for stick-shift cars. Similarly, programs have functions that perform operations, but you need to understand only the inputs you send a function and the output it returns.

In other words, you need to be able to understand math and have some basic math skills, but you do not need to be the next Einstein to be able to program.

You Must Have Studied Engineering

Many people who study engineering learn how to program, but you do not need to be an engineer to learn how to code. Engineering teaches skills that are useful to programmers, such as how to solve a problem step-by-step as well as working within and then designing around real-world constraints. These are useful skills, but you can learn them outside the engineering curriculum.

Many topics that are part of an engineering curriculum vary in usefulness for learning how to code. Topics such as algorithms can be directly applicable, especially if you're working on cutting-edge problems. Other topics, such as assembly language and computational theory, provide a good background but are rarely used by most coders.

If your goal is to push the cutting edge of computer programs, a degree in computer engineering might be useful. However, if you want to create a website to solve a problem, learning to code in three to six months is probably sufficient to start.

Many colleges offer scholarships that can subsidize or completely cover the cost of attendance for women and minorities pursuing science and engineering degrees.

You Can Learn Coding in a Few Weeks

Like any passion or profession, coding is an art and coders hone their skills over decades. Although you don't need decades of study to start coding, the amount of time needed to learn depends on your goals. For example:

- **One week:** Learn enough HTML to put text, images, and other basic content on the page. You'll be able to operate site builders to create and customize informational websites.

- **One month:** Develop your front-end CSS skills so you can position and style elements on the page. You'll also be able to edit sites built with website builders such as Wix, Weebly, or SquareSpace. For data science, you can learn to import and handle large datasets and use Python or R to find insights about the data.

- **Three to six months:** Learn front-end and back-end development skills to take a concept, build a working prototype that can store data in a database, and then code a version that can handle hundreds of thousands of users. In addition, learn how to use a programming language's external libraries to add additional functionality, user management, and version control systems such as Git so multiple people can work on a project at the same time. For data science, you'll be able to build an interactive visualization using a JavaScript library such as d3.js. Whether learning web development or data science, it will take approximately 800 hours of effort to be proficient enough to be hired for a job.

You Need a Great Idea to Start Coding

Learning to code is a lengthy process, filled with ups and downs. You might get stuck for days or see much progress. During periods of inevitable frustration, having a bigger idea or a concrete reason to motivate you to keep learning can be helpful. Instead of trying to build the next Facebook, YouTube, or Google, try to build something that solves a problem you've personally faced. Here are people who learned to code and remained motivated with a project:

- Coffitivity.com: Four college students wanted to fight writer's block by listening to ambient sound. While learning to code, Tommy Nicholas built a site that streams coffee shop sounds to add background noise to otherwise silent offices and workspaces.

- Outgrow.me: Sam Fellig is a Kickstarter enthusiast who wanted a simple way to browse and purchase items from successful crowdfunded projects. He took the leap and learned to code so he could build his website, shown in Figure 18-1, which turned into one of Time magazine's Top 50 websites of 2013.

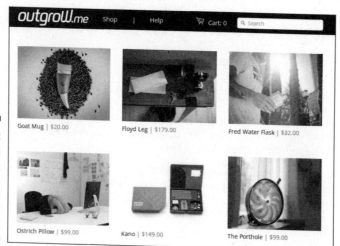

Figure 18-1:
Outgrow.me
sells prod-
ucts from
successful
crowdfunded
projects.

✔ Sworkit: Ryan Hanna liked to work out but often became bored at the gym. While learning JavaScript and Ruby, he built an app that guided users through military-style workouts in five minutes or less. The app had over 1 million downloads, and Ryan eventually sold it to Nexercise, an exercise company.

Each of these sites enjoyed a degree of popularity and were noticed by a huge number of users. If something similar happens with a site you design, it serves as a nice bonus. But even if it doesn't, you'll feel satisfied having solved your own problem.

Ruby Is Better than Python

You might wonder what language to learn first, especially given all the choices out there. You could start with Ruby, Python, JavaScript, PHP, Swift, Objective-C — the list goes on. To resolve this debate, you might search for which language is the best, or which language to learn first. You'll find articles and posts advocating one language or another. Unlike comparing TVs or toasters, a clear winner is unlikely to emerge. Sometimes you can spend more time deciding which language to learn first than getting down to learning the language.

The most important thing is to learn a few easy scripting languages first and then choose one all-purpose beginner programming language to learn thoroughly.

Usually, beginners start with HTML, CSS, and JavaScript. These languages are the most forgiving of syntax mistakes and the easiest to learn. Then, after you learn these basics, choose Python or Ruby if you are interested in web development. You'll find many online tutorials and help for both.

If you plan on doing work with a content management system such as WordPress or Drupal, consider learning PHP.

Don't spend too much time deciding which language to learn first, and don't try to learn all of them at the same time. Sometimes people hit a roadblock with one language, give up, and start learning another language. However, the end result is learning a little bit about many languages, instead of mastering a single language and being able to build a complete and functioning website.

Only College Graduates Receive Coding Offers

Both Bill Gates and Mark Zuckerberg left college before graduating to start their own technology companies. To encourage more college dropouts, Peter Thiel, the billionaire founder of PayPal and investor in Facebook, created a fellowship to pay students $100,000 to start businesses and forgo school. Still, whether you can get a coding offer without a degree varies by company type:

- ✔ **Elite technology companies:** Google, Apple, Facebook, Microsoft, Twitter, and Yahoo! are some of the world's most elite technology companies. Because of their sheer size and name recognition, they employ recruiters who screen for certain attributes, such as college affiliation. College graduates from top schools apply to these companies in overwhelming numbers. Although it is not impossible to be hired at one of these companies without a college degree, it is very difficult.

  To find out which colleges serve as feeder schools for the top technology companies, read *The Schools Where Apple, Google, and Facebook Get Their Recruits*, available at www.wired.com/2014/05/alumni-network-2.

- ✔ **Fortune 1000 companies:** Large companies such as Verizon and AT&T hire thousands of engineers a year, making their initial requirements for hiring slightly more flexible. These companies typically look for a college degree or two to three years of relevant experience with a specific programming language.

✔ **Startups and small companies:** Startups are sympathetic to non-degree holders, and many startup employees are currently in college or are college dropouts. Although startups don't require a college degree, a great deal of emphasis is given on what you've built previously and your ability to code under tight deadlines. Well-funded startups are often a good place to gain experience because they need talent to keep growing and often compensate employees as well as the more mature companies do.

✔ **Freelancing and contracting:** When working for contracting websites such as oDesk or for yourself, the main consideration is whether you can complete the job. Few employers check whether you have a college degree; a portfolio of past work, even if it was unpaid, is much more important to securing the job and conveying the confidence that you'll be able to deliver the project on time and within budget.

Interest in nontraditional candidates is growing. Companies such as `Gild.com` specialize in sourcing and scoring candidates with nontraditional markers of success, such as blog posts, Stack Exchange answers, Twitter comments, and code posted to GitHub.

You Must Have Experience

Studies have shown that there is no correlation between experience and performance in software development. For the new programmer, after you master some basic skills, your performance is affected by much more than the amount of time you've spent on a job. Despite the research, however, some companies still screen for years of experience when filling open positions.

Much of the same logic that applies to getting a coding job without a college degree applies here as well. Elite technology companies receive so many resumes and are in such high demand that they can be more selective, and look first at experienced candidates. Fortune 1000 companies usually take one of two approaches: They look for a minimum one to two years of experience, or they understand that as a new hire you'll need training and use existing staff to help support you.

Startups and small companies typically pay the least attention to the number of years of experience and more attention to your previous projects. Your contributions to an open-source project or a weekend project that attracted real users will generate plenty of interest and enthusiasm for you as a candidate. Although it can be easier to get your foot in the door at a startup, remember that the company's small size likely means there are fewer people and less money to devote to your training and support, so much of your learning will be self-supported.

Companies of any size willing to invest in developing your programming abilities will typically look for a positive attitude, a willingness to learn, and the persistence to keep trying to solve problems and overcome obstacles.

Tech Companies Don't Hire Women or Minorities

Whether in the *Law and Order: SVU* portrayal of women in technology or the national media reports of the high-powered lawsuit filed by Ellen Pao around her treatment in the technology industry, the tech industry has not had the best year for being welcoming of women and minorities.

Admittedly, the numbers show a story that has improved but still has plenty of room to grow, with the tech industry workforce made up of 25% women and 5% minority workers, which is below the national averages for both groups.

The *Wall Street Journal* has compiled publicly released diversity data from top tech companies broken down by leadership and technology positions (see Figure 18-2). Go to `graphics.wsj.com/diversity-in-tech-companies`.

Although many contributing causes have been identified, including the lack of a pipeline of candidates studying computer science or applying to tech firms, many leading companies and nonprofits are actively trying to increase the recruitment and support of women and minorities in the workplace.

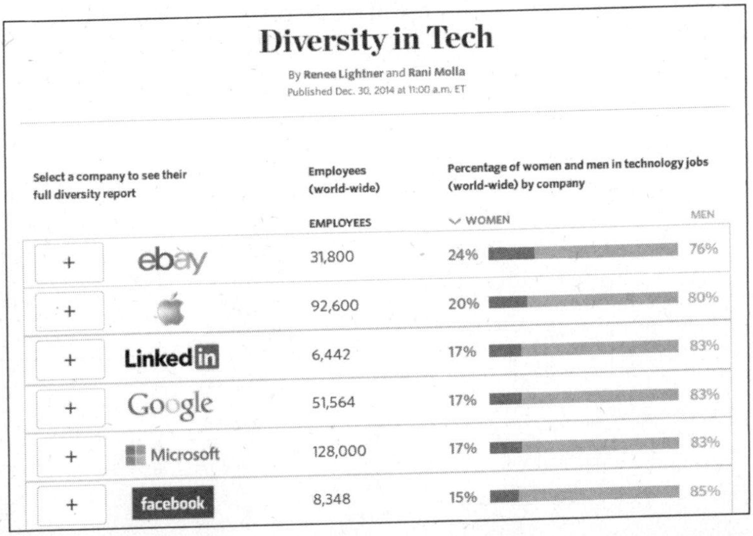

Figure 18-2: WSJ compilation of diversity in tech companies based on public filings.

Diversity in Tech

By Renee Lightner and Rani Molla
Published Dec. 30, 2014 at 11:00 a.m. ET

Select a company to see their full diversity report	Employees (world-wide)	Percentage of women and men in technology jobs (world-wide) by company	
	EMPLOYEES	⌄ WOMEN	MEN
+ ebay	31,800	24%	76%
+	92,600	20%	80%
+ Linked in	6,442	17%	83%
+ Google	51,564	17%	83%
+ Microsoft	128,000	17%	83%
+ facebook	8,348	15%	85%

On the corporate side, larger companies are creating programs that train and increase the number of pathways to join the workforce. For example, Google recently launched a $50 million campaign called Made with Code to highlight women in tech and provide opportunities for girls to learn to code.

Similarly, nonprofit organizations such as Code 2040 connect Black and Latino talent to companies. On the training side, nonprofits such as Yes We Code, Girls Who Code, Black Girls Who Code, and Women Who Code teach technical skills to increase the number of women and minorities entering the jobs pipeline.

The Highest Paying Coding Jobs Are in San Francisco

Many of the most famous tech companies, including Apple, Facebook, Google, Twitter, and Yahoo!, are located in Silicon Valley. While these and other companies in the San Francisco and Silicon Valley area hire a large number of tech workers each year, that paints only part of the picture.

Cities across the US pay tech salaries comparable to San Francisco but have a much lower cost of living, as shown in Table 18-1. Two numbers to keep in mind when evaluating a city are the average salaries paid to tech workers and the average cost of living. Salary minus rent provides a simple and rough estimate of take-home pay, though it doesn't take into account taxes, transportation, and cost of goods and services.

Table 18-1	Salary and Median Rent by City		
City	Annual Salary	Annual Rent	Salary Less Rent
St. Louis, MO	$93,829	$9,900	$83,929
Seattle, WA	$99,423	$21,492	$77,931
Austin, TX	$93,135	$18,000	$75,135
Houston, TX	$89,838	$18,000	$71,838
Washington D.C.	$98,323	$26,700	$71,623
New York, NY	$95,586	$29,100	$66,486
San Francisco, CA	$112,610	$48,000	$64,610

Sources: Dice.com Annual Salary Survey, Zillow.com median rent prices

Although San Francisco does pay the most of any city in the country, it looks less attractive after subtracting the cost of rent from annual pay. By contrast, cities such as St. Louis and Seattle offer strong salaries with a much lower cost of living.

A cost of living calculator will help you compare salaries in different cities. See, for example, the PayScale cost of living calculator by visiting `www.payscale.com/cost-of-living-calculator`.

Your Previous Experience Isn't Relevant

Coding skill is one important factor that tech companies evaluate when hiring coders. But just as important is your domain knowledge and ability to work and lead a team. For example, perhaps you're a lawyer looking to switch careers and become a coder. Your legal knowledge will far exceed that of the average programmer, and if you target companies making software for lawyers, your perspective will be valuable.

Similarly, whether you previously were in finance or marketing, the issues around managing and leading teams are similar. It is natural for a team of people to disagree, have trouble communicating, and end up short of the intended goal. Your previous experiences handling this type of situation and turning it into a positive outcome will be valued in a tech company, where much of the coding is performed in teams.

Finally, your current or previous job might not seem technical, but others like you have made the transition into a coding job. People from a variety of professions — such as lawyers, teachers, and financial analysts — have learned how to code, and found ways to incorporate their past work experiences into their current coding careers.

Chapter 19

Ten Coding Job Websites

After you've learned some coding, it's time to see what types of jobs are available and do some work to gain experience. Securing a job in any industry is never easy, but with some patience and persistence you'll be working your first coding job in no time.

The websites listed in this chapter include resources to find part-time and full-time jobs. First review the job postings so you have a sense of the types of people companies look for. Then take the plunge and start applying.

Part-Time and Contract Coding Jobs

Part-time and contract coding jobs usually involve discrete tasks with a clearly defined problem or goal. For example, you may need to write a program to pull the address information for 300 dentists from a membership directory, or fix an alignment issue on a WordPress website. When you are just starting, aim for tasks that will take between 5 and 50 hours so you don't feel overwhelmed, and that will pay $10 to $50 per hour. Many of the websites listed here allow employers to rate contractors; if you build a positive reputation, it can lead to bigger and more lucrative projects.

The websites in this section are good resources for part-time or contract coding jobs. Although each website operates a little differently, they all allow you to test your skills in a relatively risk-free environment.

One of the hardest tasks for any programmer is estimating how long a project will take, including unexpected obstacles and issues that will inevitably arise. Choosing a project with a lower hourly commitment will give you some cushion to still meet your deadline in case the programming task takes longer than expected.

oDesk/Elance

www.odesk.com and www.elance.com

oDesk and Elance recently merged to form one of the largest communities of freelancers online. Together, the company has 10 million workers in 180 countries. Although everyone works online, not everyone does coding-related tasks.

Freelancers bid on projects that are posted to the website, send messages of interest, and sometimes follow up with a phone or video chat. Multiple people bid on a single project, and the winner is chosen based on previous experience, price, and a well-written message accompanying the initial bid. Additionally, freelancers can take tests that certify their knowledge in certain programming languages and topics.

Winning that first coding project can be difficult, especially without previous experience. One way to gain experience is to bid on noncoding projects, and complete them on time while communicating well. Good noncoding projects can be in areas adjacent to coding projects, such as word processing, data entry, and manual data scraping. After you gain some experience and build your online reputation, it's easier to bid on and win coding-related projects.

Freelancer

www.freelancer.com

Similar to oDesk, Freelancer lets contract workers bid on tasks that have been posted to the website. People posting projects can also purchase optional project upgrades such as featuring a project, making a project private, and designating a project as urgent. In addition, each project can be completed by a single contractor who is paid hourly or by multiple contractors in a contest, where the contest prize is divided among the winning entries.

Keep in mind that contractors from around the world use these websites to complete projects, and variations in cost of living and market wages in different countries can result in a large spread in the project bids. Always remember to value your own time, keep in mind the budget of the project poster, and differentiate your abilities and knowledge of the product or task when possible.

CodersClan

www.codersclan.net

CodersClan is similar to oDesk and Freelancer but is designed for micro-tasks. Example tasks include creating a landing page, integrating with an API, or solving a bug in the code.

You can see recently completed tasks on the home page, and get a sense for the complexity of the average task. Contractors are paid to solve the task. On average, a task takes 30 minutes and pays $50. After a task is posted, contractors post answers to the task, and a winning answer is selected to receive payment. The person whose answer is selected receives 70 percent of the total payment, CodersClan receives 25 percent, and 5 percent goes to support a project or charity.

CodersClan tasks are crowd-sourced, so after you post an answer, you can see the responses that others have posted. In addition to seeing the types of responses that are selected as the winning answer, you can also see multiple approaches to solving a problem.

Startup Weekend

www.startupweekend.org

Startup Weekend is an event that takes place all over the world in which startup enthusiasts, technical and nontechnical, gather to launch an idea over a weekend. The event costs between $75 and $150, which covers meals, snacks, mentors, and use of an event space.

The event starts on Friday evening, when individuals pitch an idea, the audience votes on which ideas they like best, and then everyone divides into teams to work on one of the winning ideas. After teams are formed, Saturday and Sunday are spent working on the idea by talking to customers, doing market research, and building a website to test and launch the idea.

At the end of the weekend, a panel of judges, usually leaders in the community, give feedback to all the companies and choose a winning team based on the potential and execution of an idea. Over 45,000 people have participated, creating venture-backed companies such as Zaarly, FoodSpotting, and LaunchRock.

Startup Weekend is a great opportunity to practice your coding skills in a time-constrained, team-based environment. You'll have to run through the entire product process from idea conception, to creating wireframes or designs, and finally writing code to build a project that others can use. As the coder on a team, you'll need to manage constantly changing product requirements, balance feature requests with what you can build in the time available, and find agreement when team members disagree on the product. Although you won't be paid for your work, companies send mentors who provide advice throughout the weekend, which will help you develop a relationship with the company and mentor.

Startup Weekend is geared toward helping people learn how to start a company by putting theory to practice. Although a winner is announced at the end of the weekend, don't worry too much about whether you win. Focus on being a supportive team member.

Full-Time Coding Jobs

After you've completed some part-time jobs and added to your portfolio, you should feel more confident in starting to look for a full-time job. Finding a full-time job is usually more difficult than doing contract work. Companies typically evaluate you not only for your technical abilities but also for how well you will fit into the existing culture and team.

The websites listed in this section aggregate job postings and make it easy to search for and apply for full-time coding jobs.

AngelList

www.angel.co

AngelList began as a platform for startups to connect with investors before and during fundraising. Over the last four years, the company has facilitated more than $200 million in startup financing. As the number of startups using the platform increased, AngelList created a job board to help startups find candidates for jobs. Today almost 175,000 candidates and 9,000 companies, such as Yelp and Warby Parker, use the platform to find and fill startup jobs.

Job seekers create one profile and can apply to multiple companies at once. Additionally, salary and equity amounts are posted up front before you apply, so you know what to expect and can compare compensation across companies.

Indeed

`www.indeed.com`

Founded in 2004, Indeed is one of the largest job search engine sites in the world. The website, available in over 50 countries and 28 languages, aggregates job listings from thousands of sources, including company websites, job boards, and newspapers, and attracts over 180 million job seekers a month.

In addition to search services, Indeed also allows you to receive email alerts when a job posting matches your criteria and to post your resume so employers can find you. Indeed.com, and similar sites such as `careerbuilder.com` and `monster.com`, are popular with larger and more traditional companies. For example, CareerBuilder works with 92 percent of Fortune 1000 companies.

The volume of job applications companies receive after posting on a site like Indeed can be overwhelming for the HR employee who has to sort through all the candidates. You can help your application stand out by contacting the hiring manager for the position you applied to and restating your interest in the company and the position.

Hacker News

`news.ycombinator.com`

Hacker News (HN) is a discussion board for topics related to technology and entrepreneurship. Visitors can post articles published elsewhere on the Internet, and comment in a discussion-style format on any submitted articles.

Almost half its users are between 18 and 24, although the site also counts as contributors more experienced tech industry veterans such as Marc Andreessen, the venture capitalist and founder of Netscape, and David Heinemeier Hansson, the creator of Ruby on Rails.

There are three areas where jobs are posted on Hacker News:

- **HN Jobs:** Y Combinator, the parent company that manages HN, funds between 100 and 200 companies per year. Companies who receive funding post open position on the websites, available at `news.ycombinator.com/jobs`. Positions range from front-end engineers to data analysts, and most companies that post are less than two years old.

- **Who is hiring:** On the first day of each month, a post called Ask HN: Who is Hiring invites all companies, both startups and more experienced ones, to post jobs that might be of interest to HN readers. Most of the jobs posted are for technical positions, and some are for remote positions that can be performed in a city other than where the company is located. The April 2015 posting is available at `news.ycombinator.com/item?id=9303396`.

- **Who wants to be hired:** On the first of each month, developers who want a job post their location, willingness to relocate, skills, and resume. Employers reach out to candidates who might be a fit. The April 2015 posting is available at `news.ycombinator.com/item?id=9303599`.

In your HN user profile include your email address, and links to your personal website, and GitHub profile so that employers can quickly reach out to you.

LinkedIn

`www.linkedin.com`

More than 277 million people have created a profile on LinkedIn. Companies search LinkedIn members to find candidates to fill open positions, typically searching for people with certain programming skills. They reach out to individuals by using InMail, LinkedIn's messaging system for members.

Create a complete LinkedIn profile by listing past employers, your role, and a brief description of what you did. A recruiter's ability to find you is almost solely based on the keywords in your profile, so make sure to include projects from your portfolio and the languages used to create them.

In addition to companies who reach out to you, you can also search LinkedIn for companies that have open positions. See `www.linkedin.com/job/`. Unlike on job aggregators such as Indeed, companies pay to post positions, so every available position the company has may not necessarily be posted on LinkedIn. Still, LinkedIn has tens of thousands of employers using the platform. When searching potential employers, you can immediately see whether any of your immediate connections work at the company. In addition to employers, recruiters often post their positions in LinkedIn groups related to the area in which they're recruiting. Job seekers can get email digests of jobs posted in those groups from multiple companies, making it easier to find and apply for open positions.

Stack Overflow Careers

careers.stackoverflow.com

Stack Overflow is a popular question-and-answer site that developers use when trying to debug programs. The website lets users upvote answers to questions, which earns the author of the answer badges and an online reputation. The site has had almost 3 million users and 7 million questions. A question is typically answered in about 11 minutes.

Stack Overflow also has a Careers website that allows companies to recruit from this concentrated base of developers. In addition to companies posting jobs, developers can post user profiles that companies then search. Almost 200,000 developers have created profiles on the site, and although the base of profiles is smaller than LinkedIn, the profiles are created mainly by developers looking for a job.

Although you receive no compensation for contributing to Stack Overflow, answering a few questions on the website shows employers how you interact with others, your thought process, and your programming ability.

Hired

www.hired.com

The demand for developers exceeds the supply, and Hired.com, a startup founded in 2012, is currently taking advantage of this shortage. Developers apply to be listed on the Hired platform, and then companies bid on individual developer candidates.

After the companies finish bidding on a candidate, the candidate sees all the bids and accepts or decline offers to interview. If the interview process is successful, the candidate chooses the offer and company to accept and join. In its first trial run, 142 companies bid $30 million to hire 88 engineers.

Talk the Talk

Big Data

Big data: Data is usually classified as big data when it is impractical to manage with traditional software tools. What is classified as big data is always changing and is based on volume (how much data), velocity (how fast it is created), and variety (how many different data types).

Classification algorithm: Sort data into predefined labeled groups. First, the computer is given a training data set, which includes a set of data that has already been sorted, and then new data is given to be sorted based on the training data set. For example, email filters use a classification algorithm to sort newly received emails in a two groups: spam and not spam.

Clustering algorithm: Sort data into clusters without knowing the cluster labels in advance such that points in a cluster are similar to each other and points from different clusters are dissimilar. For example, to sort athletes by sport without knowing anything about the athletes in your data set, you might plot all the athletes based on height and weight, and label the clusters that are close to each other. Short and light athletes might be coxswains who steer boats, while tall and heavy athletes might be football players in defense positions.

Hadoop: An open-source framework for storing and processing big data across many computers. Instead of using one powerful computer to process data, Hadoop is a way process data across many machines.

Machine learning: Creating and using a variety of algorithms that learn from and make predictions about data.

MapReduce: Process by which a large data set is split or mapped into multiple smaller data sets that are each processed independently. Then the multiple data sets are reduced back into a single data set.

NLP (Natural Language Processing): Algorithms that analyze and convert human text and speech into a computer language. For example, NLP algorithms are used to translate text from one language to another.

R: Programming language popularly used for data analysis and statistics.

Regression: Statistical technique used to estimate the mathematical relationship between one dependent variable and one or more independent variables. The relationship is described as an equation.

Employment

409A valuation: Process in which a board of directors values the company's stock options and the option strike price in compliance with Section 409A of the Internal Revenue Code.

Capitalization table: A table that lists the equity ownership, value, and dilution of founders, investors, and employees for every external financial investment made in the company.

Cliff: A period of time, usually one year, before an employee vests any equity in the company. After the cliff, the equity usually vests monthly.

Common stock: A type of equity interest usually reserved for employees. In the event of a sale or IPO of a company, common stock holders receive their share of the proceeds, if any, after preferred stock holders.

Equity: An ownership interest in the company, usually granted as part of a compensation package in addition to cash.

Option pool: E:quity reserved for employees of the company, separate from the equity allocated to founders or investors.

Portfolio project: Coding project used to demonstrate coding ability that is shown to employers and discussed during interviews.

Preferred stock: A type of equity interest usually used by investors. In the event of a company's sale or IPO, preferred stock holders receive their share of the proceeds before common stock holders.

Strike price: The price per stock option the employee pays to exercise the option and purchase underlying equity, usually common stock.

Vesting: An employee earns the right to, or vests, the equity granted as part of a compensation package over time. The vesting schedule may vary, but companies usually use a four-year monthly vesting schedule with a one-year cliff. Using this example, if you were granted 100 options, after the first year you would receive 25 options, and then you would receive a proportional amount each month thereafter while you were employed.

Mobile

Android: Open-source mobile operating system used on a variety of cell-phones and tablets. It is currently maintained by Google and is the most popular mobile operating system in the world.

App store: A platform or marketplace used to distribute mobile apps. Popular app store include the Apple App Store, Google Play, and Microsoft's Windows Store.

Hybrid app: Using a framework such as PhoneGap, mobile apps built using HTML, CSS, and JavaScript are embedded in a native app. The main advantage of this technique is that it allows a web developer to create a native app with less time and expense and distribute it in an app store.

iOS: A mobile operating system created and developed by Apple, and used exclusively on Apple hardware such as the iPhone, iPad, and iPod.

Mobile web app: A mobile app built using HTML, CSS, and JavaScript that runs in a browser on any device. These apps may not be as fast as native apps, and can lack access to some native device functionality.

Native app: A mobile app that runs on a specific mobile platform. Apps built for iOS are coded using Objective-C or Swift, and apps built for Android are coded using Java.

Objective-C: A general purpose programming language that is over 30 years old and is used by Apple developers to create iOS native apps.

PhoneGap: A free and open source framework used to embed HTML, CSS, and JavaScript inside one or more native apps built for Apple, Android, Blackberry, and Microsoft devices.

Swift: A programming language created by Apple in 2014 that is used to build apps for iOS devices.

Infrastructure

API (application programming interface): A code library receives a standardized request using predefined inputs, and returns data in a standardized response using predefined outputs. For example, you send a request to a weather API with your zipcode, and the API responds with the current temperature.

Back end: The applications and databases that run on the server. The back end is controlled by the company that created the application.

BitBucket: A popular code repository based on Git that is owned and maintained by Atlassian, an enterprise software company.

Client: Personal computer hardware and software operated by a user that accesses a service, an application, or a website made available by a server.

Code repository: A service that hosts software code and supports version control and bug tracking, allowing multiple developers to code one program.

Database: A set of data and systems to allow users and programs to store, retrieve, update, and delete the data.

DNS (domain name server): A naming system for computers connected to the Internet that translates domain names into IP addresses.

Domain name: A string, for example google.com, used to name devices connected to a computer network such as the Internet. There are over 270 million domain names.

Front end: The interface between the user and the back end. The front end is any part of the application that receives input from or can be manipulated by the user.

Git: A version control system used for software development that is fast, protects code from corruption or accidental deletion, and does not require access to the Internet or a central server.

GitHub: The largest code repository in the world based on Git, used by over 9 million users, and home to many popular open source projects.

IP address: A numerical address used to identify every device connected to a computer network such as the Internet. For example, one IP address for amazon.com is 72.21.206.6.

NoSQL: Commonly used in big data applications, this database system can store large amounts of data without needing a schema or label for each data type.

SDK (standard development kit): A collection of software development tools, such as libraries and code editors, to create applications for a specific vendor, system, or platform. For example, the Android SDK makes it easier to develop Android apps.

Server: Computer hardware and software, usually operated by a company, which makes a service, an application, or a website available to clients.

SQL (Structured Query Language): A programming language that allows for saving, querying, updating, and deleting data in a relational database. The data must have labels and a schema (the relationships between data types) must be defined in advance.

Web Development

Agile methodology: Web and software development methodology used in situations with small teams, frequently changing project requirements, and fixed deadlines.

Bootstrap: Free open-source front-end framework for creating responsive, mobile-first websites using pre-built forms, buttons, navigation, and other interface components.

CSS (Cascading Style Sheets): A markup language that controls the look and formatting of web page content by changing text size, image size, and other attributes. CSS is also used to make a web page mobile responsive.

CSS selector: Used to style to a specific HTML tag. The selector uses the same keyword as the HTML tag, and styles any HTML tags that match the CSS selector.

Designer: A professional who designs the look and feel or interaction on the website or application.

Django: A web application framework written for Python that makes it easier to create database-driven websites.

Flask: A web development framework written for the Python programming language. Flask is typically used for small applications with simple requirements.

Framework: Works with an existing programming language, and allows developers to use prewritten code to automate common tasks.

HTML (Hypertext Markup Language): A markup language used to place text, images, and other content on a web page. Web browsers follow the HTML standard to render pages uniformly across operating systems, browsers, and devices.

HTML attribute: A parameter that modifies the behavior of an HTML tag.

HTML tag: Usually appearing in pairs, browsers apply special effects to the text between an opening and closing HTML tag. For example, the `<h1>` tag renders text in a large bolded headline. To apply that effect to the text *Hello,* you could do this: `<h1>Hello</h1>`.

IDE (integrated development environment): A software application used to code, it usually includes a code editor, compiler, and debugger. For example, Xcode is an IDE used to build iOS applications.

JavaScript: A programming language used to create interactive effects in the client browser. Recently, using JavaScript as a server-side programming language has increased in popularity.

Laravel: A free open-source web application framework for PHP.

Mobile responsive: Optimizing a website so the navigation, content, and other website components are easier to use on a mobile device and its smaller screen, virtual keyboard, and no mouse.

PHP: A general-purpose programming language designed and used for web development. PHP is used on over 240 million sites and on over 60 percent of the top 100,000 websites ranked by traffic.

Production: The currently released live version of the application or website.

Python: A general-purpose programming language used for website, data analysis, desktop applications, and games.

Rails: An open source web application framework written in Ruby, and designed to make it easier to develop web applications in Ruby.

Ruby: A general-purpose programming language, often used in combination with Rails to create websites.

Ship it: A phrase that means releasing a live version of the website or application.

Sinatra: A free open source Ruby framework that is an alternative to Rails.

Sprint: As used in agile software development, a fixed period of time — usually two weeks — during which predefined coding tasks, called a user story, are completed. A software project will have many sprints, and the code is reviewed after each sprint.

Staging: Servers used for quality assurance and testing the version of the website before sending it to production.

Story: As used in agile software development, a high-level definition of a product requirement that is small enough to finish in one sprint.

UI and UX (user interface and user experience): Describe the features, visual design, and graphics of a user interface in a website or an application.

Unit testing: Tests designed to verify that algorithms in the code work as expected and are free from errors.

Wireframe: Illustrations created by a designer that show in detail a website's layout, images, and color schemes.

Index

• Z •

About the Author

Nikhil Abraham worked for two years at Codecademy.com, where he helped companies in sectors such as technology, finance, media, and advertising teach their employees how to code. With no previous coding experience, thousands of marketing, sales, and recruiting professionals wrote their first lines of code and built functional applications. In addition to teaching, he has helped recruit developers for Codecademy, and found jobs for people who learned to code on the Codecademy platform.

Prior to Codecademy, Nikhil worked in a variety of fields including management consulting, investment banking, and law, and he also founded a Y-Combinator–backed technology education startup. He received a JD and MBA from The University of Chicago, and a BA in Quantitative Economics from Tufts University.

Nikhil lives in Manhattan, New York.

Dedication

This book is dedicated to my wife, the eternally wonderful and gracious Molly Grovak, for all her encouragement and support. Among your many talents, I'm always amazed by the number of burpees you can do and the episodes of *Keeping Up with the Kardashians* you're able to watch.

Author Acknowledgements

This book was made possible with the help from a number of people.

Thanks to all the kind people at Wiley, including Steven Hayes, for helping to advance ways people consume books, Susan Pink, for edits and advice, and Brian Benedict, for dotting the *i*'s and crossing the *t*'s for all technical matters. Also, thank you to all the editorial, layout, and graphics folks for making this book great.

Thanks to everyone who helped brainstorm, shape, or verify the content of this book. Thanks to Timor Tsentsiper and Andy Kim for answering my questions and providing advice. I'll always remember the adventure that was the first class we taught together. Thanks also to the HR professionals I spoke with, including Yoonie Kim and Sara Yu, whose years of experience helped me understand how companies recruit developers. Thank you to Drew Werner for showing me how he recruited for a technical position with a nontraditional background. And thanks to the folks at educational companies, including Eddie Washington from General Assembly and Bhaumik Patel from Thinkful. It's great to see how you're changing education in the twenty-first century.

Finally, thank you to all the people learning to code, trying to switch careers, and blogging about the good and bad parts of the journey. You're all inspiring more people than you realize.